VIETNAM

A Global Studies Handbook

GLOBAL STUDIES: ASIA

VIETNAM

A Global Studies Handbook

L. Shelton Woods

A B C ⬗ C L I O

Santa Barbara, California   •   Denver, Colorado   •   Oxford, England

Library of Congress Cataloging-in-Publication Data

Woods, L. Shelton.
    Vietnam : global studies handbook / L. Shelton Woods.
        p. cm. — (Global studies, Asia)
    Includes bibliographical references and index.
    ISBN 1-57607-416-1 (hardcover : alk. paper)
    ISBN 1-57607-417-X (e-book)

    1. Vietnam—Handbooks, manuals, etc. I. Title. II. Series.
DS556.3 .W66 2002
959.7—dc21   2002009516

06 05 04   10 9 8 7 6 5 4 3 2

This book is also available on the World Wide Web as an e-book.
Visit abc-clio.com for details.

ABC-CLIO, Inc.
130 Cremona Drive, P.O. Box 1911
Santa Barbara, California 93116–1911

This book is printed on acid-free paper.
Manufactured in the United States of America

To my friend and brother, Damon Woods

Contents

Series Editor's Foreword

It is imperative that as many Americans as possible develop a basic understanding of Asia. In an increasingly interconnected world, the fact that Asia contains almost 60 percent of all the planet's population is argument enough for increased knowledge of the continent on our parts. There are at least four other reasons, in addition to demography, that it is critical Americans become more familiar with Asia.

Americans of all ages, creeds, and colors are extensively involved economically with Asian countries. U.S.-Pacific two-way trade surpassed our trade with Europe in the 1970s. Japan, with the world's second-largest economy, is also the second-largest foreign investor in the United States.

American companies constitute the leading foreign investors in Japan.

The recent Asian economic crisis notwithstanding, since World War II East Asia has experienced the fastest rate of economic growth of all the world's regions. Recently, newly industrialized Southeast Asian countries such as Indonesia, Malaysia, and Thailand have joined the so-called Four Tigers—Hong Kong, the Republic of Korea, Singapore, and Taiwan—as leading areas for economic growth. In the past decade China has begun to realize its potential to be a world-influencing economic actor. Many Americans now depend upon Asians for their economic livelihoods and all of us consume products made in or by Asian companies.

It is impossible to be an informed American citizen without knowledge of Asia, a continent that directly impacts our national security.

America's war on terrorism is, as this foreword is composed, being conducted in an Asian country—Afghanistan. (What many Americans think of as the "Mideast" is, in actuality, Southwest Asia.) Both India and Pakistan now have nuclear weapons. The eventual reunification of the Korean Peninsula is fraught with the possibility of great promise or equally great peril. The question of U.S.-China relations is considered one of the world's major global geopolitical issues. Americans everywhere are affected by Asian political and military developments.

Asia and Asians have also become an important part of American culture.

Asian restaurants dot the American urban landscape. Buddhism is rapidly growing in the United States. Asian movies are becoming increasingly popular in the United States. Asian-Americans, while still a small percentage of the overall U.S. population, are one of the fastest-growing ethnic groups in the United States. Many Asian-Americans exert considerable economic and political influence in this country. Asian sports, pop music, and cinema stars are becoming household names in America. Even Chinese language characters are becoming visible in the United States on everything from baseball caps to t-shirts to license plates. Followers of the ongoing debate on American educational reform will constantly encounter references to Asian student achievement.

Americans should also better understand Asia for its own sake. Anyone who is considered an educated person needs a basic understanding of Asia. The continent has a long, complex, and rich history. Asia is the birthplace of all the world's major religions including Christianity and Judaism.

Asian civilizations are some of the world's oldest. Asian arts and literature rank as some of humankind's most impressive achievements.

Our objectives in developing the Global Studies: Asia series are to assist a wide variety of citizens to both gain a basic understanding of Asian countries and to enable readers to be better positioned for more in-depth work. We envision the series being appropriate for libraries, educators, high school, introductory college and university students, businesspeople, would-be tourists, and anyone who is curious about an Asian country or countries. Although there is some variation in the handbooks—the diversity of the countries requires slight variations in treatment—each volume includes narrative chapters on history and geography, economics, institutions, and society and contemporary issues. Readers should obtain a sound general understanding of the particular Asian country about which they read.

Each handbook also contains an extensive reference section. Since our guess is that many of the readers of this series will actually be traveling to Asia or interacting with Asians in this country, introductions to language, food, and etiquette are included. The reference section of each handbook also contains extensive information—including Web sites when relevant—about business and economic, cultural, educational, exchange, government, and tourist organizations. The reference sections also include capsule descriptions of famous people, places, and events and a comprehensive annotated bibliography for further study.

—*Lucien Ellington*
Series Editor

Preface

At the end of the nineteenth century Vietnam was divided into three regions and dominated by France. One hundred years later, Vietnam is united and free from outside domination. This freedom has been costly. During the twentieth century Vietnam was, at some point, invaded or dominated by France, China, the United States, and Japan. Considering the difficult past century the Vietnamese people have endured, the one word that best describes them is *resilient*. They have endured foreign and civil wars and have entered the twenty-first century with great optimism.

Americans are most familiar with Vietnam because of the war that the United States fought there from 1965 to 1973. Many movies have been made about the war. Some of the films focus on the conflict itself and others explore the scars that the war has left on individuals, families, and the government. Yet, although the scars may never disappear, it seems that the wounds have healed, and that a new generation is growing up with an appreciation for Vietnam as a country among the nations of the world. This volume is written for a wide audience of people who are interested in Vietnam, yesterday and today. It begins with a historic overview of the country and then transitions to Vietnam's current economic, social, political, and educational situations. What is most fascinating about comparing Vietnam's present to its past is the recurring theme of identity. For one thousand years the Vietnamese were considered part of China. As already noted, they were subsequently dominated by other foreign powers. In such a volatile environment, the Vietnamese have had to come to terms with their own place in the world. And now that they are at peace, they are facing their most challenging battle as they seek to become integrated into the global social and economic systems while not losing their traditional values. Many Vietnamese believe it is a war for the soul of Vietnam. In this volume I try to present the major battlefields of this current conflict.

A reference section follows the narrative portion of the book. The reference segment includes an introduction to Vietnamese language, etiquette, food, holidays, and key people and events in Vietnam's history. This portion of the book should be particularly helpful for individuals planning to spend time in Vietnam.

When I was eighteen years old I left Southeast Asia and moved to the United States. The culture shock that one experiences in such a move is almost beyond description. It was with this experience in mind that I sat down to write this volume. My hope is that this study will help Americans understand that all human beings are connected. Ethnocentrism is widespread on both sides of the Pacific Ocean. I believe that by learning about another country and its people, seeds of humility can blossom in our souls.

So many individuals helped in the production of this book. Daryl Jones allowed me to use pictures from his collection for this volume. He has been intricately involved in producing future leaders for Vietnam and I wish to thank him for his tremendous work. Lucien Ellington is the editor for this series and has been a great source of encouragement and guidance. My brother, Damon Woods, has provided keen insight into Vietnam's past, and I thank him for sharing his home and knowledge with me for so many years.

At ABC-CLIO I am particularly grateful to Alicia Merritt. Thanks for your timely words of encouragement. Carol Smith did a fantastic job of putting the manuscript into the right hands, and I wish to thank Michelle Asakawa for her excellent editing job. Scott Horst was also very helpful in finding wonderful pictures to place in this volume.

At Boise State University I wish to thank Gwen Pittam of Albertson's Library for all of her help in finding obscure texts from around the world. Guen Johnson, as always, was helpful in making life easier for the absent-minded professor. Jerome Klena and Theodore Wilbur were also very supportive in commenting on and editing portions of the manuscript.

The two people most responsible for the publication of this volume are my wife, Karen, and our son, Lindsay. Words fail to adequately express the inspiration and light they bring into my life every day so that I can spend time working on projects like this one. Thank you so much for your graciousness, support, and love.

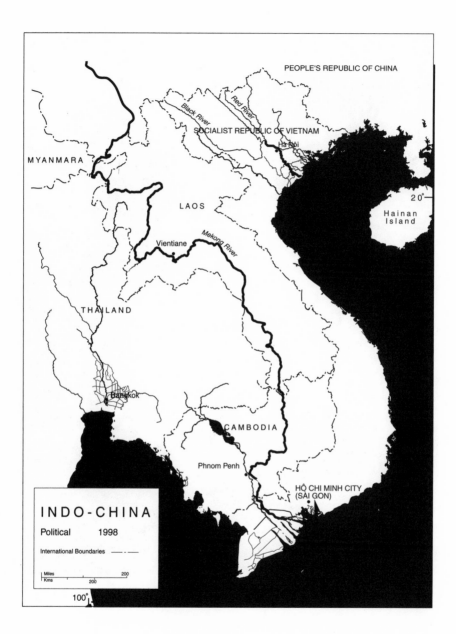

PEOPLE'S REPUBLIC OF CHINA

Black River

Red River

SOCIALIST REPUBLIC OF VIETNAM

Ha Noi

MYANMARA

20°

Hainan
Island

LAOS

Vientiane

Mekong River

THAILAND

Bangkok

CAMBODIA

Phnom Penh

HỒ CHI MINH CITY
(SAI GON)

INDO-CHINA

Political   1998

International Boundaries   — —

| Miles | 200 |
| Kms | 200 |

100°

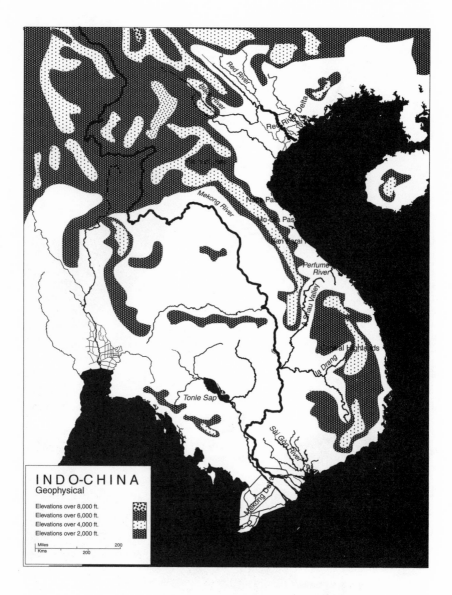

Red River

Black River

Red River Delta

Mekong River

Na... Pas...

Mo-a... Pas...

...an ... rai ...

Perfume River

Shau Valley

...al Highlands

Ia Drang

Tonle Sap

Sai Gon River

Mekong Delta

INDO-CHINA
Geophysical

Elevations over 8,000 ft.
Elevations over 6,000 ft.
Elevations over 4,000 ft.
Elevations over 2,000 ft.

Miles _____ 200
Kms _____ 200

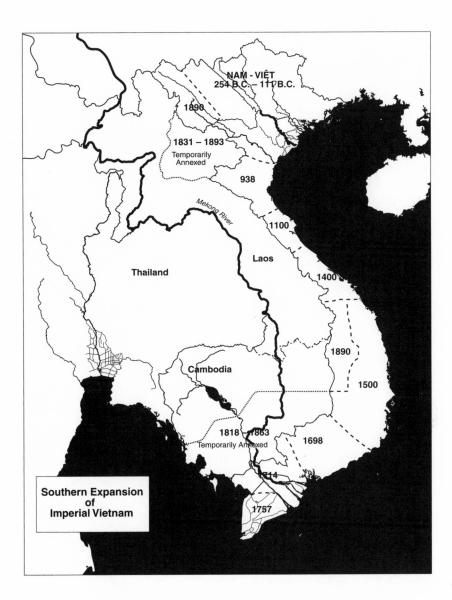

NAM - VIỆT
254 B.C. – 117 B.C.

1890

1831 – 1893
Temporarily
Annexed

938

Mekong River

1100

Laos

Thailand

1400

1890

Cambodia

1500

1818 – 1863
Temporarily Annexed

1698

1714

1757

**Southern Expansion
of
Imperial Vietnam**

PART ONE
NARRATIVE SECTION

CHAPTER ONE
Vietnam's Geography and History

For the past two millenniums, numerous forces outside of Vietnam have tried to shape that nation's society, economy, and ideology. Yet, if we want to understand Vietnam today the place to begin is with its soil. The contour of Vietnam's land and the country's location on the planet have determined the Vietnamese worldview more than all other factors. Thus we must begin our study of Vietnam by considering the land and the people who populate it. What we will find is a diverse topography and a climate conducive to planting rice—the crop that has shaped the economy and social systems of Vietnam more than any other influence.

Following an examination of Vietnam's land, the reader will be given an overview of this land's history—and what a story it is! Prior to the Common Era an agrarian society developed in northern Vietnam that centered on rice. A recurring theme in Vietnam's history is its struggle to remain independent from the world's imperialistic powers: China ruled Vietnam for more than one thousand years; during the nineteenth and twentieth centuries France incorporated Vietnam into its empire; Japan invaded Vietnam in 1940 and for all intents and purposes sought to control this Southeast Asian country; and finally, the United States determined to stop the spread of communism in Southeast Asia and supported a government in southern Vietnam from 1954 to 1975. If there is one thing we learn from this history it is that the Vietnamese are tenaciously independent, and their society is so strong that it can withstand the imperialist blows of the earth's greatest powers. Through it all, the Vietnamese have sustained their cultural identity.

THE PHYSICAL AND HUMAN GEOGRAPHY OF VIETNAM

Vietnam is a narrow S-shaped country on the eastern edge of the Indochina Peninsula. With an area of over 203,980 square miles, Vietnam is slightly larger than the U.S. state of New Mexico. The distance from Vietnam's extreme north to south is 1,023 miles, and the country enjoys more than 2,015 miles of coastline. There are two major rivers in Vietnam, the Red and the Mekong; the delta areas of these rivers are centers of agricultural activity due to the richness of the mineral deposits that come from the flowing waters. This fertile soil is needed to feed Vietnam's current population of eighty million—a population that has dramatically increased since the end of the U.S.-Vietnam War.

Imperialist powers sought to divide Vietnam into three sections, which during the early part of the twentieth century were referred to as Tonkin (north Vietnam), Annam (central Vietnam), and Cochin China (southern Vietnam). Each of these states had an urban center: Hanoi, Hue, and Saigon, respectively. One justification the French could have used in separating Vietnam into three sections is the diverse topography of these regions. Only about 20 percent of Vietnam's land is level; the remaining 80 percent is divided into highlands and forest-covered hills. Northern Vietnam is characterized by highlands that serve as a buffer from neighboring Laos and China. This area also has a 1,860-square-mile delta, which is historically the most densely populated area in Vietnam. Mountain ranges and lowlands that meet the sea distinguish central Vietnam. In fact, a section of this area is less than 31 miles wide, and so the South China Sea is a dominant part of central Vietnam's inhabitants' lives. Historically, southern Vietnam was less developed and more sparsely populated than the northern region because it took centuries for Vietnam to conquer its southern rivals; Vietnamese migration to the south was a slow process.

Among the ten countries of Southeast Asia (Myanmar, Thailand, Laos, Cambodia, Vietnam, Malaysia, Singapore, Brunei, Philippines, and Indonesia), Vietnam experienced the greatest amount of Chi-

Vietnam's landscape includes rolling hills where people build lives for themselves. (Corel)

nese influence. Geography helps to explain this fact. Sitting at the bottom of China, Vietnam was easy pickings for the powerful Chinese Han, Tang, and Ming dynasties. For more than one thousand years, China incorporated Vietnam into its empire. However, as will be discussed in detail, China's influence in Vietnam often was peripheral because it was more concerned with the trade opportunities at the port centers of northern Vietnam than it was in bilking taxes from the indigenous population. Chinese influence in Vietnam came from the top down as the Vietnamese elite incorporated the Confucian ideology of society and government; the Vietnamese eventually accepted the idea of a virtuous ruler guiding a population.

India also played an important role in shaping the early Vietnamese worldview. The Indianized state of Champa bordered Vietnam, and South Asian merchants and missionaries resided in northern Vietnam's port cities. In particular, Vietnam's religion was

The scenic highlands of Vietnam are populated by ethnic minorities. (Courtesy of Daryl Jones)

shaped by the metaphysical doctrines that came from India. This includes Buddhism and the Hindu idea of a *deva-raja,* or a god-king, whose magic powers confirmed that heaven had placed its mandate on a particular individual. Certainly Vietnam enjoyed a much more cosmopolitan atmosphere early in its history because it became the center of trade from East, South, and Southeast Asia.

Despite the international atmosphere that trade brought to Vietnam, it remained relatively ethnically homogenous. Early inhabitants of northern Vietnam are identified as a mixture of Australoid, Austronesian, and Mongoloid peoples that moved into the area from southern China. These early residents existed primarily through farming and fishing, with a range of 70 to 300 peo-

A fishing village along the west coast of Vietnam (Corel)

ple residing in each village. Today Vietnamese make up close to 90 percent of the population; the largest ethnic minority is Chinese. Living primarily in the highlands, over 50 distinct tribes add to the ethnic diversity of Vietnam. Generically termed Montagnards, these tribal peoples have historically lived apart from the lowlanders and general population. For much of their history most highland tribes survived by carving out mountain terraces to grow rice. Relying on the seasonal rains, most tribes planted just one crop annually. A few tribes live a nomadic life and create fertile ground by burning portions of a mountain, planting a crop, then moving on following a harvest. Ethnically, highlanders have distinct Malay and South Asian features and have darker skin than do the Vietnamese. Linguistic diversity also marks the highlanders as at least twelve different languages and numerous dialects are spoken among the various tribes.

As for the Vietnamese language, it is accepted as part of the Austroasiatic linguistic family. During the first millennium of the

Common Era, Vietnamese was heavily influenced by Chinese, which was the official language of the Vietnamese elite and court officials. Literature was written in Chinese during this period; but by the ninth century a Vietnamese popular script based on the Chinese character system allowed the Vietnamese to write using symbols as phonetic sounds. Four hundred years later this indigenous writing system was so developed that it became the mode for popular writing in northern Vietnam. The term given this written language was *chu nom*, "southern writing." When the Jesuits arrived in China during the sixteenth century they wondered whether the character writing system was from heaven or hell. To be sure, the beauty of character writing far exceeded that of the West, yet it took years of memorization to be literate in Chinese. Concomitantly, the European priests in Vietnam set out to simplify the Chinese and *chu nom* system of writing in Vietnam. They created a roman letter-based script called *quoc ngu*. French was introduced to the country during the nineteenth century, and Vietnamese officials were encouraged to learn this language so they could communicate with their French superiors.

RICE AND SOCIETY

One must understand rice cultivation to understand Asia. Rice is what makes Asian nations rich and poor; it unites and divides societies; it sustains large populations and is often used as the basis for taxation. From the earliest days of Vietnam's history, rice farming was the primary means of economic production. In northern Vietnam the Red River delta provided fertile territory where various strains of rice allowed the population to increase in number. One main effect of rice cultivation is that it forces individuals to work together as it is a labor-intensive enterprise. Growing rice demands that land be properly leveled and that an adequate supply of water is available. It also requires backbreaking planting of individual seedlings, a vigilant watch of the water level, and then harvesting of the crop one stalk at a time. Following a successful harvest, the rice must be dried out and then the husk

The labor-intensive nature of cultivating rice brings communities together. The group experience of rice farming helped the early inhabitants of Vietnam build a unified society. (Robert van der Hilst/CORBIS)

removed from the seed. The group experience in farming rice meant that the early inhabitants of Vietnam worked together to build a unified society.

It was imperative for farmers to work together due to the hazards of farming in Vietnam. During the dry season (November to April) water was brought to the fields through an extensive irrigation system. These canals needed constant monitoring and repair—as they still do today. Tropical weather patterns also call for communal behavior in Vietnam as climate extremes include a temperature range of 5°–37°C with an average daily humidity of 84 percent. The important job of making sure the crops receive sufficient water during the dry season is juxtaposed with the precarious situation of monitoring the water levels during the wet season (May to October). Ninety percent of Vietnam's annual rainfall—which surpasses 120 inches in some locations—occurs during the wet season. Moreover, because most of Vietnam's lowland farms are less than 3.5 feet above sea level there is a constant danger of flooding in the lowland areas. Thus, the agrarian pattern of Vietnam (65 percent of the population continues to work in the agricultural sector of the economy) demonstrates how the society was formed around the village and farmlands.

THE DIFFICULTIES IN VIETNAM TODAY

Modern Vietnam exports rice. Technological advancement in agriculture and the clearing of swamps in the Mekong River delta facilitate Vietnam's feeding of its large population while having a surplus to sell to foreign nations. The urbanization difficulties that plague the Southeast Asian cities of Manila, Jakarta, and Bangkok have thus far been avoided in Vietnam. One reason Vietnam does not have the massive urban areas that other Asian nations have is that in 1975 the government began emptying cities and forcefully placed large urban groups in state-created rural economic zones. Details of this forced relocation policy are presented in Chapter 2.

Of all the possible natural disasters, it is the annual flooding during typhoon season that continues to create problems for Vietnam. During September and October of 2000 over three hundred Vietnamese died because of flood waters, with close to $200 million of damage in six provinces along the Mekong Delta.

The real difficulty Vietnam faces today is its need to fit its ideology into a world that follows the beat of a different economic drum. Historical context helps to explain this statement. From 1945 to 1975 the prevailing ideology of northern Vietnamese leaders was Marxism. During these years Vietnam first fought the French and then the Americans in two separate wars, creating a climate of crisis because of the terrible conflicts that engulfed all of Vietnam. During this same thirty-year period South Vietnam's economy was grossly affected by the immense import of foreign goods. Also, the service sector rapidly expanded to cater to the thousands of foreign soldiers stationed there. When North and South Vietnam were united in 1975, the communist officials finally had an opportunity to implement Marxist-Leninist theory on their country's economy. Unfortunately, Vietnam's situation did not fit the needed criteria for a social revolution. There was not a large class of people who were exploited by land-owning capitalists; the economies of North and South Vietnam were artificially inflated by outside aid; a large surplus of capital would not be forthcoming from a bourgeois class; and finally, without a sizeable exploited class and minus a new surplus from an elite class, there could not be a magical new source of funds to build an industrialized society. Despite these realities, Vietnamese officials tried to force a hard-line communist economy on a united Vietnam. Results were just short of disastrous. Communist officials confiscated Chinese-owned businesses, promoted a monopoly of state-owned enterprises, and removed incentives for farmers to grow surplus crops. Compounding Vietnam's post-1975 economic stagnation was its international isolation. The United States pressured financial institutions to refuse loans to Vietnam. Vietnam's 1978 invasion and subsequent decade-long occupation of neighboring Cambodia further isolated the Southeast Asian country from the global community. Only financial aid from the Soviet Union kept Vietnam's economy afloat, and when the Soviet Union broke apart in 1989, Vietnam was forced to make tough decisions—including a withdrawal from Cambodia.

During the 1990s debate raged in the upper echelons of the Vietnamese Communist Party, and the result has been a softening of the strict state-directed economy. Thus, the major question now facing Vietnam is whether it can achieve a more open-market economy while remaining a Marxist society. Vietnam's future depends on how its leaders fit a strict Marxist political ideology into a more transparent economic system.

THE NAME *VIETNAM*

At the turn of the nineteenth century a number of Asian countries had become colonies of the European empires. Against this backdrop of slow but steady imperialistic incursions, China continued to command respect from the global community in general and the Asian states in particular. To be sure, China itself was in the throes of economic and political decline, but it would hold on for another century before internal and external factors toppled the two-millennium-year-old imperial system. Qing China (1644–1912) in the year 1800 was indeed a formidable state, with a geographical region larger than at any other period in China's history. Three emperors ruled China between 1662 and 1796, and one of the many positive results of these long reigns was political stability. However, unable or unwilling to recognize that the world was changing, the Qing bureaucratic system did not include a ministry of foreign affairs. The "Middle Kingdom" mentality, which was the prevalent worldview of the Chinese scholars, dictated that outsiders who wished to have contact with China must approach the throne with the assumption that relations were based on the good graces of the emperor, who might stoop to accept tribute from less-sophisticated—if not barbarian—foreigners. This was especially true for the Vietnamese delegates who journeyed to Peking in 1803 to offer tribute to Emperor Jiaqing.

There was reason for the Vietnamese ambassadors to fear their reception as they made their way north. In a bloody civil war between the country's Le dynasty and the Nguyen family during the late eighteenth century, the Qing court sided with the Le contingent, and in 1788 it sent a formidable army into northern Vietnam to reestablish the Le dynasty. By December 1788 tens of thousands of Chinese troops occupied Hanoi and celebrated the return of the Le emperor. The festivity was short-lived. The following month the Nguyen family attacked the Chinese army and killed over 4,000 of its troops, establishing the Nguyen hegemony over northern Vietnam. The Chinese retreated and did not return to do battle with the Vietnamese until 1979. Thus it was that when the Nguyen representatives made their way to Peking in 1803 they knew their rank disregard for Chinese support of the former Le dynasty of earlier days might be cause for the Chinese court to punish them. To stay in the good graces of the Chinese, the Vietnamese representatives identified themselves as Yueh (Viet in Vietnamese). Historically, Yueh was the designate for southern peoples on the periphery of China who recognized China's suzerainty. Thus, the Nguyen delegates introduced themselves as coming from Nan (southern) Yueh, or in Vietnamese, Nam Viet. For historical reasons, the Chinese court changed the designate to Yueh Nam, or Viet Nam. By using this term, the Vietnamese understood that they were relegating the earliest days of their history to a period when China socially, culturally, and politically dominated their lands. Although this diplomatic exchange resulted in the adoption of the term Vietnam, it also perpetuated the false notion that Vietnam's earliest history was defined by its subordinate relationship with China. In fact, Vietnamese folklore and history demonstrate that the earliest inhabitants of the area had a culture and society that were indigenous to the locale, and that Chinese political and military influence came centuries after the Vietnamese had established indigenous rule. Therefore, a proper study of Vietnam must begin with its earliest history, a time long before China dominated the region.

VIETNAM BEFORE CHINESE DOMINATION

Vietnamese point to the Hung dynasty (2879–258 B.C.E.), in the Red River basin, as the earliest political structure in the region. The apocryphal story about the establishment of the Vietnamese state centers on the mythical figure Lac Long Quan, who supposedly responded to the Vietnamese people's request to rescue them from a king in the mountains who was descending upon them. Coming out of the sea, Lac Long Quan captured Au Co, the queen of the invading king, and repulsed the intruders. The hero from the sea also taught the people agrarian methods of rice planting, and then returned to the water. An instructive aspect to this story is that it demonstrates that individuals from the sea and continent came together to form a secure, agrarian-based society. This points to an important feature of early Vietnamese civilization, which is that the region became home to a disparate number of groups from both the sea and the Asian continent.

Vietnamese scholars assert that the first culture in the region was an early bronze society that developed around the area of Me-linh. This civilization, known as Phung-nguyen, dates from the third millennium B.C.E., and for two thousand years a steady progress of its civilization included the growth of clan structures and a definite hierarchy of local power. According to one legend, two thousand years before the Common Era a man of prowess, Hung Vuong, united the various clans and established the kingdom of Van Lang—a kingdom that saw eighteen generations of Hung kings. The establishment of Van Lang coincides with the emergence of the Dong Sonian culture, which ran from the seventh century B.C.E. to 42 C.E. There were numerous changes in Vietnam during this period, but the economic and political changes are most noteworthy.

It was during the Dong Sonian era that the agricultural methods employed by the population around Me-linh graduated to a more sophisticated level. There is evidence that irrigation canals and dikes were built in relation to the tides and seasons. Increased production of crops, primarily rice, allowed the Dong Sonian society to branch out to other economic endeavors including animal husbandry (water buffaloes, chickens, pigs), weaving, leather working, and pottery. Greater agricultural technology also affected the political situation of Me-linh. As noted previously, an implication of producing rice or other such cereals or grains is the imperative of communal activity, because the construction and maintenance of rice fields and irrigation waterways demand that groups work in concert to achieve a final product. Historically the rice paddies that sustained a growing population during the Dong Sonian times were referred to as "Lac fields." Thus, between 600–300 B.C.E. northern Vietnam increased in population, due to continual immigration and a stable agrarian-based economy. The communal activity surrounding the Lac fields produced various clans that dominated particular land areas. Taxes did not go to a central area, and the Hung kings did not demand portions of the Lac lords' harvest; rather, the landowners concomitantly harvested grain while showering the Hung king with gifts.

Economic and political stability for Me-linh society was interrupted by upheaval in China. Led by Shi Huangdi, the Qin state toppled all its competitors in China during the latter half of the third century B.C.E. Fleeing before the marauding Qin army, various non-Chinese aristocratic and military leaders, including those from the southern states of Nan Yueh (Nam Viet) and Eastern Ou (Au), settled in and around Me-linh. Although the Hung king system did not survive the influx of new aristocratic families, the new outside elite did join with Lac lords to produce the kingdom of Au Lac. King An Duong, whose existence is the first verifiable figure of early Vietnamese history, built Au Lac's capital at Co Loa, 22 miles north of present-day Hanoi.

Although the Chinese Qin empire began the imperial history of that great nation, it was the shortest of all China's dynasties, lasting from 221 B.C.E. to 207 B.C.E. However, it lasted long enough to send a large army, led by General Trieu Da, against Au Lac. As with all its enemies, the Qin army swept the Au Lac king out of power and began to replace the existing political system. In the midst of this, General Trieu Da was informed in 207 B.C.E. that Emperor Shi Huangdi had died and that the Han state had overthrown the Qin empire. Rather than capitulate to the new Han emperor, Trieu Da decided to set up an autonomous state in the south, and he once again used the term Nan Yueh to describe his state. He divided the area that he had conquered into the districts of Giao-chi and Cuu-chan, which are part of present-day northern Vietnam. He colluded with the Lac lords to continue the social and economic systems that had defined the area since the seventh century. Vietnamese celebrate the memory of Trieu Da as someone who stood up against China's desire to integrate the southern states into the ever-expanding Han empire (207 B.C.E.–221 C.E.).

THE CHINESE MILLENNIUM

Autonomy was short-lived in Nan Yueh. In 111 B.C.E. the Han army defeated its southern rival and incorporated Nan Yueh into the Chinese empire. China would rule Vietnam for the next one thousand years. Han officials divided the southern area into seven districts, three of which are now part of Vietnam. Two of these three zones, Giao-chi and Cuu-chan, were already defined regions, whereas Nhat-nam was a new political unit. Initial Han interest in this area was primarily due to China's access to trade with foreign merchants in Vietnam's port towns. Valuable items, including rhinoceros horn, exotic food delicacies, and luxury goods, were brought into the Chinese market through trade along the coast of northern Vietnam. Because of their interest in Vietnam's strategic geographical location and the profitability of foreign trade, Han officials allowed Lac lords to maintain their social and political roles. There was, however, an important adjustment that Lac lords were forced to make. For more than three centuries Lac lords, as aristocratic landowners, had provided tribute to Hung and Nan Yueh kings. After 111 B.C.E., these same nobles were required to pay tribute to the Han officials, who would then reciprocate by providing seals and ribbons attesting to the legitimacy of the Lac lord rule. Although it was prestigious to receive approval from the dominating Han dynasty, this slight modification transformed the Lac lords from a landowning class to tribute-paying bureaucrats of the Han political system. Bureaucrats can be fired.

China's first one hundred years of rule in Vietnam was rather uneventful. That changed in the first century C.E. Three issues disturbed the peaceful coexistence of Han rule and Vietnamese society. First, though the Chinese were initially attracted to Nan Yueh because of the prospect of southern trade routes, the fertile land and sophisticated farming practices of the Vietnamese pointed to a source of sorely needed tax revenue for China. This resulted in a much more hands-on approach to government by Chinese bureaucrats in Vietnam. Second, an increasing number of Han families immigrated into northern Vietnam, and a clash of worldviews characterized their relationship with the indigenous population. In particular, the Vietnamese refusal to adopt a strict patriarchal society rubbed against the chauvinistic Chinese society and placed the two cultures at odds. Finally, Lac lords were the obvious targets of Han's growing economic and cultural hegemony in the area. Tribute that the Vietnamese landed elite was required to provide

Some of the older quarters in Hanoi (PhotoDisc, Inc.)

was changed to annual taxes based on the Chinese land surveys. Resentment flared into rebellion when in the spring of 40 C.E., Trung Trac, the wife of a Lac lord, led a revolt against Su Ting, the Han prefect of Giao-chi. Successful in pushing out the Han bureaucrats and military men, Trung Trac reestablished the norm of aristocratic governance of the district. It is noted in ancient Vietnamese texts that she abolished the tax system and that Lac lords subsequently sent gifts in lieu of the onerous taxes the old Han order had required.

Although the Vietnamese remember Trung Trac as an early liberator of Vietnam, it is important to note that the southern rebellion against the Han empire lasted less than two years. General Ma Yüan along with 20,000 troops easily crushed the revolt in 42 C.E. It appears that Trung Trac attracted support only as long as there was victory, and when the Han demonstrated its military might, many abandoned her. Legend has it that the Han general killed both Trung Trac and her sister, Nhi, and sent their heads to the Han emperor. Other sources claim that the two sisters committed suicide rather than surrender to the Chinese army. At any rate, this victory of the Han over the Lac lords signaled a change in Han-Viet relations—an alteration that would forever color relations between the Chinese and the Vietnamese.

For more than one thousand years Vietnam was identified as part of China. Obviously with such a long span of time the relationship between the two underwent changes based on many factors. There are, however, themes that help define the Chinese millennial rule in Vietnam. For our purposes, it is best to understand this long period by picking out these themes and using them to build a linear understanding of this epoch.

Vietnam's political and social stability, as well as the character of Chinese immigration into Vietnam, was predicated on the strength or weakness of China. For example, during four centuries following the fall of the Han dynasty (221 C.E.) at least six different dynasties, all with their capital in Nanking, attempted to bring stability to China. What we find in Vietnam during this era is relative peace and prosperity. And so a major theme in Sino-Viet relations is that during the times that China was weak at the center, Vietnam enjoyed social, economic, cultural, and political growth. However, when China was strong and could easily exercise hegemony over its southern states, Vietnam was prone to experience military and social upheaval. Concomitantly, when China was in disarray, the Chinese people fleeing south were usually from the aristocratic or upper class. They were seeking to protect their possessions and prestige against a chaotic upheaval where brigands freely looted and gave no thought to a supposed heaven-established hierarchy of power. When China was flourishing and politically stable, Chinese soldiers and officials wishing to get rich quick characterized the personnel that came to Vietnam. This was one reason why tension arose between the two states when China was robust.

China's Six Dynasties era (222–589) provided Vietnam an opportunity to develop social and economic institutions quite apart from outside scrutiny. During this period the Chinese families who had migrated to Vietnam during the chaos that brought about the Han dynasty's fall became more at home in this region than they had been in their ancestors' homelands. There was greater interaction and even intermarriage between these aristocratic Chinese families and the Vietnamese elite, including some of the former Lac lord clans. Indeed, there was little reason for these Chinese to return north after the fall of the Han because there was greater stability in the south than in the north. These Han-Viet families began expanding their influence in Vietnam through land acquisition. Between the fourth and fifth centuries the number of households in Vietnam that paid the land tax (families that owned some land) dropped from 25,000 to 10,000, indicating that there was a transfer of land ownership along with the emergence of what westerners would call feudal lords—individuals who owned large estates where landless tenants engaged in subsistence farming and paid rent for land use.

Predictably, one might even say inevitably, several of these large landowners sought to completely throw off any vestige of Chinese rule in Vietnam. Ly Bi was one of these rebels. Descended from a Chinese family that had migrated to Vietnam in the first century C.E., Ly Bi in 543 rebelled against China and declared himself emperor of Nam Viet. His capital was in the Red River delta, but his rebellion was short-lived, and in 547, proving that even a weak China was stronger than a pretender in the south, the Chinese killed Ly Bi. Legend has it that Ly Bi's devout followers continued to press for independence for fifty years, which leads some historians to call this the earlier Ly dynasty. One year before Ly Bi's death, Trieu Quan Phuc, leading an army of 20,000, also declared his rebellion against China's hegemony. He made his headquarters on an island in the dense swamps of the Hong River. Moving at night and retiring to the swamps before daybreak, Quang Phuc wreaked havoc on the invading Chinese armies. Yet, this upstart was also defeated, giving insight to another theme in Sino-Vietnam relations: that no matter how severe its own domestic problems were, China still had the ability, resolve, and strength to crush rebellions in Vietnam. Thus, during the Six Dynasties period China was strong enough or had sufficient interest in Vietnam to squash revolts, and its leaders allowed social and economic changes to take place as long as they were done under the rubric of China's suzerainty.

Vietnam's relative stability during the Six Dynasties era was somewhat shaken at the beginning of the seventh century, when China moved into its golden era of the Tang dynasty (618–907). As noted earlier, the implications of a strong unified China were more negative than positive for Vietnam. The status quo was replaced with some sweeping changes including the incorporation of Vietnam into the protectorate of Annam (Pacified South). Tang Chinese coming to Vietnam were primarily from the bureaucratic and military classes. The bureaucrats' goals were to keep peace, make money, and return to the north. For the soldiers it was often more advantageous to stay in Vietnam, and many intermarried with the indigenous population and remained in the south. Overall, however, the three centuries of Tang intrusion in Vietnam witnessed the ebb and flow of outside influence while local beliefs and cultural patterns grew even deeper in society.

Early relations between Vietnam and Tang China saw various revolts among Vietnam's indigenous tribal mountain dwellers against the encroaching northern hegemony. These highlanders retreated into Vietnam's remote mountainous areas. Various factions in the twentieth-century Indochina Wars sought the support of these tribes.

One consequence of China's grandeur during the Tang dynasty was that its capital, Changan (now Xian, Shaanxi), was the greatest cosmopolitan area on the planet. Some historians estimate that foreigners made up one-third of the city's population, which included Nestorian Christians, Islamic traders, Taoist priests, and fire-worshipping adherents of Zoroastrianism. It was during this period that Buddhism became an entrenched world religion in China. Vietnam was affected by Buddhism's popularity in Tang China because of the great number of Chinese monks that made pilgrimages through Vietnam to the flowering Buddhist states in Southeast Asia. These monks were not the first to preach the teachings of the Buddha in Vietnam, but the overt acceptance of this faith by the Chinese court increased the credibility of this foreign religion in Annam.

VIETNAM'S TRANSITION TO INDEPENDENCE

The dissolution of the Tang dynasty in 907 provided opportunities for peripheral states, like Vietnam, to assert their independence. Various bureaucrats and generals throughout China carved out their particular spheres of influence. In southeast China during the tenth century, Liu Kung was the leader of the southern Han polity. Anxious to reassert Chinese rule in Vietnam, he commissioned his son, Liu Hung-ts'ao, to lead a naval expedition against the independent-minded Vietnamese in the year 938. Ngo Quyen, the Vietnamese military leader, rallied the local population in an effort to repel the Chinese attack. Quyen correctly guessed that the route of the approaching Chinese army would be through the Bach-dang River, and he ordered poles to be embedded in the riverbed at a height just under the high-tide water surface. Luring the Chinese boats into the river at high tide, Quyen regaled as the boats became stuck among the poles when the tide shifted. He thus defeated the Han attack—they did not return.

The Battle of Bach-dang River, as it came to be known, signaled the beginning of Vietnam's independent history during the Common Era. In an extremely symbolic move, Quyen moved Vietnam's capital from Dai-la—a capital associated with China's rule in Vietnam—to Co-loa. This latter area had been the residence of Vietnamese leaders before China incorporated Vietnam into its empire. Unfortunately, Quyen was more successful on the battlefield than he was in the palace. Despite taking the name "king," he continued to use the Chinese system for political legitimacy. When he died in 944 at the age of forty-seven, chaos shaped the political landscape of Vietnam. It was in to this political intermission that the controversial figure Dinh Bo Linh (r. 965–979) stepped on to the stage of Vietnam's history.

Unlike preceding rulers in Vietnam, Dinh Bo Linh's credentials were rather meager. A leader of the buffalo-watching children in his village, he emerged as a local leader whom village elders rallied to support. One reason for Linh's rise to power is that the conventional mode of political legitimacy was changing from Chinese rule to a more local hero type of construction. Following the overthrow of both established and potential leaders in Vietnam, Bo Linh spurned the previous capitals of Dai-la and Co-loa and centered his power at Hoa-lu. This area differed from former capitals in that it was not on an open plain and was much easier to defend. This indicates that Bo Linh was willing to choose a more rustic setting for his capital because the basis of his power was military might. Indeed, he is known to have placed wild beasts and vats of boiling water in the center of town to warn would-be lawbreakers that they would be eaten or boiled as punishment.

Paralleling Bo Linh's consolidation of power in Vietnam was the reemergence of a united China under the Song dynasty. Despite having taken the title of "emperor" (a title that the Chinese believed belonged only to the head of their state), Bo Linh sought official recognition by Song officials and received it. This diplomatic acknowledgment was given in light of Vietnam's distance from Song power, the numerous domestic issues the newly established Song dynasty had to deal with, and the fact that Bo Linh sought recognition not for himself but for his son (who had the title of "king"). As China acquiesced to these requests, Bo Linh proceeded to organize a 100,000-man army. Extending down to local militias, this army was a reminder that Vietnam faced a formidable potential enemy to the north. Historical reality pointed to the need for the Vietnamese to have a strong army. The emphasis on a strong army—including a local militia—would remain in Vietnam long after Linh passed from the scene. However, Linh's army was not sufficient to stop Vietnam from imploding following his assassination in 979. Like the post-Quyen rule, post-Linh Vietnam fell in on itself, with various factions claiming suzerainty over the entire region.

During the tenth century, Vietnam flirted with political autonomy, but rulers such as Quyen and Bo Linh were more transitional figures than individuals who could establish a lasting political legacy for Vietnam. Perhaps the Vietnamese needed these experiments in political economy to throw off the longstanding Chinese political paradigm that had been placed on them. Indeed, it would not be until the year 1009, under the leadership of Ly Cong Uan, that Vietnam would find its political bearings and establish a truly independent dynasty that would last for several centuries.

THE LY DYNASTY

If Quyen and Bo Linh's reigns were the seeds of Vietnam's political break from China, the Ly dynasty (1009–1225) was the budding of indigenous political, bureaucratic, and religious patterns in Vietnam. During the tenth century Vietnamese kings needed political legitimacy to ward off rebellions and civil disorder. Thus, China's approval of a particular ruler was indispensable for potential Vietnamese leaders. Given the historical context of Vietnam in the tenth century and the fact that China remained the paramount power in East and Southeast Asia, it was natural for Vietnamese leaders to seek China's approval of their realms. For some of these reasons, Vietnamese kings sought the assistance of Buddhist monks to work as intermediaries between China and the newly created southern state of Dai Viet. As each decade passed, these monks' influence on Vietnam's politics grew. Various kings acknowledged the need for the Buddhist monks to endow heavenly blessing and approval on court politics and leaders. Born into this situation was Ly Cong Uan (974–1028), an orphan who was shown pity by Buddhist monks who raised him in their temple. Said to have a propensity for learning, mercy, and martial prowess, Ly Cong Uan was placed as the commander of the palace guard in Hoa-lu. In 1009, when an inept king died, the Buddhist monks exerted their religious and political influence and placed Ly Cong Uan on the throne, thus establishing the Ly dynasty (1009–1225).

Scholars argue about the nature of this important Vietnamese dynasty: Was it a full-fledged China-imitating kingdom, or something quite distinct from anything Vietnam had seen before? The answer may lie somewhere between these two. One cannot simply ignore the enormous influence China would have to have on any social or political entity so connected (historically and geographically) to itself. There was the idea of a leader who was owed patronage and honor. However, the basis of power for Ly Cong Uan and subsequent Ly kings was not so much the nebulous mandate of heaven that Chinese emperors claimed; rather, these Ly kings were accorded honor, respect, and obedience because of their spiritual prowess and their interaction with the local gods found in nature. A Ly king was followed because he had convinced his constituents that he was, in some sense, a spiritual superman. Supernatural phenomena—such as a crooked pillar being made straight when the king looked at it—identified a king as an individual whom the gods were pleased to work through.

At least two important implications follow this new pattern of political legitimacy in Vietnam. First, it demonstrates that the Vietnamese were in touch with other governing patterns in their neighboring Southeast Asian states. This is evident because this was the type of political legitimacy that dominated other eleventh-century

Buddhism has affected more than just the spiritual life of Vietnam; Buddhist monks helped to bring the Ly dynasty into power. This is a picture of the White Buddha statue in Vietnam. (Brian A. Vikander/CORBIS)

Southeast Asian states. O. W. Wolters, a legend among Southeast Asian scholars, calls this political paradigm the "Great Man" or "Man of Prowess" government. If the Ly dynasty followed this pattern, it is clear that there was significant interaction between Vietnam and other Southeast Asian states. A second implication of the spiritual nature of the Ly kings was that their hegemony was probably limited to areas surrounding the capital, while other leaders who might also claim spiritual and political leadership controlled the areas further away from the capital. Therefore, it was paramount for Ly kings to work in concert with other indigenous leaders to create a state strong enough to stave off northern aggression while concomitantly pushing out their southern neighbors so as to expand the Vietnamese state.

Ly Cong Uan, posthumously known as Ly Thai To, worked to establish the Ly dynasty by moving—once again—the capital, this time to Thang-long, and by encouraging the building of numerous temples and rice paddies around the area. His tax system relied on nonessentials that complimented the agrarian-based economic system. It is said that he did not center his taxes on rice and other grains because he wanted to shift the tax burden away from the farmers and onto the community of traders and merchants. Social, religious, economic, and political stability encouraged the first Ly king to move south and seek greater territory at the expense of the Cham and Cambodian kingdoms. The mostly acrimonious relationship Vietnam had with its southern neighbors eventually resulted in three Cham provinces being turned over to Vietnam in 1078 and finally, in the fifteenth century, in the complete destruction of the Cham political entity. These incursions by the northern aggressors would be remembered through the centuries and continue to taint Cambodian-Vietnamese relations into the twenty-first century.

Although historians disagree on the effectiveness of Ly Cong Uan's rule, there is unanimity regarding the second Ly king, Ly Phat Ma (posthumously known as Ly Thai Tong, r. 1028–1054). Born in 1000 as the first son of Ly Cong Uan, Ly Phat Ma was raised to understand the importance of leadership, spirituality, and the need for vigilance against the Chinese. His twenty-six-year reign is considered the height of Ly power in Vietnam. Careful to keep both his subjects and the gods happy, Ly Phat Ma changed the name of his reign six times to fit the immediate situation. He personally led the expedition south against the Cham kingdom and returned with an enormous amount of plunder and promises for tax reduction. Ly Phat Ma's incursions south and the consequent growth of Vietnam's boundaries over the next decades fit the dynastic cycle pattern seen throughout the world, particularly in China—that is, a dynasty would begin and would grow due to the charismatic leadership of strong kings but would reach an apex of power and then begin to disintegrate due to corruption at the center and weak kings. Fortunately for Vietnam, it was while the Ly dynasty was on the upswing that China in 1076–1077 sought to reassert its influence in their former southern provinces. The subsequent battles were indecisive, causing China to acknowledge that Vietnam was not an extension of China. Ly Can Duc, the last strong Ly king, died in 1127. Lacking an heir, a nephew of his was selected to rule, and from this point on the Ly emperors were but puppets of court advisers, officials, and relatives.

THE TRAN DYNASTY

The Ly dynasty died a slow death, yet in its demise lay the seeds of a new dynasty. For decades the Tran clan had wielded influence at court over the Ly kings. Thus, the Tran transition from de jure leadership to overt rule took place without major political disruption. Once in power, Tran leaders instituted three policies to avoid the economic and political blunders that cost the Ly kings their kingdom. First, to prevent dispute about succession and inordinate court influence by maternal clans, the Tran kings chose their brides from within their own extended families. They also understood the importance of not leaving the throne to a child, who could be easily manipulated. Moreover, Tran kings began the practice of abdicating to serve as "senior kings" once their predecessor died, thus allowing the next generation to establish itself at court.

Ruins from the Champa Kingdom. Champa was Vietnam's historic enemy. In the fifteenth century Vietnam finally demolished the Champa kingdom. (Corel)

The second Tran policy shift had to do with both political and economic centralization. Whereas Ly kings had allowed powerful outside families to hold large farms near the capital, Tran leaders used their influence to become the dominant landowning group in the Red River plain. This dismantled the influence of rival clans in the area and bolstered the annual income of Tran lords.

Finally, Tran kings understood that one failing of the Ly dynasty was an inadequate bureaucracy. To bolster the recruitment of the finest candidates for government service, they instituted the examination system, which was modeled after the millennium-old Chinese system. Candidates were tested on their knowledge of Chinese classical literature. Among other things, this literature emphasized the cultivation of morality and virtue through right action and proper ritual activity. What emerged from this was an elite scholarly class that would transcend the ebb and flow of dynasties and would, in fact, be the moral guiding force for the rank and file.

The Tran kings faced two major external crises. The first bolstered the Vietnamese confidence in their ability to remain a free people, and the second crisis brought such chaos that not only did the Tran dynasty come crashing down, but China also reasserted its suzerainty over its old southern province.

During the thirteenth century Vietnam faced a formidable external threat. The Mongols, once a disparate group of nomadic clans north of China, had united under Genghis Khan. Under the leadership of Kublai Khan, the grandson of the great Mongol unifier, the Mongols successfully conquered China and established the Yuan dynasty (1276–1368). Turning his attention farther south, Kublai demanded that the Vietnamese acknowledge Mongol hegemony over their land. Rather than agreeing to this, the Tran court ordered histories to be written that demonstrated that Vietnamese kings had political authority and precedent to reject any type of outside rule. Mongol forces responded by invading Vietnamese territory in 1257, 1284, and 1287. Mongol soldiers captured an abandoned Thang Long, but they found out what twentieth-century French and American soldiers later learned, that is, holding Vietnamese territory does not necessarily mean victory.

Wracked with disease, thin supply lines, and a scorched earth policy that further alienated the Vietnamese population, the Mongols withdrew after their first two invasions. Their final push for Vietnam included an army of 300,000 with a naval flotilla of over four hundred ships. Borrowing the tactics of Ngo Quyen, General Tran Hung Dao ordered iron-tipped stakes placed in the bed of the Bach-dang River—stakes that would be just below the water surface during high tide. Lured into the mouth of the river by Vietnamese decoys, the Mongol navy found itself stuck when the tide went out, and it was destroyed. This victory added to the indigenous legends of Vietnamese triumph over any and every foreign invader.

Unfortunately for the Tran kings, these would be the last great victories they would experience. One century later the Tran dynasty faced a second external enemy—the Chams to the south. Weak Tran kings did not successfully repel their southern enemies, and in 1371 Cham invaders looted Thang Long. Responding to the chaos, the Vietnamese general Ho Quy Ly placed himself on the throne and proclaimed the end of the Tran dynasty and the birth of the Ho dynasty (1400–1407).

This short-lived dynasty was doomed at the outset due to Ho's alienation of the feudal lords. He limited the amount of land an individual could own and also issued decrees in Vietnamese rather than Chinese, which demonstrated his indigenous preferences over and against the Vietnamese scholarly elite, who preferred official communication in the Chinese script. Scholars and feudal lords asked China to intervene and overthrow the Ho dynasty.

At the beginning of the fifteenth century, China was a good friend to have. Four decades earlier, in 1368, the Mongol dynasty had been torn down, and China entered into its final indigenous dynasty, the Ming (1368–1644). By 1400 Ming China was in full bloom. It responded to the southern chaos and requests from the Vietnamese elite and once again incorporated Vietnam into China's empire.

For twenty years Ming governors administered Vietnam as if the country was a province of China. The Vietnamese leadership who requested China's aid quickly found out that they had jumped from the wok into the fire. Ming administration of Vietnam was harsh. Many Chinese came to the area with the intention of economically exploiting the Vietnamese and then returning north to enjoy Ming China's cultural sophistication. Vietnamese were forced to pay taxes on all products, and corvée labor added to the humiliation of outside rule. Even local customs were disrupted by Chinese rule. Hair and clothing styles had to conform to Chinese patterns. Chewing betel nut, a common practice in Vietnam, was forbidden. Despite China's attempts to influence all of Vietnamese life, the only class of people thoroughly affected by Ming China rule was the Vietnamese scholars. The majority of the population continued to teach their children the local language, culture, and folklore. For all of their pomp, the Chinese effect on Vietnam during this twenty-year period did not successfully alter the Vietnamese worldview. When the foreign Ming politicians and soldiers were defeated in 1428, the Vietnamese settled down to once again enjoy indigenous rule.

THE LE DYNASTY

Vietnam does not lack heroes because, among other things, every time a foreign power invaded Vietnam, a new opportunity for a revolutionary figure emerged. In the early fifteenth century Le Loi (1385–1433) was added to the pantheon of Vietnamese heroes due to his revolutionary action against the occupying Chinese forces. A scholar-official from a wealthy landowning family, Le Loi served his constituents until the oppressive nature of Ming China's rule in his country became unbearable. Exploited and angry Vietnamese flocked to Le Loi's growing band of anti-Chinese revolutionaries, and in 1428 they successfully defeated the Ming army. Anxious to demonstrate his benevolent nature, Le Loi returned the surviving Ming officials and soldiers to China with the hope that peaceful relations between Vietnam and its northern neighbor would replace the past two decades of acrimonious interaction.

Confucian ideals were ingrained in Vietnam by this time, so it was natural, if not necessary, for Le Loi to demonstrate that heaven had given him the mandate to rule. Taking the name Le Thai To, he established the Le dynasty (1428–1788). Although the first decades of the Le dynasty demonstrated an increased stability throughout Vietnam, it was the fourth emperor of the Le dynasty, Le Thanh Tong (1441–1497, r. 1460–1497), who has the distinction of bringing numerous positive changes to Vietnam.

Ascending to the throne at nineteen years of age, Le Thanh Tong reorganized the bureaucratic structure under the rubric of six ministries (Rites, War, Justice, Interior, Public Works, and Finance). A thorough census of land and people was ordered to facilitate proper taxation and relief for the landless. Dynamic expansion of Vietnam's territory necessitated that a new census be taken every six years to include new lands for taxation. Le Thanh Tong addressed the chronic problem of landless farmers eking out a miserable existence as he encouraged the building and maintenance of dike and irrigation systems on virgin soil so the poor could find relief from exorbitant tenant rates. A larger military also facilitated continued expansion south and the destruction in 1470 of Vietnam's old rival—the Champa empire. Le Thanh Tong created *don dien,* military stations in the south to expedite the flow of the landless northern populace into the southern region. These military stations were turned into villages after political stability in the area was assured, and then the soldiers would move on and create new frontier posts.

Another legacy from the Le dynasty's fourth emperor was his promulgation of a penal code, The Hong Duc Code (1483). This code sought to systematize civil and criminal laws throughout Vietnam. Although there are obvious Confucian overtones in its 721 articles, there is also a distinct Vietnamese flavor to it. In particular, the code demanded that women possess property rights and enjoy equal inheritance laws with their male counterparts. Women were also given the right to divorce their husbands. Such laws demonstrated a higher view of women by Vietnamese against the more male-centered patterns expressed in Chinese society.

The three decades following Le Thanh Tong's death witnessed ten different rulers ascending to the throne. The weakness at the political center created opportunities for powerful families to manipulate the throne. From 1517 to 1527 Mac Dang Dung (r. 1527–1530) dominated the Le emperors, and finally in 1527 he seized the throne and proclaimed the establishment of the Mac dynasty (1527–1592). Two powerful aristocratic families, the Trinhs and the Nguyens, would not be party to this coup and remained loyal to the Le family.

Related in marriage to the Le emperor, Nguyen Kim (1467–1545) attacked the Mac forces and settled the Le emperor in Thanh Hoa province. By the time of his death, all of southern Vietnam remained in the hands of the Le emperor, who became more of a figure that the Nguyen family could rule through. Nguyen Hoang, a son of Kim, allied with his brother-in-law, Trinh Kiem, and together they ousted the Mac pretenders in 1592. Rivalry between the Trinh and Nguyen clans eventually led to a division in Vietnam, with the Nguyens in control of southern Vietnam and the Trinhs ruling north of Thanh Hoa province. Paradoxically, both families claimed to be supporters of the Le emperor. Vietnam's seventeenth century was characterized by incessant civil war between these two families.

On paper, the Trinh appeared to be more formidable than the Nguyen. With an army of 100,000 troops, 500 elephants, and 500 large junks, the Trinh greatly outnumbered its southern rival. In addition, the north had a much longer legacy of governance and more sophisticated agricultural development. Yet the Nguyen held their own in this civil war due to three factors. First, the local population was eager to defend its lands. Much like the South in the U.S. Civil War, the southerners fought tenaciously to hold on to their institutions and lands. Second, the vast open lands in the Mekong Delta that the Vietnamese had gained in their war with Champa was fertile soil for farming. This land attracted a range of characters including over 3,000 Chinese who fled from the new Manchu-led Qing dynasty (1644–1912) in China. Finally, the Nguyen, though inferior to the Trinh in numbers, were superior to its northern enemy in terms of weapon sophistication. This is because the Europeans more readily aided the Nguyen in this civil war. After two major battles in 1661 and 1672, the Trinh and Nguyen families settled down to a hundred-year truce. Emerging from this truce would be Vietnam's last dynasty. But before we get to this, it is helpful to understand the context of European intrusion into Asia and Vietnam.

Europeans had visited Vietnam during the days of the Roman empire, but a millennium passed before steady interaction took place between the two regions. A renewed interest in the East was one by-product of the Christian crusades. Although European Christians did not enjoy great military success during their holy wars, they were introduced to new spices: specifically, nutmeg, clove, and mace. These spices from the small islands in modern-day Indonesia made their way to Christian lands through trade in Constantinople, Baghdad, and Alexandria. Up until 1453, the Christians received these spices mainly through the markets of Constantinople. However, in that year the city fell to the growing Islamic empire, and the Moslems now had a monopoly on the precious spice commodity. Rather than acquiescing to this onerous trading situation, the Portuguese began exploring the western coast of Africa in search of a passage to the spice islands, or to lands where spices could be bought from non-Moslem traders. In 1498 Vasco da Gama reached the southern tip of Africa. Ten years later the Portuguese were on the west coast of India, where they established two colonies, Goa and Cochin. In 1511 the Portuguese captured Malacca, an important trading fort on the southern tip of the Malay Peninsula. Because Malacca controlled the traffic through the Malacca straits, the Portuguese thanked God and their guns for the new land that was theirs. They immediately began to move north to China, Japan, and Vietnam.

Antonio Da Faira was the first European to attempt a permanent settlement in Vietnam when he made Faifo (Hoi An) his headquarters for trade in 1535. The port town, fifteen miles south of Da Nang, housed merchants from Holland, China, and Japan. He had hoped that Faifo would take on the same importance as Malacca or Goa, but Faifo never lived up to the dreams of Da Faira.

It is said that there were three motives for European explorers to come to Asia: God, glory, and gold. To be sure there was money to be made in spice trading, and many merchants gambled that a little inconvenience would land them a future full of wealth and titles. By 1680 the Portuguese, Dutch, English, and the late-arriving French all had set up shop in Vietnam's port town of Pho Hien with the intention of using this as a base for trade in East Asia. The Vietnamese, however fragmented, were even more wary of Europeans than they were of each other. Inhospitable Vietnamese and nascent wars in Europe convinced these merchants that there was little to be gained in Vietnam, and by 1700 European traders abandoned the country.

Although gold and glory did not come to the seventeenth-century Europeans in Vietnam, Catholic missionaries enjoyed success in the conversion of tens of thousands to the Christian faith. Next to the Philippines, Vietnam became the most Christianized nation in Asia between the seventeenth and twentieth centuries. Of the earliest missionaries in Vietnam, the best known is Alexander de Rhodes (1591–1660). Rhodes was born in the southern

French town of Avignon and joined the Society of Jesus as a young man. As a Jesuit priest, he was sent to Thang-long in 1627. Of Rhodes's many gifts, his linguistic abilities stand out. After six months in Vietnam he was able to preach in the local language and eventually mastered Chinese, Japanese, Hindustani, and Persian. With the help of various colleagues, he created *quoc ngu*—a romanized system of writing the Vietnamese language. He wrote the first catechism in quoc ngu, and later published a Vietnamese-Latin-Portuguese dictionary. In the court of the northern Trinh lords, Rhodes baptized over six thousand converts, but his success might have been his undoing in Vietnam. Confucian scholars convinced the Trinh lords that the Christian message was subverting society and threatening the moral norm of polygamy in Vietnam. Rhodes was expelled from northern Vietnam in 1630 and moved to the Nguyen-controlled portion in the south. He was not welcome in this region and was forced to settle on the Portuguese island of Macao near the southern China port of Canton. Rhodes's life-long dream was the mass conversion of Vietnamese to the Christian message. He believed the answer would be a seminary where indigenous men could train for the priesthood. He repeatedly returned to Vietnam at the risk of his life. In 1645 he was caught and sentenced to death. He spent three weeks in prison and was released—though several of his companions lost their lives. Rhodes was so frustrated by the Catholic Church's lack of progress in Vietnam that he visited the Vatican and sought to replace the declining Portuguese influence in the area. Rebuffed by church authorities, Rhodes returned to France and lobbied for greater French commercial and religious action in Vietnam. Although he was not successful, the idea of Vietnam being a rich jewel in the French crown was kept alive. Rhodes died in 1660 while on a mission to Persia.

THE TAY SON REBELLION

During the eighteenth century Vietnam was plagued by economic and social difficulties. Despite the century-long truce between the Trinh and Nguyen families, conditions for the poor worsened during this period. Taxation, already a major burden on the poor, increased during the Le dynasty. Both of the dominant families sought an upper hand in the country and had to support their armies through heavy taxation. New taxes on commercial activities targeted the nonagrarian segment of the population. The scholar-official class was the only group spared the crippling tax increases because scholars could own property without paying taxes on it. In fact, during the eighteenth century, officials increased their land holdings as they bought out small farms from a population that could not afford to pay revenue. As the tax-free lands grew, the greater share of the duty fell to the peasants. Irrigation and other waterworks fell into disrepair, resulting in massive flooding and famine.

Economic pressures led to numerous local revolts between 1730 and 1770. These uprisings were usually spontaneous, localized, and centered on economic issues rather than an idea of creating a new dynasty. In 1771, however, three brothers raised their standard against the existing power structure. Their local rebellion spread over the entire state and eventually brought about the fall of the Le dynasty.

The Tay Son rebellion began in modern-day Nghia Binh province in 1771. Three brothers, reportedly aggrieved by accusations leveled at their family, rebelled against continued inept governing by the southern Nguyen lords. Their battle cries included the need for social justice and the redistribution of land to poor farmers. They stormed Saigon and killed all the Nguyen family members they could find. In addition, they went after the Chinese merchants in the area. It is estimated that more than ten thousand Chinese were murdered. This was because of their association with the Nguyen lords and the reported exploitation in which the Chinese merchants were engaged. Individuals from all walks of life joined the revolution. Food was taken from storage bins and distributed to the poor. Taxes were reduced or abolished, and the Tay Son brothers granted protection for Catholic priests. By 1778, the Tay Son rebels controlled southern Vietnam. They continued to support the Le emperor, but they also had their eyes on northern Vietnam. By 1786 they had overthrown the Trinh family, and the Tay Son brothers installed themselves as kings of northern, central, and southern Vietnam— all the while claiming that the Le emperor was their final authority. Eventually, the Le emperor grew tired of his puppet status and fled to China, whereupon the Qing court decided to send an army to reestablish the Le dynasty.

One fatal mistake the Tay Son rebels made in the south was that they did not completely eliminate the Nguyen family. Nguyen Anh (1761–1820), the nephew of the Nguyen lord who had been killed by the Tay Son rebels, escaped to the Mekong Delta where he rallied the retreating Nguyen forces and planned a counterattack. Control of Saigon changed hands several times during the 1770s. Finally in 1773 Nguyen Anh's navy was destroyed and once again the Tay Son contingent governed southern Vietnam. Meanwhile Nguyen Anh and his army were in full retreat. Their eventual destination of refuge changed the course of world history.

Nguyen Anh and his army fled to Phu Quoc in 1783. This Siam Gulf island was also the locale of the Catholic Church's seminary. The title "seminary" might conjure wrong images, because in truth the school was a group of wobbly structures where about forty Chinese, Vietnamese, and Thai men trained for the ministry. The leader of the seminary was Pigneau de Béhaine (1744–1798), a French priest who was instrumental in bringing France and Vietnam closer together. The eldest of nineteen children, Pigneau left the humble home of a tanner and dedicated himself, against his father's wishes, to the priesthood. At the age of twenty-four he was sent to the Siam Gulf seminary as a missionary for the French Society of Foreign Missions. In 1768, two years into his work at the seminary, he was forced to relocate to Malacca due to severe persecution. Recognizing his hard work, Pope Clement XIV assigned Pigneau to India and gave him the title Bishop of Adran. This ancient Middle Eastern city fell to the Turks during the crusades. Perhaps more symbolic than real, Pigneau could not receive a bishopric in the Far East because of the established Portuguese ecclesiastical monopoly in the region. However, the Frenchman's heart was in Vietnam, and in 1775 he returned to

Phu Quoc to take up his teaching duties. Within this context, Nguyen Anh, fleeing for his life in 1783, parlayed an agreement with Pigneau wherein the bishop would act as Nguyen Anh's emissary to the court of Louis XVI. As security, Nguyen Anh allowed his five-year-old son, Prince Canh, to travel to France with the cleric.

Pigneau believed an opportunity for religious freedom in Vietnam would accompany Nguyen Anh's victory over his rivals, so he sailed to the French citadel of Pondicherry on the east coast of India. Unable to garner support for his project in India, Pigneau next traveled to Paris with Prince Canh and laid out the project to the French monarch. In exchange for military support, Nguyen Anh promised Pigneau that he would cede the island of Poulo Condore and part of the strategic Tourane (Da Nang) port to France. Louis XVI hesitantly agreed to aid Nguyen Anh and sent Pigneau back to Vietnam via Pondicherry, where he was to pick up the needed military supplies. It was a ruse. Once at Pondicherry, Pigneau found that there would be no French government support for Vietnam. Undeterred, Pigneau raised private funds for two ships and ammunition, and he hired French deserters and other mercenaries to fight for Nguyen Anh. In 1789 the two ships with Pigneau and the now-Christian Prince Canh returned to Vietnam and assisted Nguyen Anh in his battles against the Tay Son brothers.

Pigneau, who died of dysentery in 1799, did not live to see Nguyen Anh's victory over the Tay Son government. Following his triumph, Nguyen Anh established Vietnam's last imperial dynasty, the Nguyen dynasty (1802–1954). It was in June 1802, after consolidating north and south Vietnam, that Nguyen Anh took the very symbolic reign name of Gia Long. Gia was taken from the southern city Gia Dinh (Saigon), and Long was from Thang-long (Hanoi) in the north. For the first time in Vietnam's history one court would rule the area from the Chinese border to the Gulf of Siam. In his tribute to China, Gia Long presented his country not as Dai Viet but as Nam Viet. For the Qing court, the name Nam Viet conjured bad memories of General Trieu Da, and so it reversed the name and recognized its southern neighbor as Viet Nam.

An incredible opportunity lay before Gia Long, but there were also ominous storm clouds looming over all of Asia. At the turn of the nineteenth century Qing China was past its prime. To be sure, China still commanded regional and global respect, but the world was changing, and soon the balance of power between the East and West would shift in favor of the West. Reasons for this shift included the advance in western technological sophistication, especially the use of steam to drive engines; the growth of western free markets and capitalism; and all the innovations blossoming in the Western Industrial Revolution.

Vietnam, like the rest of Asia, was aware of these newfangled machines, but at the turn of the nineteenth century the myopic and xenophobic nature of Asian governments did not allow them to foresee the implications of these changes. Indeed, in 1800 East Asia continued to enjoy a large surplus in trade with the West— mainly due to tea and silk. Foreign devils or barbarians, the terms Vietnamese and Chinese used in referring to westerners, were oddities and at times curious—if not laughable—objects, but they were considered irrelevant. With this attitude, Gia Long set about to organize his state following the Qing model. It was a recipe for disaster.

To a greater degree than any of his predecessors, Gia Long attempted to implement the Confucian ideology and the Chinese bureaucratic system to Vietnam's political and social life. Vietnam closed in on itself just as Qing China had done. Regional and international commerce were discouraged because the Confucian worldview looked at merchants with suspicion. Gia Long established his capital at Hue and, like the Qing emperors in Peking, resided in a newly built forbidden city where he would be removed from the people. Laws protecting the rights and properties of women were reversed, and an onerous duty of corvée labor—sixty days a year—was placed on the farmers. Tax levels rose to the level of the pre-Tay Son era. In 1807 the civil service exam was reinstated, and the scholarly mandarin class was ordered to wear Chinese robes to show its scholarly distinction.

Although Gia Long remained thankful to Pigneau for his earlier support and demonstrated his gratitude by providing the French priest with an elaborate funeral, the emperor never forgave Pigneau for his work in converting Prince Canh (who died in 1801). Gia Long did not trust religion—whether Buddhism, Daoism, or Christianity. He especially feared Christianity because of its association with the French. Thus, his choice for a successor was not Prince Canh's eldest son; rather, Gia Long chose Minh Mang, one of his sons from a concubine, because he knew this son embraced the isolation policy on which the Nguyen dynasty was founded. Gia Long's decision was also based on the fact that there were numerous troubles throughout Vietnam. The golden age Gia Long had hoped for never came to fruition in Vietnam. During his tenure as emperor there were 105 peasant-led uprisings against the Hue-based court; all the while, Christianity continued to spread throughout Vietnam.

Minh Mang (r. 1820–1841) was about thirty years old when he succeeded his father to the throne. He understood the crises Vietnam faced and did his best to plug the nascent political and economic leaks that would eventually destroy the Nguyen dynasty. Irrigation projects were instituted to relieve the distress most farmers experienced due to heavy taxes and a self-absorbed imperial court. Minh Mang did not tolerate the propagation of the Christian faith. He outlawed this foreign religion, though this edict was not strictly enforced. In foreign affairs, he surprisingly encouraged the growth of commerce, and extended Vietnam's influence in neighboring Cambodia. Xenophobic to the core, Minh Mang continued to ignore the need for a foreign affairs department in the government.

Among western observers, Minh Mang's anti-Christian laws signaled a dangerous future for European-Vietnamese relations. Not only did the second Nguyen emperor outlaw Christianity, in 1825 he also made it illegal for a foreign priest to visit Vietnam. His anti-Christian laws were ill-timed. An increasing number of French diplomats, merchants, and navy personnel were moving into Vietnam, and in France a religious revival was underway as a response to the earlier secular revolution and the Napoleonic wars. During Minh Mang's reign the French Sociétés Missions Etrangerés reported that there were close to half a million Catholic Vietnamese. Entire communities and villages in Vietnam had become Christian as they received support from the church and freedom from the yoke of a Confucian ideology that discouraged social change. In his final years, Minh Mang sent two mandarin scholars to France to negotiate an agreement with the European state. Bolstered by a more militant Catholic Church that was growing closer to a French navy anxious to increase its position in Asia, the French government refused to meet with Minh Mang's ambassadors. An important diplomatic opportunity was lost. Minh Mang died in 1841 knowing that trouble with France was in store for future Nguyen leaders.

Thieu Tri (1810–1847, r. 1841–1847) could not have chosen a worse time to take the reigns of power in Vietnam. It was during 1841 that Asia was rudely awakened to the fact that it was helpless against the West's weaponry and imperialistic advances. It is true that parts of Asia, the Philippines and India in particular, had earlier been incorporated into the Spanish and English empires. Yet Asians confidently pointed to the grandeur of China, the Middle Kingdom, as proof of the status quo in their world. Britain's smashing victory over China in the 1841 Opium War demythologized the invincibility of Asia in general and China in particular. On the heels of its victory, Britain forced China to pay twenty-one million ounces of silver (a portion of this money was to pay for the British opium that the Chinese had destroyed). China also was forced to open five ports on its eastern seaboard to trade, revise its mode of trade, and finally the Qing government had to cede the island of Hong Kong to her majesty's government. American, French, and other western powers enjoyed the fruits of Britain's victory with a laissez faire economic philosophy in these new open ports. Gone was the time when government-sponsored East India companies enjoyed a monopoly of trade in Asia. Capitalism was the word of the day, and the race was on to find markets and raw materials. Certain monopolies could be secured by creating colonies and protectorates over other states, and western powers jostled for colonies throughout the world. France, feeling that it was a latecomer to the collecting colonies game, believed that Vietnam would serve as a perfect base for economic ventures in East and Southeast Asia. Immediately following the Opium War, a permanent French naval squadron was stationed in the South China Sea.

Aware of China's humiliating defeat, Thieu Tri was guardedly optimistic that he could learn from the West. Yet, Vietnam was shackled by an ideology that was xenophobic and inward looking. France, in contrast, was more than cautiously optimistic about its economic and religious prospects in Vietnam. In 1843 the French navy received tacit approval to intervene in Vietnam to recover imprisoned missionaries. The navy took this carte blanche order to bully its way into Vietnam's internal affairs. One example of its action is seen in the port of Tourane (Da Nang). In 1847 two French warships bombarded the Da Nang shoreline, killing a good number on shore as well as destroying five Vietnamese ships. Its justification for this action was to gain the release of a priest who had actually been set free several weeks before. Thieu Tri railed against the French following this bombardment, but there was little he could do. He died within a few weeks of this incident.

At mid-nineteenth century Vietnam needed a visionary leader to handle the global changes and domestic crises the country faced. This is what Vietnam needed, but what it got was a pessimistic, sickly, fatalistic emperor—Tu Duc (r. 1847–1883)—the last emperor of a free Vietnam. In fact, Tu Duc ascended to the throne through court intrigue. The rightful heir to the throne, his older brother Hong Bao, was a victim of political plotting that denied him his deserved position. Tu Duc inaugurated his reign with stepped-up persecutions of Catholic priests and the church's laity. Unlike his father, Tu Duc did not act cautiously with regard to the French. He commanded that all Vietnamese Christians be branded on the cheek with the characters *ta dao,* or infidel. He ordered foreign priests to be drowned and indigenous clerics be sawed in half lengthwise. Yet, his antiforeign policies did not change the perception most of his subjects had of him. He was unpopular and he knew it.

Tu Duc's religious persecution was publicized in France, and pressure was put on Louis Napoleon, who proclaimed himself Emperor Napoleon III in 1852, to take military action. With a Spanish Catholic wife, Eugenia, Napoleon III saw only advantages in attacking Vietnam. He would receive support from the Catholic Church, and France's naval officers, diplomats, and merchants would boast that France was in the thick of the imperialistic game. In 1858 French troops captured Da Nang and the following year Gia Dinh. French invaders expected a swell of support from the Vietnamese Christians, but this did not happen. Rather, beset by cholera, typhoid, stiff local resistance, and dwindling supplies, the French withdrew from Da Nang while they clung to portions of Gia Dinh. France responded to these setbacks in 1861 by sending seventy ships and 3,500 men to reinforce their comrades in Gia Dinh. Bloody battles around the area of Gia Dinh placed the French in control there. In June 1862 Tu Duc signed the Treaty of Saigon.

Observers were shocked at the generous terms the French received in this treaty: Gia Dinh and its surrounding three provinces were ceded outright to France, French warships were entitled to free passage up the Mekong River to Cambodia, three ports were open to trade, missionary activity was legalized, and Vietnam paid a handsome indemnity for losing the war.

In retrospect, there are three important reasons for Tu Duc's capitulation to the French. First, the southern region of Vietnam was still perceived as the frontier by the Vietnamese. For example, of the 1,024,338 male taxpayers in the official 1847 census, only 165,598 lived in its southern provinces. Also, only one of the fifty-six men who earned the doctorate degree in the imperial exam system between 1822–1840 was from the south. Second, Tu Duc was an unpopular emperor. Internal rebellion led by his older brother shook the court's stability and added to Tu Duc's pessimism and paranoia. The court was afraid to call for all-out support against the French because it was possible that the people would not answer the call from the detested emperor. Finally, Tu Duc faced greater problems in northern Vietnam, where a Christian-led rebellion threatened the stability of this vital region. He needed to have troops and to give his full attention to the north and so quickly made peace with the French in the south.

Tu Duc's gamble paid off as he brutally crushed the rebellion in the north, killing thousands of Christians in the process. He renegotiated with the French, and in exchange for returning the three southern provinces to Vietnam, Tu Duc allowed the French to claim a protectorate status over the six provinces that made up Cochin China. The French then pushed their way up the Mekong River, and in 1863 the Cambodian king was also forced to accept a French protectorate over his country. Siam, Cambodia's neighbor to the west, accepted this new political situation because the French ceded two western Cambodian provinces to Siam.

France was not satisfied with its position in Asia. Herbert Spencer's doctrine of social evolution spread like wildfire through Europe, and the French believed that they had a mission to civilize the Vietnamese. Although this was the dominant rhetoric to justify imperialism in Vietnam, an undeniable motive for France's deeper claws in the Asian country was the belief that Vietnam would serve as a stepping-stone to a more lucrative relationship with China. Thus, in June 1866 a party set out from Saigon to discover whether the Mekong River would facilitate trade in and out of southern China. France's Garnier was part of this two-year expedition, and his two-volume *Voyage d'Exploration* beautifully illustrated the amazing scenes along the Mekong River. Although the explorers concluded that the Mekong could not be traversed by boat into China, Garnier believed that trade could be conducted between China and Vietnam via the Red River. He mapped out a Red River route that ran from China's southern Yunan Province to Vietnam's port of Haiphong.

French intrusion in the Tonkin area, including Garnier's storming of Hanoi in 1873, forced Tu Duc to sign yet another treaty with France in which he recognized France's sovereignty, rather than the previously agreed-to protectorate status, over

Cochin China. He opened the Red River to French traders. Anxious to push through the implications of this treaty, Garnier set out to remove any obstruction between Hanoi and the port towns. However, the increased French trade in the mountainous region that separated China and Vietnam led to local resistance. Chinese soldiers fleeing the turmoil in their own civil war, the Taiping Rebellion, at times aided the disgruntled Vietnamese. In 1873, as Garnier made his way to the coast, they killed him. Garnier's head was placed on a pole and paraded throughout the surrounding villages.

Nine years later, the French once again tried to create stability in the Tonkin area; this time they were led by Henri Riviere and six hundred troops. He met the same fate as Garnier. The difference this time, however, was that when France heard that Riviere's head was carried from one village to another as a trophy, popular outrage led the government to forcefully teach the Vietnamese a lesson. French forces attacked Hue itself. Gravely ill during 1883, Tu Duc died in July of that year with French guns closing in on Hue. Probably sterile, Tu Duc did not have children, and debate raged at court as to a successor as well as how to deal with the French. Within a year of Tu Duc's death three emperors were enthroned and deposed, further destabilizing the shaky imperial court. Meanwhile, France would not wait for imperial political stability at Hue and were delighted with the internal chaos. The court was forced to sign a treaty in August 1883, one month after Tu Duc's death, wherein the Vietnamese recognized a French protectorate over Tonkin and Annam while Cochin China remained a part of the French empire. France would handle Vietnam's foreign relations, and the Vietnamese emperor would have limited power. One year later, in June 1884, the scholar officials recognized this humiliating situation and signed the Treaty of Protectorate, agreeing to French suzerainty over their lands. Once again all of Vietnam was in the hands of a foreign nation, only this time it was not with a contiguous northern neighbor; it was a nation across several oceans.

FRANCE RULES VIETNAM

During U.S. president William McKinley's tenure in office (1897–1901), Rudyard Kipling, the English proponent of western imperialism, addressed the poem, "White Man's Burden" to the American public. His purpose in doing this was to encourage the United States to colonize the Philippine Islands—a possession the United States had bought from Spain after the Spanish-American War. The poem's content demonstrated the prevailing views of many western nations. Various terms such as "benevolent assimilation" described the methods these imperialistic nations employed in their colonies. Colonial goals, policies, and administration differed based on a myriad of contingencies including geography, economic objectives, and the goodwill of the mother country. Some colonial masters were genuinely interested in the welfare of their colonial inhabitants while others dominated and exploited the countries they governed. In Vietnam, however, French policies were primarily self-serving, with an ultimate goal of profiting the mother country at the expense of the Vietnamese.

Despite the draconian French rule in Vietnam, it took the Vietnamese more than half a century and two world wars to throw out their colonial masters. Numerous factors made it difficult for the Vietnamese to unite against the French. The following pages briefly outline the obstacles that prevented the immediate ouster of the French from Vietnam.

First, not all Vietnamese opposed their European overlords at the outset of French rule. Many Vietnamese scholars believed, based on Confucian ideology, that Tu Duc and the family line of Gia Long had lost the mandate of heaven to rule. In the Confucian worldview, internal and external disasters often portend a dynastic change, and during the mid-nineteenth century Vietnam experienced pestilence, famine, floods, and a cholera epidemic in 1865 that took the lives of more than a million Vietnamese. Tu Duc could not prevent French incursions into Vietnam. The court leaned toward negotiating with the foreigners rather than fighting the more

This Catholic church at the base of a mountain in Vietnam is a reminder of the French influence in Vietnam. (Catherine Karnow/CORBIS)

powerful outsiders. Thus, during the reign of Tu Duc it was not filial for Vietnamese to oppose the increased aggression of the French because the court's policy was amelioration rather than confrontation. Perhaps if the Vietnamese could foresee what the French would do to their country there would have been greater resistance at the outset.

France set out to firmly take hold of its Asian possession, and, just as the British Colonial Office administered the Malaya Straits Settlement after 1867, the French in 1887 created the Indochinese Union (ICU). Cochin China was thus made a colony and Annam, Tonkin, and Cambodia were labeled as French protectorates, with Laos added to the ICU as a protectorate in 1893. For the French, it would be easier to administer this area if they could project a divided Vietnam. Hence they did not refer to the Vietnamese as such but rather as Cochin Chinese, Annamese, and Tonkinese. In Annam and Tonkin they replaced the emperor's adviser with a French resident superieur stationed at Hanoi, thus stripping the emperor's court of any power. France was not interested in allowing the Vietnamese to directly rule themselves in a modern type of state. They kept the existing bureaucratic system where the people's voice was not heard. Examinations for scholars continued until 1918, and the idea of a democracy was not immediately introduced to the Vietnamese. A telling statistic that illustrates the French stronghold on Vietnam is that in 1925 there were five thousand French bureaucrats in the ICU. At this same period there were fewer British administrators in India—a country whose population was more than 300 million, ten times larger than the ICU populace.

Paul Doumer (1897–1902), the governor-general of the ICU, and later the president of France, was typical of the French rulers in Asia. He believed that the colony should pay for itself—including the salaries of all the ICU French administrators. The state monopolized the sale and taxation of salt, alcohol, and opium. Moreover, land accumulation was the goal for the French in Cochin China. French colons (colonial settlers) were sold large tracts of land in the Mekong Delta where they set up plantations. A few Vietnamese elite families were also given generous terms for this delta land. By 1920, at least 90 percent of the rubber plantations in Vietnam were French owned and Vietnam was a major exporter of rice—something that had been forbidden by most Vietnamese emperors. High taxes, forced corvée labor, and French domination of the economy had devastating effects on Vietnamese farmers. By 1930, 57 percent of the rural population in Cochin China was landless, with almost two million more northern farmers in the same economic strait.

Throughout the first decades of French rule there were numerous petty revolts against the harsh conditions placed on the court and farmers. In July 1885, for example, Ton That Thuyet, the emperor's regent, raised a revolt against the resident superieur in Hanoi, took the boy emperor Ham-Nghi out of Hue, and called for a general uprising against the French. The so-called *can vuong* (aid the king) movement captured the support and interest of many Vietnamese even after the French had captured the emperor and exiled him to Algeria. These nineteenth-century uprisings might be properly termed pre-nationalistic in nature because those in revolt did not fight for a nation-state called Vietnam. As a new century dawned, however, so too did the spread of new ideas, and the Vietnamese nationalist movement was born.

VIETNAMESE NATIONALISM

The French did not emphasize education in Vietnam. There was in fact a diminution of literacy during their first decades of rule. By 1900 a generation had been raised in this colonial state with the strong foreign hand in firm grasp of Vietnam. Individuals were not permitted to leave their district without identification papers, and it was illegal to have an assembly or to publish without French approval. Vietnamese nationalism gave birth under these circumstances. A review of the lives of its two main leaders, Phan Boi Chau and Phan Chu Trinh, demonstrates the complexities, promises, and problems of Vietnam's early nationalist movements.

Phan Boi Chau (1867–1940) was born into a northern Vietnamese family of scholars. He was working his way up the examination ladder when in 1903 he founded the Restoration Society, with the intention of returning Cuong De, one of Prince Cahn's (the eldest son of Gia Long, who had accompanied Bishop Pigneau to France) descendents to the throne. In 1906 he brought the prince to Japan. This proved to be an inspiring time for an Asian to be in Japan because during the previous year Japan had fought the Russian empire and had crushed its Baltic fleet at the spectacular naval battle of Tsushima Straits. An Asian nation had stood up against a western empire. Japan also inspired other Asians because of its rapid transformation into a modern state. Indeed, in 1868 Japan had just emerged from a semifeudal state where for more than two and a half centuries the Tokugawa house had ruled as shoguns from Edo (Tokyo), while more than two hundred *daimyos* (military governors) ruled over semiautonomous *hans* (prefectures) throughout the land. By 1906, however, Japan boasted a modern

This statue in Hue, with its elegant nature and prestigious craftsmanship, is a reminder of the dominance that Hue once played in Vietnam's political life. The Nguyen emperors made Hue their home. (PhotoDisc, Inc.)

constitution with a two-house Diet, a prime minister, cabinet, and a state that between 1895–1905 had defeated both China and Russia. Japan served as an example of an Asian "first-class" nation. While in Japan, Phan Boi Chau organized more than one hundred Vietnamese students who were studying in that foreign land. Of great significance is the title of this organization, Viet Nam Cong Hien Hoi (Vietnam Public Offering Society); this title demonstrates that there was by this time a growing desire to achieve a united Vietnam state and an integrated Vietnamese people.

French pressure on Japan forced the exportation of Phan Boi Chau. He moved to southern China and again found himself inspired, this time by Dr. Sun Yat-sen, the leader of Chinese nationalism who was then in southern China working to overthrow the ancient imperial system based in Peking. There Phan Boi Chau abandoned his idea of restoring the monarchy and in 1912 transformed the Restoration Society into the Modernization Society. Although this society's objective was to create a modern indigenous government in Vietnam, Phan Boi Chau believed that sensational acts in Vietnam, such as terrorist bombings and assassinations, would spur Vietnamese expatriates to contribute money to the cause. It did not. What it did do was heighten French paranoia in the ICU. In 1916 the French exiled emperor Duy Tan (r. 1907–1916) to Reunion Island in the Indian Ocean. In 1925 Phan Boi Chau was captured by French agents in the international section of Shanghai, brought to Vietnam, and placed under house arrest until his death in 1940.

There were major differences between the two main icons of early Vietnamese nationalism. Phan Chu Trinh (1872–1926) was born in Quang Nam, which is further south than Phan Boi Chau's birthplace, and he came from a military family. Phan Chu Trinh pursued his interests in politics at a time when the social revolutionary writings of Rousseau and Montesquie were made available to the Vietnamese through Chinese translations. Also, the increased use of romanized Vietnamese in the Tonkin area provided a greater audience for the spread of new ideas. Unlike Phan Boi Chau, Phan Chu Trinh did not believe the answer for Vietnam was a monarchy restoration or even immediate French withdrawal. Rather, he believed that a bright future for the Vietnamese would be based on learning from the French and holding the French accountable to their civilizing mission, which meant that Vietnam would become a modern state mirroring its colonial mother. ICU bureaucrats considered Phan Chu Trinh's writings subversive and imprisoned him in 1908. He was later exiled to France but received permission to return to his homeland in 1925, where he died a year later. His funeral became a demonstration against the French and verified that by 1925 there was a nationalistic fervor in Vietnam.

These two patriots of Vietnamese nationalism were from central and northern Vietnam, where France held a protectorate status. Cochin China, in contrast, was a colony—directly ruled by France—and so residents there experienced a different degree of French control. As noted earlier, large portions of land were sold to French colons and to rich Vietnamese families. Manufacturing in Cochin China was minimal, mainly cement and textiles for domestic use, and the economy was in the hands of a few. During World War I, however, more than 100,000 Vietnamese were shipped to fight in Europe or work in the war effort, and while the war occupied the colonial mother's attention, many Vietnamese took this opportunity to fill in the vacuum of French interest in Vietnam. Bui Quang Chieu, a French-trained agricultural engineer who was part of the pro-French landed elite in Cochin China, founded the Constitutional Party in 1917. He did this with the hope that it would pressure the colonial council of Cochin China—the bureaucratic apparatus of Cochin China since 1880—to be more liberal in its policies. Specifically, the Constitution Party lobbied for greater representation on the council (of the twenty-two members, only six were Vietnamese); higher salaries for Vietnamese officials; a move away from the scholar-official form of domestic rule to a more modernized bureaucracy; reform of the naturalization law, which made it difficult for Vietnamese to become French citizens; and a crackdown on the growing Chinese domination of Cochin China's economy. The French, like the British in Malaya, gravitated to the Chinese population when it came to economic interests because the Chinese were less likely to fuss about independence. Furthermore, the overseas Chinese had a network of economic allies that allowed them to flourish wherever they were living. The council took some of these requests under advisement and raised the number of Vietnamese representatives on the council from six to ten.

The first two-and-a-half decades of the twentieth century witnessed an emergence of nationalism in Vietnam. Its early leaders' successes and failures would serve as guideposts for future revolutionaries. In particular, the failure of these early leaders to incorporate the farmers in their movements would be rectified in the future. One single leader did not emerge during this period that would eventually lead Vietnam to freedom. That missing individual was biding his time and was making ready his life to free his brothers and sisters. We know him as Ho Chi Minh.

THE VNQDD AND HO CHI MINH

"If we want the Vietnamese nation one day to achieve freedom and independence, then before all else the Vietnamese people must have community spirit and action. But if we want to have community spirit and actions, is there anything better than to preach socialism among the Vietnamese people?" (Steinberg 1987, 318). These words, penned by Phan Chau Trinh in 1925, express the rhetoric that Vietnamese revolutionaries were tossing around during this period. French officials tried to stop such talk through arrests and intimidation; yet, the more they suppressed the emerging nationalism, the faster it grew. Socialism was only one of the many ideologies expressed by Vietnamese nationalists, though the ultimate goal of each philosophy was national freedom. Likewise, the various nationalist organizations drew their inspiration from a wide range of countries. However, though China had undergone decades of humiliation since the 1841–1842 Opium War—including the worst civil war in human history; defeat at the hands of the British (1861), French (1887), and Japanese (1895); the debacle of the peasant-led 1900 Boxer Rebellion; and a fragmented country governed by regional warlords—China was still the nation Vietnamese turned to for a political paradigm. By the mid 1920s China's charismatic nationalist leader, Dr. Sun Yat-sen, had assembled a formidable army at Canton with the intention of sweeping north to unite China into a republic. His nationalist party, the Kuomintang (KMT), grew to the point that the communist Soviet Union ordered the newly organized Chinese Communist Party (CCP) to move south and join the KMT. Sun Yat-sen welcomed Soviet advisers and support but insisted that the CCP members shift their allegiance to the KMT. This they did, on order from Moscow, but they clandestinely remained communist ideologues hoping that their numbers would grow in the future.

On the eve of the KMT's northern expedition, Sun Yat-sen succumbed to cancer, and the party's mantle of leadership fell to its leading general, Chiang Kai-shek. The generalissimo did have spectacular success in uniting China. Once in control of the coun-

Ho Chi Minh is still revered as Vietnam's leader against imperialist powers. Here people are lined up to visit the Ho Chi Minh Mausoleum in Hanoi. (Bohemian Nomad Picturemakers/CORBIS)

try, he turned on former CCP members because of his hatred for communism and his doubt whether they had ever really renounced their deep-seated beliefs when they joined the KMT at Canton. In Shanghai, where the CCP was strongest, trains full of KMT soldiers entered the city in April 1927, and the subsequent "Shanghai Spring Purge" of CCP members resulted in the execution and imprisonment of numerous communists. Eventually, the communists were also pushed out of the southern provinces. In 1926–1927, led by Mao Zedong, the communists marched more than five thousand miles until they settled in Yanan in north-central China.

Vietnamese nationalist observers had varied interpretations of the KMT-CCP interaction. One group, led by Nguyen Thai Hoc, believed that the KMT paradigm was the answer for Vietnam, and so it chose the name Viet Nam Quoc Dan Dang (VNQDD, the Vietnamese Nationalist Party) for its organization. Its original members were from a book club in Hanoi, and they developed secret codes and elaborate oaths of loyalty. New recruits had to be vouched for by two members, and it myopically followed the Chinese KMT model. VNQDD membership came mainly from disgruntled soldiers in the north. In an effort to recruit southern and rural members, the VNQDD authorized the 1929 assassination of the French official Bazin, whose harsh tactics for recruiting labor for southern plantations were well known. This was a mistake. Not only did this act infuriate the French, it also demonstrated the lack of peasant support for the VNQDD as no uprising took place in the rural south. Following Bazin's assassination, hundreds of VNQDD members were arrested and killed. Nguyen Thai Hoc escaped the initial arrests and sought to regroup by stockpiling weapons and ordering an all-out rebellion against the French. This too failed, and the leaders of the VNQDD, including Nguyen Thai Hoc, were caught and sent to the guillotine.

An important implication of the VNQDD's failure is that it opened the door to organizations that sided with the CCP rather than Chiang Kai-shek's anticommunist party. Ho Chi Minh led the Vietnamese who followed the CCP model.

In professor William Duiker's definitive biography of Ho Chi Minh, he writes that "At the heart of the anti-French resistance movement was the central Vietnamese province of Nghe An. . . . The soil is thin in depth and weak in nutrients, and frequently the land is flooded by sea water. Perhaps that explains why the inhabitants of Nghe An have historically been known as the most obdurate and rebellious of Vietnamese" (2000, 14–15). It was in this province of Nghe An that in May 1890 a boy was born to a family of little means. They named him Nguyen Sin Cung but changed his name to Nguyen Tat Thanh (He who will succeed) when the boy turned eleven. Early on, Thanh's propensity was to study rather than play. He was educated at the national academy in Hue and became a teacher, though larger goals brought him to Saigon, where in 1911 he took a job as a cook's assistant on a French ship. He traveled to North America, Africa, and Europe. After spending some time in London, he moved to Paris, where he took the name of Nguyen Ai Quoc (Nguyen the patriot). He was drawn to the writings of Marx and Lenin and in 1919 attempted to meet with U.S. president Woodrow Wilson at the Versailles Peace Conference. Wilson's Fourteen-Point Program, which included national self-determination, coincided with Quoc's hopes for a free Vietnam. Wilson did not meet with the Vietnamese patriot, and one of the many failures of the Versailles Conference was the lost opportunity to address the exploitation that Vietnamese experienced at the hands of its colonial mother.

Quoc was influenced by Lenin's 1920 "Thesis on the National and Colonial Questions." In that same year Quoc became a founding member of the French Communist Party (FCP). Three years later he moved to Moscow, where he attended the Fifth International Communist (Comintern) Congress. Then in 1924 he moved to Canton, where Sun Yat-sen was organizing China's nationalist party. While in Canton, he trained two hundred Vietnamese and provided a guide for revolutionary techniques that would fit Vietnam's political and social situation. This group became the Vietnamese Revolutionary Youth League, and it began a Vietnamese revolutionary newspaper, *Thanh Nien* (Youth). Following Chiang Kai-shek's Shanghai Spring Purge, Quac moved back to Moscow, where he renewed earlier contacts and continued his study of Marxism. Quoc also changed his name to Ho Chi Minh (He Who Enlightens).

Meanwhile in Vietnam, several communist organizations had been born and, in fact, were in competition with each other. The Comintern criticized these competing Vietnamese communist parties, and in 1930 each group was asked to send representatives to Hong Kong so a united party could emerge. Ho Chi Minh was asked to preside over the assembly. The result was the formation of a unified Indochina Communist Party (ICP). A Central Committee was formed with nine members: three from Tonkin, two from Annam, two from Cochin China, and two from the Vietnamese community in China. The transcending stated goals of the ICP were to remove France from Indochina and to create a government where exploitation of people would cease.

The ICP was born into a troubled world. World markets were

devastated by the global depression, and Vietnam was not spared economic hardship. French investors withdrew from Vietnam, the world market price for rice was slashed in half, and rubber exports in 1930 brought in one-fourth what they had in 1928. The rich made sure they survived the economic storm, while the farmers had to bring in the same amount of annual tax despite the bottom dropping out of the global economy. This meant farmers had to produce double the amount of rice they did prior to the depression just to pay their taxes and debts. Urban centers experienced upheaval as the incidence of strikes increased; in 1927, for example, there were seven strikes, whereas two years later there were 98 in a year's time.

Nghe An province, the noted hotspot for Vietnamese resistance, was hard hit by this economic predicament and was ripe for communist infiltration. Nghe An villages were turned into soviets, village taxes and debts were lowered, and farmers were given a voice in local council meetings. By September 1930, the French were aware that a potential disaster was brewing in Nghe An. They responded with a remarkable display of force and brutality. Foreign Legion soldiers broke up the budding soviets while French planes dropped bombs on civilian targets. Over one thousand ICP suspects were arrested, and hundreds were sent to prison to serve long sentences.

Ho Chi Minh, still in Hong Kong, was arrested by the British. He spent two years in prison and then in 1933 returned to the Soviet Union, where he spent the next years recovering physically and politically. While recuperating, Ho studied at Moscow's Lenin Institute, and his reputation grew inside and outside of Vietnam through his writings.

WORLD WAR II AND VIETNAM

World War II began on July 7, 1937. It is true that German troops did not march into Poland until September 1, 1939, and that U.S. military bases at Pearl Harbor, Hawaii, were not attacked by the Japanese until December 7, 1941, turning the war into a truly global conflict. But the seeds for the bombing of Pearl Harbor were planted on July 7, 1937, when Japanese troops moved from their stations in Manchuria and invaded China. Japan's anticipated quick victory over China proved illusory as Chiang Kai-shek and the KMT Army traded space for time and moved in to China's vast interior, using Chongqing in Sichuan Province as its headquarters. Japan was stuck in an Asian land war, and its enemy held on because of the supplies it received from so-called neutral countries via Burma and Vietnam. Thus it was that on September 23, 1940, Japanese troops moved into northern Vietnam with the tacit approval of the French. This was only possible because earlier in that month the former French government had fallen to the German-dominated Vichy government, and there was little the colonial bureaucrats could say or do to the advancing Japanese. This prompted Japan's Emperor Hirohito to note that Japan's incursions into north Vietnam were akin to stealing from a house that was on fire. The United States responded to the plight of the Vietnamese by placing a scrap metal embargo on the Japanese, warning the Japanese that they should not venture into Annam or Cochin China.

Ho Chi Minh rightly perceived that this might be an opportune time for the ICP to make headway in Vietnam. France was weakened by its war in Europe, and the United States seemed serious in its warnings to Japan. After being absent from Vietnam for thirty years, Ho returned to his country in February 1941 and took up residence in a cave at Pac Bo near the Sino-Vietnamese border. Several months later the Eighth Plenum of the ICP convened, which resulted in important decisions that would affect the history of Vietnam and its national struggle. It was agreed at the plenum that national freedom took precedent over ideological or class struggle and that the ICP would work with any organization that shared a vision of nationalism. Furthermore, the leaders agreed that guerrilla warfare, urban and rural personnel, and nonconventional warfare would be called upon to dislodge the French and Japanese from Vietnam. At the meeting, the League for the Independence of Vietnam (Viet Nam Doc Lap Dong Minh Hoi, or Vietminh for short) was established as the organization that would fight with all like-minded Vietnamese for national liberty.

Ho was right about the Japanese. They were not content to stay in Tonkin, and by July 1941 they occupied all of Vietnam. They continued to do this with the acquiescence of the Vichy government. Japan's interest in Vietnam was secondary. It did need some of the raw material Vietnam afforded, but this country was merely to be a springboard from which Japan would move further south into the oil-rich Dutch East Indies. Oil was key because in 1941 the United States supplied the Japanese with 85 percent of its oil. But as Japan moved into all of Vietnam, the United States placed an oil embargo on Japan as well as froze all Japanese assets in the United States. Inevitably this led to Japan's raid on Pearl Harbor.

From Vietnam, Japan preached its antiimperial doctrine of "Asia for Asians" with a promise that it would create a Greater East Asian Co-Prosperity Sphere where all Asians would be free under the protection of Japan. The Vietminh were not fooled. Behind Japan's rhetoric was perhaps something worse than European hegemony: Japan's domination of Asia. Although Vietnam was nominally still under French control, Vietminh operatives spread their message and influence wherever they could. They received a setback when Ho was captured by a Chinese general and imprisoned for two years (1942–1944), but they did not abandon their ultimate goal while they waited for the release of their leader.

Upon his release and return to northern Vietnam, Ho made contacts with United States personnel in the area to express his desire to work with them to defeat the Japanese. He also made it known that should the Japanese withdraw, France had lost its authority to rule over Vietnam. This was especially true after March 1945, when the Japanese declared the abolition of the 1885 Vietnam-French treaty and declared a fully independent Vietnam. Again, the Vietminh were not deceived. This independent Vietnam was in reality a country under the supposed leadership of Emperor Bao Dai, the reigning Nguyen emperor, but in truth

Japan ruled the country and the Nguyen emperor was its puppet. French bureaucrats and military personnel were swept away into prisons, and Japan took control of the country.

Vietnamese nationalists were opportunistic. They saw that Japan was straining to hold on to its Pacific possessions and that the noose was growing tighter around Japan's islands, which meant that a sick and dying imperialist power was losing its grip on Vietnam.

Allied powers met at Potsdam, Germany, in July 1945 to map out strategies following the war's end in Europe. Although Vietnam was a side issue on the Potsdam agenda, it was discussed. The resolution was that the British would accept the Japanese capitulation south of the sixteenth parallel, and China's KMT Army would take the Japanese surrender north of the sixteenth parallel. What was not known at the conference was that the war in the Pacific was about to come to an abrupt close through the use of nuclear weapons. The allied powers at Potsdam also failed to recognize how powerful the Vietminh had become in Indochina.

In early August the ICP met for its Ninth Plenum and, working in concert with the Vietminh, declared that preparations should be made for a general uprising. The timing was perfect, as close to half a million Vietnamese had died of starvation in recent months, and economic chaos ruled the country. Starvation and famine were the results of Japan's draconian laws that made Vietnamese farmers grow crops such as hemp to support the Japanese war effort. Rice that was grown was either given to the Japanese occupying forces or stored for the rich Vietnamese who collaborated with the Japanese. Vietminh soldiers began their campaign in earnest, entering villages and redistributing rice to the starving while speaking of a new dawn for a free Vietnam.

Following Japan's surrender in August 1945, the Vietminh filled the political vacuum throughout Vietnam; this is known in Vietnam as the August Revolution. On September 2, 1945, Ho Chi Minh declared the founding of the Democratic Republic of Vietnam (DRV). He began the declaration by quoting from the U.S. Declaration of Independence, which some took as a sign that he wished to work with the United States and certainly desired the United States to recognize the new country. There was reason to hope that this would happen. President Franklin Roosevelt had often stated that France was no longer welcome in Indochina and that the European nation had not helped the Indochina peoples.

The August Revolution had achieved mixed results. The northern area was completely under Vietminh control, and in central Vietnam, Bao Dai was forced to abdicate and move to Hanoi to act as an adviser in the DRV government. Cochin China was another story. Disparate groups filled the political vacuum in the area, including the two popular religious organizations, Cao Dai and Hoa Hao. Founded by Ngo Van Chieu in 1919, the Cao Dai "High Tower" was a syncretic religion based on the teachings of major world religions, and by the end of World War II it was the fastest growing religion in the south. Most of its followers were sympathetic to the French and supported their return to power. A young Buddhist mystic, Huynh Phu, who preached against idols and expensive ceremonies, established the Hoa Hao in 1939. Simplistic in its teachings, the Hoa Hao attracted many poor peasants to its cause, and following World War II they came to see the Vietminh as rivals rather than allies. More devastating for the Vietminh, however, were the British actions in Cochin China. Led by British General Douglas Gracey, the British entered the area and presumed that the French, once released from prison, would retake the reigns of power in Vietnam. The British proceeded to facilitate the French resumption of political power in southern Vietnam.

Meanwhile in the north, a Chinese army of almost 200,000 descended on Hanoi and absconded everything they could. Ho tried to cooperate with the KMT generals, but he understood that he would have to negotiate with the French to have any hope of Vietnam's immediate independence. Consequently, he invited the French back to northern Vietnam to replace the undisciplined Chinese army. In March 1946 the French and Ho came to an agreement. The French would recognize the DRV as an independent state and would agree to a future plebiscite in Cochin China; in

return the DRV would agree to be part of the proposed French
Union and would allow a small contingent of French soldiers in
northern Vietnam. Several months later Ho traveled to France to
work out the final details of this agreement. He was profoundly disappointed at the reception he received: He was shunted off to
Fontainbleau, where the French sent second-tier politicians to
speak to him. Despite Ho's protest that Cochin China was part of
Vietnam, he reluctantly signed an agreement that allowed the
French to remain in control of southern Vietnam while French
soldiers and merchants continued to hold special positions in the
DRV region.

Ho returned to Vietnam a discouraged man. The French meanwhile wanted to demonstrate to the Vietnamese that they still controlled sectors of Vietnam's land and economy. When Vietnamese
inspectors tried to verify shipments in northern ports, angry
French businessmen called for their nation's navy to enforce
France's position in the area. Meanwhile, French soldiers strolled
through Hanoi and Hue as if they continued to control the area.
It was just a matter of time until rows turned into bloody confrontations. That happened in November 1946, when French
ships bombarded the Vietnamese section of the port city of
Haiphong. Weeks later the entire northern area was in chaos, and
the first Indochina War (1946–1954) broke out.

THE FIRST INDOCHINA WAR

Because of superior weaponry, the French quickly recaptured
the urban areas in Vietnam following the bombing of Haiphong.
Yet, the People's Army of Vietnam believed that its tactics would
eventually lead to a glorious victory. The military's confidence was
based on the leadership of its general, Vo Nguyen Giap—a man with
many talents and a tragic past. Giap was from a peasant family and
had been drawn to the independence movement as a young man.
In 1930 he joined the ICP, and he eventually received his law degree
from the University of Hanoi. Following his graduation he taught
history at the Thang Long school in Hanoi, where he was partic-

ularly interested in great historical generals and battles. He married Nguyen Thi Minh Giang, whose sister Nguyen Thi Minh Khai had been an earlier romantic interest and rumored wife of Ho Chi Minh. While Giap was assigned to work with Ho on the Sino-Vietnamese border at Bac Po, the French imprisoned his wife and young daughter; while in prison they both perished. This would leave an emotional scar on Giap and make his resolve to defeat the French even stronger.

During the First Indochina War, Giap understood that the Vietminh could not defeat the French in conventional warfare. Preparing for a long war, Giap insisted that all Vietnamese be taught to read in order to understand what the fight was about. He also used guerrilla warfare to continually harass the French and planted spies in the French quarters of Hanoi. An ominous pattern emerged wherein the French would hold the main urban centers and portions of the countryside; yet, as soon as the French would leave a particular rural area, the Vietminh would recover it and make it a base for nationalistic activities.

The localized stakes in the fight between the Vietminh and French became global when the Cold War divided the world between the capitalists and communists. More importantly for Southeast Asia, and Vietnam in particular, the Chinese civil war between the nationalists and communists resulted in an astounding victory for the CCP. Mao Zedong declared the founding of the People's Republic of China on October 1, 1949. The United States, which had actively supported Chiang Kai-shek, now lost China as an ally. Half a year later, North Korea's communist army invaded South Korea. Once again the world's attention was on the struggle between the clients of the Soviet Union and the United States. In this context, the United States became keenly interested in the French effort against the communist-led Vietminh in Indochina. During the first Eisenhower-Nixon administration, the United States began to send a tremendous amount of aid to the French fighting force in Vietnam.

Giap knew that the French were anxious to fight a conventional battle with the Vietminh. He began to send troops into Laos from the northwestern portion of Vietnam, believing that the French would do all they could to stop the Vietnamese from supplying their fellow communists in Laos. General Henri Navarre ordered 15,000 French troops to occupy a valley town called Dien Bien Phu, close to the Laos-Vietnam border. He hoped that this would draw out the Vietminh, where a conventional battle would prove French military superiority. His plan worked, but it was a nightmare for the French. Giap ordered Vietminh troops to occupy the hills surrounding Dien Bien Phu. With sheer willpower, sacrifice, and muscle the Vietminh carried heavy cannons up the mountain trails and surrounded the area with artillery. The jungle foliage made the Vietminh and their weapons impossible to see from the ground and air, and the advantage of aircraft that Navarre believed would make the difference in a conventional battle proved to be irrelevant. Moreover, heavy fog in the valley and continual rainfall during the monsoon season made it impossible for the planes to drop supplies to the beleaguered French army. On May 6, 1954, the French army at Dien Bien Phu surrendered to the Vietminh. One day later, at Geneva, Switzerland, previously scheduled talks between the Vietminh and the French began.

One would imagine that the Vietminh had all the advantages going into the Geneva talks. Dien Bien Phu was labeled the greatest defeat of a colonial army in Asia, the French nation was growing tired of the "dirty war," and the Vietminh's main ally—the People's Republic of China—was a participant in the Geneva talks. Unfortunately for the Vietminh, they could not translate victory on the battlefields to victory at the negotiating table. Weeks passed at Geneva with little headway made between the French and Vietminh. Meanwhile, the French Parliament ousted Prime Minister Laniel and voted in Mendès-France, who had been a vocal critic of the slow-paced movement of the Geneva negotiators. On June 17, 1954, the new French prime minister promised that an agreement would take place within four weeks or he would resign.

Under this pressure, Mendès-France turned to Zhou En-lai, the affable leader of China's delegates at Geneva. Working behind the scenes, the two leaders decided the fate of Vietnam and then brought the proposal to the Vietnamese. Shocked and disappointed, the Vietminh delegates listened as Zhou outlined the agreement. An immediate cease-fire was called for. Vietnam would be divided at the sixteenth parallel (this was renegotiated to make it the seventeenth parallel), with the Vietminh in control of the northern portion of the state. Southern Vietnam remained under the control of noncommunist elements in Emperor Bao Dai's government. The unification of Vietnam was to be based on a plebiscite conducted two years following the Geneva conference. Adding insult to injury for the Vietminh, Zhou En-lai insinuated that China would like to open up relations with Bao Dai's government in southern Vietnam. The participants went home, the French left Vietnam, and the United States moved in to prop up the fledgling new southern state of the Republic of Vietnam (RVN), known to most of the world as South Vietnam..

THE SECOND INDOCHINA WAR

Emperor Bao Dai remained in France and under pressure from the United States appointed Ngo Dinh Diem as the RVN's new prime minister. Diem was somewhat of a strange choice. Born into a Catholic mandarin family with high connections at the imperial court, Diem grew up surrounded by the trappings of the court and scholars. He earned his law degree at the University of Hanoi and for a period eschewed politics altogether. In the mid-1940s he was asked by Ho to join the ICP, but Diem, a Catholic, was devoutly religious and disagreed with the communist ideology. He was also embittered by the Vietminh's assassination of his brother. Following the war, he moved to the United States, where he sought religious training and solitude. U.S. advisers considered Diem's main credential for the prime ministership to be that he was staunchly anticommunist. His devotion to the Catholic faith was also a plus for many Americans. Thus, they supported Diem as he took the reigns of power in his native land.

Within a year, an orchestrated election deposed Bao Dai as the RVN's supreme leader, and Prime Minister Diem became the leader of the Republic of Vietnam. It was at this time that Diem had many opportunities to bring relief to the Vietnamese rural population, but his policies did more to isolate the farmers than improve their situation. He continued to allow large landowners to exploit the services of the landless tenant farmers, and he uprooted entire villages to make sure communists would not infiltrate them. Diem was wedded to the Confucian ideal of a virtuous ruler and saw himself fulfilling the role of a sage king holding a nation together. Unfortunately, this meant that he granted favors to family members—as filial piety required. His brother, Ngo Dinh Nhu, was appointed minister of the interior and ruthlessly cracked down on any organization or individual who disagreed with Diem's policies. Nhu and his wife, Madame Nhu, were the most unpopular aspect of Diem's regime, but the prime minister refused to oust his brother.

Diem's unpopularity with the general public actually helped the spread of communist influence in the south. Because neither the United States nor South Vietnam signed the Geneva Accords, Diem ignored the dictate that a plebiscite was to take place in 1956. He had no intention of reunifying Vietnam—unless Ho would agree to surrender the North to the South—and that was not going to happen.

In the north, the DRV was working its own magic with its people. The DRV instituted a land policy that redistributed the land from the rich landowners to the landless population who had suffered for years. This campaign was a brutal blow to the rich landowning class, many members of whom were killed. Moreover, more than a million Northerners, mostly Catholics, were transported south after the Geneva conference, and their former lands were used to alleviate the food shortage that the north had earlier experienced. Receiving limited aid from both the USSR and the PRC, the DRV established a solid government in Hanoi and organized its urban and rural areas.

In the south, land reform was a sham. Rather than crack down on the establishments that were exploiting the people, the government focused its efforts against advocates of justice for the poor and landless. Tens of thousands of individuals who disagreed with the government were killed, tortured, or thrown into jail. Dissenters derided Diem and his regime as puppets that governed on behalf of the United States. Secret antigovernment organizations in the south began to plot against the government and carry out terrorist attacks. Rather than acknowledging this problem, the Diem government claimed that all these upheavals were due to the communists who were trying to destabilize the southern government. In fact, the Vietminh had created a nationalistic organization in South Vietnam and called it the National Liberation Front (NLF). Diem's advisers pejoratively termed the Southerners who joined the NLF as Vietcong—an abbreviation for Vietnamese communists. The Vietcong quickly found support among the rural peasants in southern Vietnam. By 1963 it was estimated that close to two-thirds of RVN rural villages were controlled by the Vietcong.

The United States established an overt operation in southern Vietnam to counteract the NLF's successes and sent numerous diplomats and advisers to prop up its Military Assistance Command Vietnam (MACV). With military assistance and advice, the Hamlet Program was instituted in the Mekong Delta. This plan resulted in the construction of new villages that would be secure and safe from Vietcong infiltration. Thousands of these new villages sprang up throughout South Vietnam. This program demonstrated the shortsightedness of many U.S. programs in the RVN. First of all, to construct such villages meant that thousands of farmers would be taken off their land to build the necessary structures. Yet these new villages could not hold all those who contributed to their construction, and so millions worked without any reward. For those who did get to live in these barbed-wired-surrounded hamlets, the rewards did not outweigh the heartbreak of being taken away from ancestral lands where sacred burial grounds had been abandoned. To be sure, there were some advantages for the Vietnamese who lived in these hamlets. American aid for these villagers included the introduction of new strains of rice that produced greater harvests, new equipment for farming, and medical supplies.

Diem, like many leaders in history, believed that he alone had his people's best interests in mind. Unfortunately, this meant that he was unmovable on issues where he should have been flexible. This was particularly true regarding religion. As noted earlier, Diem was a devoutly religious man from a devoted Catholic family. One of his brothers was the bishop of Hue, and, in his younger years Diem himself had entertained the thought of studying for the priesthood. Diem never married, and his life was a moral example—he truly was the virtuous leader called for in Confucian ideology. Catholicism was not the dominant religion of Vietnam, however, and as the insurgency movement in the south grew in scope, any organization not in line with Diem became a target for persecution. This included the popular Cao Dai and Hoa Hao faiths. It was, however, the Buddhist religion that bore the brunt of persecution at the hands of Diem's family. During August 1963 raids were conducted against Buddhist temples and reporters caught the brutality on film. A dramatic event took place on June 11, 1963, when a Buddhist priest immolated himself in the center of Saigon to protest the persecution of the Buddhist faith. Rather than show sympathy toward the Buddhists, Diem's sister-in-law Madame Nhu noted at a news conference that these sacrifices were nothing more than "barbecues." U.S. advisers encouraged Diem to be more sympathetic toward the Buddhists and hinted that he should replace his brother with someone more in touch with the Vietnamese people.

As Diem's intransigence became even firmer, military leaders began to plot an overthrow of the government. When this cabal approached the U.S. advisers they were met with approval. Diem knew that there were traitors in his regime and wondered what side the Americans would take. In an August 7, 1963, interview with Marguerite Higgins, an American journalist in Saigon, Diem noted that he was aware of the plots against him:

> But now I hear hints that this aid may be withdrawn if I do not do exactly what the Americans demand. Isn't there a certain arrogance in these demands? America has a magnificent economy and many good points. But does your strength at home automatically mean that the United States is entitled to dictate everything here in Vietnam, which is undergoing a type of war that your country has never experi-

enced? If you order Vietnam around like a puppet on a string, how will you be different—except in degree—from the French? I am not unaware that some Americans are flirting with elements in my country that perennially plot against me. These elements cannot succeed without the Americans, and they know it. (Riley 1987, 288)

Diem's premonitions about U.S. acquiescence of a coup were correct. On November 1, 1963, Diem, the leader U.S. advisers and money had put in to power, was overthrown by generals in the Army of the Republic of Vietnam (ARVN) while U.S. officials stood by. The following day Diem and his brother Nhu were killed while in captivity.

A shift in leadership did not change the growing problems in South Vietnam. U.S. support increased in the hopes that the new military leaders would be more willing to listen to advice and more competent in fighting the growing influence of the Vietcong. The ARVN increased in number, but they were matched by an increased presence of North Vietnamese advisers and cadre soldiers. To send supplies and support to their southern comrades, the North Vietnamese constructed a road along the Laos/Cambodian/Vietnamese border and transported weapons, food, and soldiers south. The so-called Ho Chi Minh Trail cut through extremely dense jungle, making it impossible to spot the trail from the air. Nonetheless, the United States tried to stop this movement by bombing areas they thought were part of the path.

By 1964 it was clear that Vietnam was a major political issue in the United States. The U.S. government had supported the RVN for a decade and had sent an enormous amount of supplies to the ARVN. These policies were extensions of earlier strategies. During Dwight Eisenhower's tenure as president, the United States provided aid for the French and then propped up the Diem regime. President John Kennedy approved of the U.S. bombing of Laos because the communist organization in the area, known as the Pathet Lao, was growing and there was a fear that they had already united with the Vietminh. Vietnam was where the United States decided to make a stand against the exportation of communism. Advisers claimed that if South Vietnam fell to the communists, Laos, Cambodia, Thailand, Malaysia, Burma, and the rest of Southeast Asia would fall like dominos. Yet the dilemma that Americans faced in Vietnam was that there appeared to be only two options: to become directly involved in the fray by sending troops, or to withdraw completely. Some U.S. observers, journalists in particular, believed that there was no end in sight to the fighting and wrote that it was futile to prop up an unpopular RVN government since the Vietcong promise of economic equity was growing more attractive to Southern farmers caught between ideological, religious, and military battles.

During August 1964 U.S. ships increased their presence in North Vietnamese waters as they provided support for clandestine ARVN maneuvers on islands off the DRV coast. North Vietnamese patrol boats tried to drive off the much larger U.S. ships in the Tonkin Gulf. The U.S. ships destroyed these Vietminh boats and then withdrew from the area, but they were ordered to return with several more ships for support. Although it has never been confirmed, U.S. radar operators on the returning ships claimed that they were then attacked by the North Vietnamese. This prompted President Lyndon Johnson to order the bombing of North Vietnam. The United States Congress passed the Gulf of Tonkin Resolution, which gave the president authority to do all in his power to stop any aggression against United States personnel in Vietnam. In essence it was a blank check, and it led to the decisions to increase the bombing raids and to send U.S. soldiers to Vietnam.

Ho Chi Minh and the DRV were taken aback by the U.S. bombings of their country and the dispatch of U.S. military personnel to support the ARVN. At the Twelfth Plenum of the Central Committee (December 1965) a strategy was introduced that demonstrated that North Vietnam would not be content with a divided country. With the ARVN already demoralized by 1965, DRV leaders determined that Saigon was weakened enough to bow to steady pressure. North Vietnam's efforts were encouraged by support from the Soviet Union and the People's Republic of China. It appeared that Vietnam was going to be a pawn in a much larger game, and Ho was willing to play his part.

At the outset of direct hostilities between the United States and Hanoi, there were opportunities for negotiation, but both parties had prerequisite conditions before serious negotiation could begin. The DRV insisted that U.S. planes stop dropping bombs on its land before it would consider negotiations, whereas the U.S. government insisted that the DRV cease from sending supplies and personnel south via the Ho Chi Minh Trail. These two prerequisites were not resolved between 1965–1968, and the fighting escalated to the point that by 1967 there were more than half a million U.S. troops in Vietnam.

Beyond the many men, women, and children who lost their lives during the Vietnam War, other important issues surfaced because of the conflict. In South Vietnam the economy was completely transformed during the war. The population of urban areas, particularly Saigon, increased as over four million rural folk fled to the cities to escape the frontier battles. These cities became rest and relaxation centers for the U.S. soldiers, who had money to spend and a horrific war to forget—if only for a weekend. Prostitution, a black market of foreign goods, and overpopulated urban centers made their marks not only in an economic transformation of South Vietnam but also in a social one. The United States was throwing money at the South Vietnam problem, and where it landed was, at times, anyone's guess. ARVN generals falsified the number of soldiers under their command in order to receive monetary compensation for these paper soldiers. Of course this meant that the actual ARVN soldiers fought in undermanned units and then were castigated for losing battles.

North Vietnam's economy and society were also transformed because of the war. During the 1950s the DRV leadership had followed the Chinese pattern of taking land away from the rich and giving it to the poor, eliminating an entire class of landowners. In China, however, the redistribution of land did not produce the dramatic economic results for which Mao had hoped. During 1959 Mao launched the radical economic program entitled the Great Leap Forward, where private property was abolished and the entire population was called to work in large communes where life was regulated "for the good of the nation." The DRV believed that similar radical action was needed based on the crisis in the south. Between 1958 and 1964 the majority of North Vietnamese farmers lost their private plots of land and were incorporated into more than 30,000 different agricultural cooperatives. Within each cooperative roughly eighty-five families worked in concert to produce food for the government. By the early 1960s the DRV became aware of the growing animosity between the Soviet Union and the PRC and it tried to balance each country off the other. DRV leadership began to lean toward the less radical Soviet advisers because of the success of the power plants and other industrial complexes that the USSR had helped to build in the DRV. Communism was not going to be engendered by rhetoric, and the Soviets demonstrated to the Vietnamese that Mao's radical view of continual revolution was not producing economic prosperity in the PRC.

By 1967 it was clear that the Vietnam War had become a bog for the United States—a prediction that the journalist David Halberstam had made as early as 1965 in his book *The Making of a Quagmire.* The war grew more unpopular both in the United States and in South Vietnam. Troop morale among the ARVN was low because of its corrupt leadership. Disillusionment among U.S. troops grew due to the lack of clear military objectives, racial tensions, drug use, and the seeming omnipresence of an enemy they could not identify. In that same year South Vietnam created a new constitution that provided for open elections and a multiple-party system. Freedom of expression remained limited, however, and antiwar and various Buddhist candidates were barred from running for president. Nguyen Van Thieu, a former general in the ARVN, won the South Vietnam presidency, but the military candidates received less than 35 percent of the vote. Following the elections, large crowds demonstrated against the winners because widespread election fraud was uncovered. Nevertheless, Thieu held on to power, and the war effort increased with perceptible gains for the ARVN and U.S. forces.

Thieu's focused effort on destroying Vietcong presence in rural and urban areas was relatively successful. However, this meant that the anti-Thieu elements in the south grew more dependent on personnel and supplies from the north. In early 1968 the Vietcong and Vietminh armies planned a concerted attack on the major cities of South Vietnam. They believed that a general uprising would follow these attacks and that the ARVN and U.S. soldiers would be defeated and withdraw from Vietnam. The offensive was planned around Tet—the Lunar New Year celebrations of late January/early February. Paradoxically, the Tet Offensive was at the same time the worst defeat and greatest victory of the war for the communists. It was a military disaster for the Vietcong because of the immense loss of soldiers during the operation. Moreover, the human sacrifice did not translate into military victories. The ARVN and U.S. soldiers were able to hold on to the cities. Only Hue fell into the hands of the communists, though it was fully recovered in a matter of days. Worse yet for the Vietcong, the general uprising it believed would occur among the anti-American and anti-Thieu elements did not take place. However, images of the Tet Offensive filmed by American television crews—including the fight in and around the Saigon U.S. embassy and an ARVN official summarily executing a suspected Vietcong sympathizer—were shown on the evening news in the United States, prompting an increased mood of skepticism in the United States. Just prior to the Tet Offensive, American generals and leaders had spoken about the light at the end of the tunnel and the inevitability of Vietcong defeat. Walter Cronkite, the most popular American broadcaster, concluded that Tet demonstrated that the most the United States could hope for in Vietnam was a stalemate. Tet also had an effect on President Johnson's advisers, who questioned the wisdom of sending more troops to a war in a country that held no promise of victory. President Johnson decided that he would not seek or accept his party's nomination for the 1968 presidential election, leaving the morass of Vietnam for the next president.

Following Tet, North Vietnamese officials and generals delivered an optimistic report to the party faithful. They understated the losses of the attack and painted an unrealistic picture of a great

victory in the south. However, the end of their report made it clear
that the fighting in South Vietnam was just beginning:

> Although the enemy is suffering defeat and is in a passive and con-
> fused situation, he still has strength and is very stubborn. In his death
> throes he will resort to more murderous and savage actions. . . .The
> struggle between the enemy and us will become fiercer, particularly
> in areas adjoining the towns and cities. . . .However, it must be clearly
> realized that this will be but the enemy's convulsions before death,
> his reaction from a weak, not a strong position. The situation will con-
> tinue to develop in a way favorable to us and detrimental to the
> enemy with the possibility of sudden developments which we must
> be ready to take advantage of in order to secure final victory. (McMa-
> hon 1995, 350)

Some speculate that the Tet Offensive was launched so that
Vietnam would be reunited before Ho Chi Minh's death. Ho's health
was precarious during the latter 1960s, and he often traveled to
China to receive medical attention. In terms of important political decisions, Ho was still consulted, but by the late 1960s the
real power lay with Le Duan (1908–1986), who was the general
secretary of the Vietnamese Communist Party from 1960 until
his death in 1986. Following Ho's death on September 2, 1969,
Le Duan's influence on the upper echelon of the VCP grew even
greater. The overriding goal of North Vietnam remained the unification of the country. Le Duan was a master at bringing together
the various factions in the north, while in foreign affairs he continued to play the two powerful communist countries, the USSR
and PRC, off of one another. By 1969 this became more difficult
as tension between the Soviets and Chinese led to open battles
on the USSR-PRC border. The two powerful nations courted
Vietnam, but Le Duan continued to seek aid from both countries.
Foreign affairs also had changed for the DRV when in 1968
Richard Nixon became the thirty-sixth president of the United
States. Nixon promised his constituents that he would bring
about an honorable peace in Vietnam. Aided by his national
security adviser, Henry Kissinger, Nixon sought numerous avenues
to bring peace to Vietnam. In early 1969 peace talks were opened
in Paris and the four parties (United States, South Vietnam,

North Vietnam, and NLF) jockeyed for the best deal each could get. Negotiations were slow, tedious, and frustrating, and meanwhile each party tried to win on the battlefield what they could not at the peace talks.

Extensive U.S. bombing of North Vietnam continued during the negotiations, but the war entered a new phase in 1970. Cambodia, Vietnam's western neighbor, had remained neutral throughout the 1960s because its leader, Prince Norodom Sihanouk, embraced all foreign governments as long as they did not impinge on Cambodia's sovereignty. This neutrality frustrated the Americans and the ARVN because they believed that the Ho Chi Minh Trail ran through Cambodia and that the North Vietnamese were using Cambodian territory as base camps from which they launched attacks on South Vietnam. On March 18, 1970, President Nixon and Henry Kissinger decided to begin secret bombing operations on Cambodian territory. Although the immediate results of this secret bombing campaign were minimal, the long-term consequences of this decision would prove disastrous in later years. Sihanouk protested these bombing raids, and while he was on a trip outside of Cambodia a coup pushed him out of power. The Cambodian government was now directed by pro-U.S. elements in the Cambodian military. ARVN and U.S. troops invaded Cambodia but found that the so-called huge North Vietnamese bases did not exist—or could not be found. An important consequence of these actions was that the miniscule communist element in Cambodia, the Khmer Rouge, received legitimacy because the exiled Sihanouk called on the Cambodian people to reject the pro-American puppet government and to align with the Khmer Rouge.

As the peace talks stalled and the Cambodian plan deteriorated into massive bombing raids, Nixon surprised the world by announcing in 1971 that he would visit the PRC—a country that the United States had yet to recognize. U.S. officials hoped that if the United States would make certain concessions to China, the PRC would pressure the North Vietnamese into a peace settlement. In fact what Nixon's trip did in Vietnam was to further alienate the

PRC from the DRV. North Vietnamese officials could not forget that Zhou En-lai had betrayed the DRV at the 1954 Geneva conference. Following Nixon's visit to the PRC, Le Duan and the VCP made a definite shift toward the Soviet Union as its closest brother-in-arms.

Major points of contention at the Paris Peace Talks were North Vietnam's insistence that U.S. troops be withdrawn from the RVN and the U.S. insistence that the North Vietnamese recognize the Thieu government and withdraw all of its troops from South Vietnam. Finally a compromise was reached in 1973 wherein the United States agreed to withdraw its troops from South Vietnam and allow North Vietnam to keep its troops in South Vietnam. For its part, North Vietnam agreed to recognize the Thieu government and agreed to return captured prisoners to the RVN and the U.S. governments. The United States did not consult President Thieu on some of the most important decisions, and the RVN leadership sensed that they had been sold out by their American allies. Indeed, it was only a matter of time until the NLF and the North Vietnamese army overran the RVN government. The United States did not completely abandon South Vietnam following the signing of the peace agreement; rather, it continued to send enormous amounts of money and material. However, with the impending impeachment of President Nixon and the national economic oil crisis, Southeast Asian politics took a back seat to pressing domestic issues. On April 17, 1975, the Khmer Rouge entered Cambodia's capital of Phnom Penh and ousted the pro-U.S. government. Thirteen days later the DRV government in Saigon was toppled by North Vietnamese troops, and the process of reunification of North and South Vietnam began.

THE SOCIALIST REPUBLIC OF VIETNAM

After one hundred years marked by imperialism, division, and civil war, Vietnam was in a new situation following the unification of its country. When South Vietnam fell to the communists in 1975 there was anticipation and trepidation regarding what a united Vietnam would be like. South Vietnam's economy was completely different than the state-controlled North, and the effects of the war on the entire country were staggering. In North Vietnam, twenty-nine out of thirty provincial capitals were damaged and nine were completely destroyed. In South Vietnam, society and the economy centered on the cities and the American-supported service sectors in the urban areas. One observer described the situation in these terms:

> The legacy of the U.S.-Thieu regime was an economic and social malaise of unknown proportion: an economy that was on the verge of bankruptcy; a threatening famine in the northern provinces of Central Vietnam; more than three million unemployed people, excluding the army of a half-million prostitutes about to be out of work; six to seven million refugees who had been forced by wartime activities to flee their native villages into the cities, etc. (SarDesai 1997, 332)

In an effort to put a face of unity on all Vietnam, the country was dubbed the Socialist Republic of Vietnam (SRV) in 1976 with Hanoi as its capital, and Saigon was renamed Ho Chi Minh City. The massive bloodshed that some predicted would take place after the South's defeat did not occur, but this does not mean that there were not severe growing pains immediately following the reunification. The southern citizens were forced to attend study sessions so they could be taught the doctrines of Marx and a state-controlled economy. For those who had collaborated with the Americans—merchants, prostitutes, soldiers, and bureaucrats—reeducation camps were erected where the North Vietnamese would make sure that all vestiges of capitalistic notions would be replaced by communist ideology. Though torture tactics did not mark these camps, the inmates were forced to do hard labor for years on end. Human rights groups protested the demeaning aspects of these outdoor prisons. In fact, seven years after the establishment of the SRV, more than 120,000 people remained in these hard-labor prisons. Reeducation camps were only part of North Vietnam's strategy to remake South Vietnam in its image. To push people out of the urban areas, special economic zones were created, and in one year alone (1976), more than 600,000 people were forced out of Ho Chi Minh City on to these new "farm lands." In truth, many of these economic zones were nothing more than mosquito-infested swamps that people would have to shape into farms. These relocations were forced on the urban people because a vast majority of them did not want to leave the cities.

Two other groups also were harmed by the reunification of Vietnam. Paradoxically, the NLF, Vietcong, and the provisional government that the southern communists had established were pushed aside by the more dominant northern officials. Southern cadres believed that North Vietnam ignored all their years of sacrifice, and longstanding animosity between the north and south did not die with the formation of the SRV. Finally, the reemergence of ethnic hostility against the Chinese merchant class resulted in hostile actions against an entire class of people following the unification of Vietnam. During 1976 the SRV government made a decision to align itself with the Soviet Union, which meant a conscious decision to reject China's aid and advice. Two years later the SRV denied the Chinese in Vietnam the privilege of dual citizenship. As the economy slumped, SRV officials began to blame Chinese businesses for the failure of the state-run financial system. Property was seized from Chinese-owned stores and companies. Many Chinese were forced into the reeducation camps, losing not only their wealth but also their health. This initiated a clandestine exodus of people out of Vietnam. For individuals and groups under SRV persecution the best alternative was to leave Vietnam. However, as it was illegal for anyone to leave Vietnam without government permission, thousands of people began to secretly buy their way onto boats that would take them to Hong Kong, Thailand, Malaysia, the Philippines, and anywhere outside of the Vietnam area. Heartbreaking stories of the "boat people" began to emerge from this situation. At times the boats would be adrift for days with little or no food and water for its passengers. It was not unusual for these boats to be stopped by pirates, who would rob everyone aboard of their possessions and rape the female passengers. Tales of persecution and hardship in Vietnam made the SRV government an international pariah. The United States made sure that the world financial institutions and nations trading with the United States would not provide any aid to Vietnam. This caused Vietnam to rely even more heavily on the Soviet Union's support, and Vietnam limped along with a wrecked economy.

The SRV's first major international crisis involved its neighbor Cambodia. As noted earlier, the Phnom Penh government fell to the Khmer Rouge on April 17, 1975, and this radical communist organization had an agrarian utopian plan that would remove all of Cambodia's urban residents and place them in the rural areas to work the soil. Mass murders took place during the Khmer Rouge reign in Cambodia; some estimate that one-third of the nation died between the years 1975–1978. Pol Pot, Ieng Sary, and other Cambodian leaders received support from the PRC, and a close relationship was formed between Kampuchea (the name the Khmer Rouge gave to Cambodia) and China. For China's leaders this represented a perfect opportunity to ensure that they remained a thorn in the side of Vietnam and the Soviet Union. Once again, Vietnam became a pawn in a much larger political game. During 1978 increased Khmer Rouge incursions into Vietnam alarmed the Hanoi leaders. Moreover, Cambodian citizens and some runaway Khmer Rouge soldiers sought asylum in Vietnam, and their stories of starvation, mass murder, and torture alarmed the SRV leadership. On December 25, 1978, Vietnam invaded Cambodia, and in a three-week blitzkrieg the SRV army pushed the Khmer Rouge out of Cambodia. Red Cross camps were set up on the border of Cambodia and Thailand, and with the help of international aid—including the United States—the Khmer Rouge officials and soldiers were given shelter in Thailand. The international community condemned Vietnam for invading Cambodia, even though this foray certainly saved thousands of Cambodian lives.

The People's Republic of China was particularly outraged as its patron was ousted by Vietnam. Now recognized by the United States, the PRC decided to teach its southern neighbor a lesson, and in February 1979 the China's People's Liberation Army invaded northern Vietnam. Large battles were fought with heavy losses on both sides. It is rumored that General Vo Nguyen Giap, the hero of the Dien Bien Phu Battle, was demoted following the Chinese invasion because of the many losses that the Vietnamese army sustained during the battles. China, believing that it had shown its determination to support its allies and punish its enemies, then withdrew its troops. The United States and the United Nations continued to recognize the Khmer Rouge government as the legitimate organization for Cambodia.

Vietnam was sensitive to accusations that its only reason to invade Cambodia was to spread its hegemony in Laos and Cambodia, and so it set up a government in Phnom Penh that was run by Cambodians. Schools and hospitals were reopened as the Vietnamese sought to bring normalcy to a society that had been destroyed by Khmer Rouge policies. Paradoxically, the Vietnamese found themselves in the same quagmire that the Americans had faced earlier. As the Khmer Rouge continued to receive recognition and aid from the international community, particularly from China, there was a constant threat that if the Vietnamese quit Cambodia, the Khmer Rouge would return and then the SRV would face a hostile neighbor to its west. For ten years the Vietnamese continued to occupy Cambodia and to fight against the Khmer Rouge in the western Cambodian provinces. Land mines in Cambodia began to outnumber the population of the country.

With a weak economy, the only way Vietnam was able to sustain its operations in Cambodia was by massive support from the Soviet Union. Vietnam was the USSR's proxy in its continued hostilities against the PRC, while the Khmer Rouge remained China's surrogate in its battle against Vietnam and the Soviet Union. It is dangerous to rely so heavily on one source of aid, as the SRV learned in 1989 as Mikhail Gorbachev began dismantling the Soviet Union. In June 1989 Gorbachev visited China. The PRC leadership insisted that normal relations between China and the former Soviet power was predicated on the cessation of Russian aid to Vietnam. When this aid did dry up, Vietnam was forced to withdraw from Cambodia, but with the help of the United Nations a government was set up in Phnom Penh that proved to be friendly to Vietnam.

The economic implications of a united Vietnam and a foreign war in neighboring Cambodia are dealt with later in this book. It should be noted here, however, that by the 1990s, Vietnam had reached such a difficult economic situation that a shift was made and individuals were given freedom to grow food on rented land and sell their surplus food at independent rates. State-owned enterprises were forced to compete in a more open-market economy. The term Vietnam's government used for this new economic and social situation was *doi moi,* or renovation through liberalization of the economy. The international situation also improved for the Vietnamese: In 1993 the United States did not vote against foreign aid for Vietnam, in 1994 the U.S. trade embargo was lifted, and finally on July 11, 1995, the SRV and the U.S. normalized relations. Now Vietnam stands on the precipice of a new age where its people are not faced with a civil war, colonial status, or an unyielding ideology. After decades of war, Vietnam has peace.

References

Balaban, John. *Vietnam: The Land We Never Knew.* San Francisco: Chronicle Books, 1989.

Cady, John Frank. *The Roots of French Imperialism in Eastern Asia.* Ithaca, N.Y.: Cornell University Press, 1954.

Chapuis, Oscar. *A History of Vietnam: From Hong Bang to Tu Duc.* Contributions in Asian Studies, Vol. 5. London: Greenwood Press, 1995.

Cima, Ronald J., ed. *Vietnam: A Country Study.* Area Handbook Series. Washington, D.C.: United States Government, 1989.

Duiker, William J. *Historical Dictionary of Vietnam.* Asian Historical Dictionaries, Vol. 1. Metuchen, N.J.: Scarecrow Press,1989.

———. *Ho Chi Minh: A Life.* New York: Hyperion, 2000.

———. *Vietnam since the Fall of Saigon.* 2nd ed. Athens, Ohio: Center for International Studies, 1985.

Griffiths, Philip Jones. *Vietnam Inc.* New York: Collier Books, 1971.

Groslier, Bernard Philippe. *Indochina.* Translated by James Hogarth. New York: World Publishing, 1966.

Haines, David W. "Reflections of Kinship and Society under Vietnam's Le Dynasty." *Journal of Southeast Asian Studies* 15, no. 2 (1984): 307–314.

Halberstam, David. *The Making of a Quagmire.* New York: Random House, 1965.

Hickey, Gerald Cannon. *Sons of the Mountains: Ethnohistory of the Vietnamese Central Highlands to 1954.* Binghamton, N.Y.: Vail-Ballou Press, 1982.

Higham, Charles. *The Archaeology of Mainland Southeast Asia: From 10,000 B.C. to the Fall of Angkor.* Cambridge World Archaeology. New York: Cambridge University Press, 1989.

————. "The Later Prehistory of Mainland Southeast Asia." *Journal of World Prehistory* 3, no. 3 (1989): 235–282.

Hodgkin, Thomas Lionel. *Vietnam: The Revolutionary Path.* New York: St. Martin's Press, 1981.

Jamieson, Neil L. *Understanding Vietnam.* Los Angeles: University of California Press, 1993.

Jones, John R. *Vietnam Now.* Bourne End, England: Aston Publications, 1989.

Karnow, Stanley. *Vietnam: A History.* New York: Viking Press, 1983.

Kien, Nguyen. *Vietnam: Fifteen Years after the Liberation of Saigon.* Hanoi: Foreign Languages Publishing House, 1990.

Marr, David G., ed. *Vietnam.* World Bibliographic Series 147. Santa Barbara, Calif.: ABC-CLIO Press, 1993.

————. *Vietnamese Tradition on Trial, 1920–1945.* Los Angeles: University of California Press, 1981.

McLeod, Mark W. *The Vietnamese Response to French Intervention.* New York: Praeger, 1991.

McMahon, Robert J., ed. *Major Problems in the History of the Vietnam War.* 2nd ed. Lexington, Mass.: D. C. Heath, 1995.

O'Neill, Robert J. *General Giap: Politician and Strategist.* New York: Praeger, 1969.

Reid, Anthony. *Southeast Asia in the Age of Commerce, 1450–1680. Vol. One: The Lands below the Winds.* New Haven, Conn.: Yale University Press, 1988.

Riley, Philip F., ed. *The Global Experience: Readings in World History since 1500.* Englewood Cliffs, N.J.: Prentice-Hall, 1987.

SarDesai, D. R. *Southeast Asia Past and Present.* 4th ed. Boulder, Colo.: Westview Press, 1997.

Spenneman, Dirk H. R. "Evolution of Southeast Asian Kettledrums." *Antiquity* 61 (1987): 71–75.

Steinberg, David Joel, ed. *In Search of Southeast Asia: A Modern History.* Rev. ed. Honolulu: University of Hawaii Press, 1987.

Tarling, Nicholas, ed. *The Cambridge History of Southeast Asia: From Early Times to c. 1800.* Cambridge, U.K.: Cambridge University Press, 1992.

————, ed. *The Cambridge History of Southeast Asia: The Nineteenth and Twentieth Centuries.* Cambridge, U.K.: Cambridge University Press, 1992.

Taylor, Keith W. "Authority and Legitimacy in Eleventh-Century Vietnam." Pp. 139–176 in *Southeast Asia in the Ninth to Fourteenth Centuries,* edited by David G. Marr and A. C. Milner. Singapore: Institute of Southeast Asian Studies, 1986.

————. *The Birth of Vietnam.* Los Angeles: University of California, 1983.

Thrift, Nigel, and Dean Forbes. *The Price of War: Urbanization in Vietnam, 1954–1985.* London: Allen & Unwin, 1986.

Trung, Thai Quang, ed. *Vietnam Today: Assessing the New Trends,* 1990. London: Taylor & Francis, 1990.

Tucker, Spencer. *Encyclopedia of the Vietnam War: A Political, Social, and Military History.* 3 vols. Santa Barbara, Calif.: ABC-CLIO, 1998.

Ulack, Richard, and Gyula Pauer. *Atlas of Southeast Asia.* New York: Macmillan, 1989.

Vella, Walter F. *Aspects of Vietnamese History.* Asian Studies at Hawaii, Vol. 8. Honolulu: University of Hawaii Press, 1973.

Vien, Nguyen Khac. *Vietnam: A Historical Sketch.* Hanoi: Foreign Languages Publishing, 1974.

Whitfield, Danny J. *Historical and Cultural Dictionary of Vietnam.* Metuchen, N.J.: Scarecrow Press, 1976.

Wolters, Oliver W. *History, Culture, and Region in Southeast Asian Perspectives.* Singapore: Institute of Southeast Asian Studies, 1982.

CHAPTER TWO

Vietnam's Economy

Economic textbooks usually contain many graphs, tables, charts, and endless lists of numbers understood only by a select few. Although a few specific statistics will be mentioned in this chapter, this section on Vietnam is presented in a narrative style. That being said, some telling facts help set the stage for understanding Vietnam's present economic situation.

A quick glance at present-day Vietnam is potentially discouraging. With approximately eighty million people cramped on a small strip of land that hugs the coast of South China Sea, Vietnam is one of the planet's most densely packed populations. Thirty million people, or about 37 percent of the population, live under the poverty level. Out of a workforce of thirty-five million people, 60 percent are unemployed or underemployed.

The Vietnamese government paradoxically encourages the growth of its agrarian sector of the economy while at the same time it is attempting to reduce the role of agriculture in the economy. Party officials want the country's industrial sector to overtake the prominence of agriculture. Because 75 percent of Vietnam's population lives in the countryside, many have felt the brunt of the government's decision to focus on industrialization. Farmers claim that the government has completely ignored the importance of developing the rural agrarian sector of the economy. There are many poor, unemployed, and frustrated Vietnamese.

A casual observer might say that the above-noted data points to an economically weak Vietnam. In truth, local officials and international monetary agencies are quite optimistic about Vietnam's current economic state. How can this be? There are other statistics that might help answer this question. Between 1964 and

Rice farming has been the foundation of Vietnam's economy for over two thousand years. (Brian A. Vikander/CORBIS)

1972 the United States and its allies exploded fifteen million tons of bombs in Vietnam. That is twice the amount used in all of Europe and Asia during World War II. During the Second Indochina War, the United States sprayed defoliants on 20 percent of South Vietnam's jungle areas.

It also scattered these cancer-causing chemicals over more than 35 percent of South Vietnam's mangrove forests. Furthermore, more than one-third of South Vietnam's population was relocated during the war, and almost all of North Vietnam's industrial and transportation infrastructures were destroyed. It is estimated that three million Vietnamese died during the war. Three years after the 1975 unification of Vietnam, it once again found itself at war in neighboring Cambodia—a war that lasted for more than a decade.

These introductory remarks illustrate that one should be cautious when studying Vietnam's economy. Relative to more prosperous states, Vietnam's current economic situation seems weak and fragile. However, given the context of its recent past, there is reason to be optimistic about Vietnam's future prospects.

HISTORICAL CONTEXT

Vietnam's political officials did not have a coherent plan for uniting the North and South Vietnamese economies following their 1975 victory. For decades, Vietnam's economic goals were tied to the transcending objective of winning wars. Once U.S. military personnel returned home following the U.S.-Vietnam War, South Vietnam's economy was in shambles because service-oriented jobs were bereft of big-spending clients. Capitalism had been encouraged in South Vietnam during the war, and the main architects of its economy were Chinese entrepreneurs. The South Vietnamese Chinese community was the economic foundation of the increasingly urbanized society. When it became apparent that the anticapitalist DRV would win the war, South Vietnam's Chinese business folk began exporting their capital. They were wise in doing this because, after the war, the DRV confiscated capitalist businesses in South Vietnam. In a matter of weeks, the entire economic structure of South Vietnam was demolished. A vacuum was created with nothing to fill the void.

Following the lead of other Marxist states, Vietnam's leaders approached the state's economy by use of five-year plans. The first Five-Year Plan (1960–1965) applied only to North Vietnam. Due to the war, more than ten years passed before the Second Five-Year Plan (SFYP, 1976–1980) was implemented. Before the SFYP was instigated, the VCP tried to weed out what they termed the "comparadore bourgeoisie" and the "feudal landholding class." This anticapitalist operation began on September 11, 1975, and lasted until December 1976. Again, the main targets were the wealthy and those with ties to the former regime.

When the national congress met in December 1976 and announced the implementation of the SFYP, the language it used was ominous. Its plan was to "concentrate the forces of the whole

A woman tries to make a living by selling fresh fruit on the streets of Hanoi (Steve Raymer/CORBIS)

country to achieve a leap forward in agriculture [and] vigorously develop light industry" (Tri 1993, 78). These words echo the sentiments the Chinese communist leaders had expressed in the late 1950s when they launched China's Great Leap Forward. China's irrational agricultural campaign resulted in the most devastating famine in human history and cost the lives of an estimated thirty million people. Fifteen years later Vietnam was proposing its own Great Leap Forward. Its goal included the manufacture of light industry to help raise the nation's agricultural output. The aim set in the SFYP was an annual increase of 18 percent in food production. Although this may seem unrealistic, the VCP was basking in the glory of having just defeated the planet's strongest nation. Confidence in projected economic attainments was rooted in the improbable defeat of the United States.

The politburo ordered that agricultural cooperatives replace South Vietnam's private farms. For the first time in southern

Vietnam, farmers were forced to pool their labor and land for the state. The results were disastrous. Just two years later, 10,000 of the 13,246 cooperatives collapsed under the pressure of disgruntled farmers and due to some of the worst weather Vietnam had ever experienced. Even more troublesome for the government was that expected foreign economic aid did not materialize because of the continued political hostility between the United States and Vietnam. By 1979 Vietnam was also considered an international outlaw because of its invasion and occupation of Cambodia. International banking organizations were pressured by the United Nations to snub Vietnam.

Socialist farming was an "all for one, one for all" enterprise. People worked on parcels of land that belonged to the community—or the state. Pooled labor on state-owned agricultural land proved to be a losing economic enterprise for Vietnam. Again, this mirrored the agrarian failures in China's collective experiments of the late 1950s.

Harsh weather and the use of unscientific methods for increasing grain output contributed to the disappointing results of Vietnam's cooperative programs. However, from an ideological viewpoint, there was not a great deal of incentive for farmers to work hard or be creative in their jobs. Everyone received their quota from the communal lands while the taxes flowed out of the village to the state.

At the end of the SFYP the VCP was sobered by the stark reality of failure. For most of the five years, food production had actually decreased. In 1980, Vietnam's total food production was 14.4 million tons—well short of the goal of 21 million tons. During the SFYP the total increase of food output was 6.45 percent, while the population grew by 9.27 percent! Vietnam was forced to import 9 million tons of food because malnutrition and starvation were widespread. During the SFYP, the average output of rice *dropped*—from approximately 1,936 pounds per acre to 1,840 pounds per acre.

One success that the VCP could be proud of at the conclusion of the SFYP was that it had wiped out any entrepreneurial business spirit in southern Vietnam. By early 1978, the VCP boasted that it had closed 1,500 private businesses and turned them into 650 state-owned enterprises employing 130,000 people. What the VCP did not add to this report, however, was that it had taken the strongest aspect of Vietnam's southern economy, private industry, and transformed it into money-losing government-run industry.

Vietnam's Third Five-Year Plan (TFYP) spanned the years from 1981 to 1985. The apparent crises in all sectors of the economy prompted the government and the VCP to reassess their policies. Although the government continued to encourage the collectivization of all farmland, it also implemented a system similar to the "Household Responsibility System" established in China during this same period. In Vietnam, a subcontracting system was established where individual families were given their "own" plot of land that they could cultivate. This was a radical departure from the collective land programs.

The TFYP's subcontracting system provided more motivation for farmers to work hard. They were required to pay a certain amount of their land's yield to the cooperative, but the family was permitted to keep everything above that amount. They could sell surplus grain to the cooperative or take it to free markets and make money as small-time merchants.

The VCP had good reason to fear this new economic incentive. There was a hint of capitalism in the subcontract system. Nonetheless, Vietnamese families positively responded to the opportunity to generate an income outside of the state-sanctioned cooperative. Families began to make handicrafts at home and sell them in open markets. Entrepreneurial farmers received permission to raise animals and sell them at market prices. By 1983, the private funds from these activities supplied up to 60 percent of Vietnamese farmers' revenues. Vietnam's population was slowly weaning itself from state handouts.

By the end of the TFYP, the subcontracting system began to lift Vietnam out of its economic nosedive. Agricultural production had increased by more than 30 percent in monetary terms, and the

Many rural homes are transformed into small factories to help supplement the family income. (Courtesy of Daryl Jones)

availability of food grew by 20 percent. Rice paddy production rose by more than 30 percent. Despite these amazing numbers, the SRV faced even more difficult economic trials in 1985 than it had five years earlier.

Vietnam's population grew at an astounding 13.8 percent during the TFYP. This development offset Vietnam's economic gains. In fact, the optimistic financial predictions of Vietnam's top officials proved false. The Vietnamese had been told in 1976 that in ten years every home would have a radio, a refrigerator, and a television set. In 1985, a Vietnamese family was fortunate to have even one of these products in their home. By United Nations estimations, Vietnam's per capita income was $101 in 1976. It had slipped to $91 in 1980 and rebounded slightly to $99 by 1982. In 1985 health officials in Vietnam estimated that Vietnamese were receiving less than 80 percent of their daily needed calories. During the same year, children's birth weights had dropped to alarmingly low levels. A professional Western observer estimated in 1985 that 10 percent of Vietnam's children died from gastroenteritis. This malady is a direct result of malnutrition.

At the VCP sixth congress, held in December 1986, the main issue of discussion was the state's weak economic situation. This historic congress turned into a self-criticism exercise on the part of the VCP. In an unprecedented move, the proceedings of the congress were broadcast on radio stations throughout Vietnam. Top VCP officials were forced to retire because of the state-controlled economy failures. Several officials noted that the only economic bright spot in Vietnam was the subcontracting system. The socialist transformation of the economy was declared a failure and a new renovation program that the VCP termed *doi moi* was established. This program was an attack on the centrally planned economy. The goal was to take the positive aspects of the entrepreneurial farmers' spirit and extend them to other areas of society and the economy.

An immediate consequence of doi moi was the government's willingness to allow individuals to create businesses for profit. The SRV also lowered foreign and domestic trade restrictions. State-owned factories, most of which were not profitable, were given notice that their government subsidies would be reduced and eventually eliminated. Businesses would succeed or fail based on entrepreneurial activities—a very capitalistic-sounding notion.

These ambitious reforms ran into immediate problems. First, managers of state-run factories were unprepared to function in an open-market system. The "open-market" system gives greater freedom to individuals who wish to start and operate a business. Apart from the factory administrators, millions of workers who depended on the state subsidies had to find jobs. In the mid-1980s, unemployment and underemployment reached their highest levels in Vietnam's recent history. At the same time, inflation plagued Vietnam's economy. The banking system was also beleaguered by the government's ineffective monetary and economic policies. Altogether, inflation and a decline in food production caused near-famine conditions for three million Vietnamese during the late 1980s.

The VCP responded to these crises by trying to accelerate doi moi policies. The result was disastrous. By April 1988 a kilogram of rice cost 600 dong. Two years before the same amount had cost 30 dong. The seemingly uncontrollable inflation wiped out the savings for those Vietnamese fortunate enough to have some money set aside. Desperate times called for desperate measures. The VCP encouraged the creation of small entrepreneurial businesses. During the first half of 1987 it is estimated that 3,000 such companies, employing 30,000 Vietnamese, were formed. Agricultural cooperatives were reduced in number and size. Close to 50 percent of the communist workers on these cooperatives lost their positions and were also thrown into the new competing market.

By 1989, Vietnam's government had adopted a somewhat open-market economy with regard to rice production, even though this was not in keeping with earlier socialist concepts of labor and land. However, the combined effect of relaxing trade restrictions and giving farmers autonomy over Vietnam's agricultural land produced an astounding reversal of fortune for Vietnam. In 1989, Vietnam exported 1.4 million tons of rice. This accounted for 20

Traffic congestion is part of Hanoi's modern landscape. (Steve Raymer/CORBIS)

percent of Vietnam's foreign exchange earnings for 1989, or about $315 million. By the early 1990s Vietnam had became the world's third leading exporter of rice (only Thailand and the United States exported more rice). Liberalization of state-run coffee farms also transformed many farmers' lives. In 1980, 90,000 hectares in Vietnam were used for coffee cultivation, every hectare in state hands. By 1988, coffee land use had more than doubled to 190,000 hectares. Of even greater significance, however, was that only 8 percent of this land was under direct control of the state.

By 1990, increased foreign investment along with substantial growth in Vietnam's agricultural sector pointed to better times for the Vietnamese. Yet, Vietnam was hit with two devastating setbacks that once again crippled all of its economic strides. Between 1980 and 1990, aid from the Soviet Union had sustained Vietnam's economy. It also had allowed Vietnam to continue its occupation of Cambodia. Eighty percent of Vietnam's fertilizers and more than two-thirds of its oil came from the Soviet Union.

The Soviet Union and Vietnam enjoyed a patron-client relationship from the late 1970s up until 1990. In 1978, Vietnam formally joined the Soviet-sponsored Council for Mutual Economic Assistance (known as Comecon). This was an organization founded in 1949 to economically assist socialist countries. In the 1980s, Comecon included the states of Bulgaria, Czechoslovakia, East Germany, Cuba, Mongolia, the Soviet Union, Hungary, Poland and Romania. Economic cooperation between these nations extended to favorable trading practices and the extension of foreign loans. Vietnam was given particularly favored treatment because of the Soviet Union's lead in extending generous loans to the only Southeast Asian Comecon member.

All this benevolence disappeared when the Soviet Union collapsed. Vietnam was in an awkward position of trying to maintain friendly relations with its former closest allies, who had abandoned the socialist ideology to which Vietnam still clings. With the disintegration of the Soviet Union and East Germany, Vietnam's strongest economic friends no longer existed. In its place, Vietnam was saddled with a $15 billion debt and the prospect of securing loans outside of the Comecon. Vietnam faced an immediate short-age in almost every sector of its economy, including fertilizers, fuel, cotton, and steel.

The second major foreign blow that Vietnam endured at the end of the 1980s was also related to its ally, the Soviet Union. Before the Soviet Union collapsed, its leader, Mikhail Gorbachev, visited China in June 1989. While there, Gorbachev met with China's leader, Deng Xiaopeng, in an effort to improve relations between the two countries. During the course of these talks, Deng Xiaopeng made clear that one condition for better relations was that the Soviet's client state, Vietnam, must withdraw from Cambodia. Fol-lowing these talks, the Soviet Union communicated to Vietnam's leaders that it would be in Vietnam's economic and political inter-est to pull out of Cambodia. Vietnam was not in a position to dis-agree with its most powerful economic supporter. Withdrawal from Cambodia began in 1989.

This retreat coincided with the crumbling of Eastern Europe's socialist states, Vietnam's rapid inflation, and the demise of many state-run enterprises. As a result of all this, more than a million Vietnamese workers in state-run organizations were laid off between 1988 and 1991. More than 150,000 Vietnamese workers returned from collapsed socialist countries during 1991, and 13,000 Vietnamese who had left Vietnam by boat during the 1970s and 1980s were returned to Vietnam. Added to this grow-ing list of repatriates and the growing army of unemployed Viet-namese were more than a half-million soldiers returning from their tours in Cambodia. An embarrassing problem for Vietnam was a growing discontented unemployed population in a state that promised work for all people.

RECENT ECONOMIC INDICATORS

Vietnam limped through the 1990s as the VCP alternately moved from liberal to conservative economic policies. Foreign trade and investment in Vietnam was volatile throughout the 1990s. More recently, however, foreign companies have been attracted to Vietnam because of a large educated, but relatively inexpensive, labor force. There are potential natural resources in Vietnam, such as gas and oil, which might prove lucrative for companies who can extract these materials. The SRV maintains a socialist ideology while it tries to maintain a partially open-market economy. The constant tension for the SRV is in deciding how much economic freedom the government should allow entrepreneurs and foreign companies to have. Corruption has also become a major problem in Vietnam as communist leaders are in positions to gain from emerging businesses. Foreign companies also find that there are numerous bureaucratic departments they must pass through, and pay, in order to work in Vietnam. The VCP is aware of this corruption; an estimated 20,000 party members were reprimanded for dishonesty during the first half of the 1990s. However, the problem of corruption continues to grow.

One encouraging economic development for Vietnam during the 1990s was the normalization of relations with the United States. American companies, like their European, Asian, and European counterparts, are now free to do business in Vietnam. Overseas Vietnamese in the United States, many of whom fled Vietnam after the war, are now able to return to their homeland. Although most Vietnamese Americans desire to remain in the United States, they now are allowed to send money to their relatives in Vietnam. These remittances have provided an economic boost in both Vietnam's rural and urban areas.

Vietnam's tourist trade has grown because of normalized relations between Vietnam and the United States. Many former U.S. military personnel who served in Vietnam during the 1960s and 1970s have made it a point to visit the now peaceful Southeast Asian country. Hotels and resorts throughout Vietnam have experienced a dramatic rise in business because of the growth in the tourism industry. This has also created employment opportunities in the service sector of Vietnam's economy.

Given these changes, the national congress met for the ninth time during April 18–22, 2001, and developed an economic plan for 2001–2010. Its goals and recommendations were based on statistical data from the year 2000. This data is noted herewith and is followed by a brief study of Vietnam's future economic plans:

Population: 78 million

Labor force by occupation: 65 percent agriculture; 35 percent industry and services

Unemployment rate: 25 percent

Population below the poverty line: 49 percent

Gross domestic product: $134.8 billion

Gross domestic product composition by sector: agriculture: 28 percent; industry: 30 percent; services: 42 percent

Purchasing power per capita: $1,770

Exports: $9.4 billion

Main export products: crude oil, marine products, rice, coffee, rubber, tea, garments, shoes

Main export partners: Japan, Germany, Singapore, Taiwan, Hong Kong, France, South Korea

Imports: $11.4 billion

Main import products: machinery and equipment, petroleum products, fertilizer, steel products, raw cotton, grain, cement, motorcycles

Main import partners: Singapore, South Korea, Japan, France, Hong Kong, Taiwan.

External debt: $25 billion

Economic aid: $2.2 billion in credits and grants by international donors

The general goal for the SRV, with regard to its economy strategy for 2001–2010, is to bring Vietnam out of underdevelopment. The year 2020 is the targeted date for making Vietnam a modern industrialized country. To accomplish this, the SRV intends to double the country's gross domestic product (GDP) by 2010. Projected strategies to achieve this include a dramatic increase in exports. Furthermore, the above-noted balance in the economy needs to shift so that the agricultural sector of the economy accounts for 16 percent of the GDP, industry 40 percent, and services 42 percent. The SRV has specific strategies for each of these sections of the economy.

AGRICULTURE AND RURAL VIETNAM

Vietnam's agriculture and the countryside are so intertwined that when the SRV sets objectives for major changes in the country's agricultural development, it must also address rural economic transformation. Vietnamese officials face staggering challenges as they attempt to modernize rural Vietnam. Raising the standard of living in rural areas, where 75 percent of the Vietnamese people reside, means addressing 90 percent of the nation's poverty-level population.

An immediate agricultural problem for Vietnam is the sparse amount of arable land. In 2001 the average farm in Vietnam was less than two acres in size. This meager amount of land is not large enough to occupy the energies of one family. Unfortunately, there are few economic opportunities for the farmers to supplement their income. A dilemma faced by the SRV is how to raise its agricultural output while trying to decrease the number of people involved in the agrarian sector of the economy. To make these large economic and social transformations, the SRV has developed a four-point program.

First, Vietnam's agricultural production must continue to grow. During the 1990s, Vietnam's farming output increased at an annual rate of 4.9 percent. Based on research, the SRV concluded that 87 percent of this expansion was due to greater labor supply and growth in capital. Two other reasons for agricultural growth were the greater availability of land and gains due to scientific advances. For SRV officials, the most disturbing aspect of this increase was that technology accounted for only 4 percent of the growth. This is not surprising given the sparse capital allocated for experimentation. Less than 2 percent of Vietnam's public agricultural budget is devoted to research. In comparison, Thailand and Malaysia, two of Vietnam's Southeast Asian neighbors, spend 10 percent of their agricultural budget in this area.

Given the limited resources that the SRV can draw upon, it does not look like there will soon be an outpouring of funds for technology. Nevertheless, the government recognizes that more attention must be given to research and development in the agricultural sector. Officials also continue to encourage the growth of private enterprise in agriculture. This extends to firms that manufacture and sell fertilizers and seeds.

A Vietnamese merchant selling painted baskets (Steve Raymer/CORBIS)

According to SRV publications, diversification is the second necessary modification needed to increase Vietnam's agricultural production. Rice accounts for 60 percent of Vietnam's agricultural land. This will have to decline if Vietnam's projected goal of a monetary output of $2,000 per 2.5 acres is to be realized. There are, however, historical and societal barriers in trying to get farmers in Vietnam to grow something besides rice. From the beginning of Vietnam's existence, rice was its principal crop because this grain sustains life. Cash crops might make the farmers wealthier, but there is a greater risk in planting a crop that cannot guarantee subsistence.

With more than two thousand years as precedent, the Vietnamese know how to grow rice. Farmers spend their youth helping their parents build paddies, transplant rice seedlings, nurture the crop, and harvest the rice stalks. Even apart from their own experience, farmers draw upon written and oral instructions on how to overcome destructive insects, drought, flood, and a score of other potential hazards surrounding the production of rice. Officials realize that in order to encourage farmers to abandon their rice crops for cash crops they will have to provide inducements. Current government-sponsored incentives to farmers include providing additional land for farmers who choose to grow crops other than rice, giving subsidized credit for start-up farms that produce cash crops, and providing free technological information and instruction for farmers who voluntarily diversify their products.

Vietnamese officials believe that the third needed change in the agricultural/rural sector of the economy is the promotion of rural off-farm employment. The growth of nonagricultural careers for the rural population is a pattern for every industrialized country. In Asia, Japan is a model for this type of employment transition. When Japan moved from an agrarian-based economy to a modern industrialized society between 1870 and 1900, its rural population moved into the urban areas to labor in the factories. Vietnamese officials plan to decrease the number of farmers in its rural areas between the years 2001 to 2010. Unlike Japan, however, it is the SRV's goal to keep the rural nonfarmers in the

During the 1990s, Vietnam became a leading world exporter of rice. This rice mill is just one of hundreds that are scattered throughout the country. (Michael S. Yamashita/CORBIS)

countryside. To do this, Vietnam will have to create a rural industrialized economy.

The SRV will have to overcome three major hurdles if it hopes to produce an industrialized rural economy. First, the government does not have the needed funds to invest in urban industrialization, much less rural modernization. During the first five-year plans, the Vietnamese government ignored this basic lack of funds for accomplishing its goals. Unreasonable projections coincided with an irrational belief that the farmers' ingenuity and hard work would compensate for the lack of capital and scientific methods. Fortunately, the SRV has moved beyond these presumptions, knowing that it will have to find funds from domestic or foreign sources if it intends to have an industrial sector in Vietnam's rural areas.

A second challenge with regard to the development of its rural areas is the poor condition of Vietnam's transportation infrastructure. This is where Vietnam's backwardness is most apparent. More than half of Vietnam's rural areas are inaccessible to large vehicles. Without this basic infrastructure, one can hardly speculate when more modern tools of technology, such as communication and multiple sources of energy, will be accessible to Vietnam's rural population.

Third, the SRV must assist the underprivileged areas of Vietnam if it intends to have a balanced economy. The poorest among the poor in Vietnam are ethnic minorities. In Vietnam's thirteen most destitute provinces, the provincial population consists of more than 60 percent who are under the poverty level. In twelve of these provinces, more than 50 percent of the inhabitants are ethnic minorities. This statistic is even more surprising given that Vietnam's ethnic minorities represent only 15 percent of the nation's population. If Vietnam is to alleviate the hardship in its highland regions, it will have to focus on research and investment among its ethnic minority farmers. Agricultural practices in the upland farms are dated, but they persist because there are no alternatives. For example, if upland farmers had effective fertilizers, they could reuse plots of land rather than burning portions of a mountain to use the land for only one season. During 2001 to 2010, Vietnam intends to turn the liability of the agriculturally nonproductive highland areas into farms that will assist its minorities.

INDUSTRY

Beginning in the 1950s party officials proclaimed that Vietnam was on the fast-track to industrialization. The capital needed to accomplish this transformation was supposed to come from the agricultural sector of the economy. Political crises and wars were blamed for preventing the fulfillment of this goal. Nevertheless, North Vietnam received economic aid from the Soviet Union, and heavy industrial projects were developed in the region. Historically, South Vietnam was technologically behind when com-

The modern skyline of Ho Chi Minh City demonstrates an increased modernization in Vietnam. (John R. Jones; Papilio/CORBIS)

pared to the North. The manufacturing gap between these regions grew even wider during the Second Indochina War. Although the Soviet Union continued to assist in developing North Vietnam's large industries, South Vietnam's economy was bolstered by the services that it offered U.S. personnel.

The reunification of Vietnam did not bring immediate changes to Vietnam's weak industrial sector. After the first five years of reunification, from 1975 to 1980, there was minimal growth in industrial output. During the next five years, Vietnam's manufacturing growth was uneven. Expansion in paper products represented the greatest improvements. Other noteworthy gains included processing of saltwater fish, processed sugar, and brick production.

By 1991 the industrial sector of Vietnam's economy equaled 22.8 percent of the nation's total output. During this same period, about 11 percent of the labor force was engaged in industrial works. Consumer goods grew from 55 percent in 1981 to close to 70 percent ten years later. During the 1990s, the government's strategy to increase industry included reshaping 400 state factories. As has been done with Vietnam's agricultural lands, the SRV seeks to privatize numerous state-run industries. Those companies slated for privatization include businesses engaged in steel production, shipbuilding, manufacturing of cement, food processing, and sugar production.

VIETNAM AND FOREIGN AID

Although the 1990s saw many shifts in Vietnam's economy, the greatest change was its improved relations with the larger global community. There were two developments that previously hindered Vietnam from enjoying positive relations with numerous countries. First, the United States and Vietnam did not enjoy cordial relations for more than two decades following Vietnam's political reunification. On the Vietnamese side, there were accusations that the United States had reneged on promised aid to Vietnam. American officials pointed to evidence of U.S. personnel missing in Vietnam and the Vietnamese government's refusal to cooperate in locating them. Vietnam suffered through more than twenty years of economic cold war with the world's largest economy because of a hangover from a much larger conflict.

The second reason for its alienation was Vietnam's invasion and occupation of Cambodia. The United Nations and other international organizations considered Vietnam a rogue nation due to its violation of Cambodian sovereignty. Consequently, Vietnam's closest geographical neighbors did not cooperate with the perceived outlaw country.

Fortunately for Vietnam, the final decade of the twentieth century witnessed a dramatic improvement in its foreign relations. In 1995 Vietnam became part of the Association of Southeast Asian Nations (ASEAN). This organization was created in 1967 with Indonesia, Malaysia, the Philippines, Singapore, and Thailand as its charter members. As it has developed, ASEAN has provided a network for economic cooperation among Southeast Asia countries. With more than half a billion people in the ten Southeast Asian member countries and an area rich in natural resources, ASEAN has provided Vietnam with an opportunity to expand its exports and imports.

More cordial relations with the United States during the 1990s also strengthened Vietnam's economy. In 1993 President Bill Clinton eased government-imposed sanctions against Vietnam; the following year he announced the lifting of the U.S.-Vietnam trade embargo. Just several weeks before Vietnam was invited to join ASEAN, the United States announced the normalization of relations with Vietnam. Numerous American companies quickly established business offices in Hanoi and Ho Chi Minh City.

Increased participation in global trade, however, has not provided much relief for Vietnam's feeble economy. Very few foreign companies have had a positive experience in Vietnam. Incessant corruption by local, regional, and national officials hinders the supposed free-market system that Vietnam advertises. One example of the frustration local and foreign investors experience is evidenced in the highly anticipated Vietnam stock market. After promising that such an organization would be a reality, government officials opened Vietnam's first stock market in late July 2000. Only two firms were listed at the Securities Trading Center: Refrigeration Electrical Engineering, and Cables and Telecommunications Material. On the first day of trading only four thousand shares were exchanged because the government placed a ceiling on the price of the shares. This type of interference makes most investors skeptical about this organization's viability.

Thus, though Vietnam is economically in a much better position than it was during the 1980s, it continues to limp behind even its weakest neighbors. If it is to have a vibrant business sector, the SRV will have to commit to a truly free market system. For this to happen, the VCP will have to further separate itself from the open market system. Until this happens, Vietnam's direction will remain in limbo.

References

BBC World Service. "Communist Vietnam's First Stock Exchange Opens." BBC News. http://news.bbc.co.uk. July 28, 2000.

Beresford, Melanie, and Phong Dang. *Economic Transition in Vietnam: Trade and Aid in the Demise of a Centrally Planned Economy.* Northampton, Mass.: Edward Elgar, 2000.

CNN. "Vietnam Market to Open, No Trade Immediately." http://www.cnn.com. July 19, 2000.

Commission for External Relations. "Strategy for Socio-Economic Development 2001–2010." The Communist Party of Vietnam. http://www.cpv.org. April 22, 2001.

Communist Party of Vietnam. "The Eighth National Congress." http://www.cpv.org. June 28–July 1, 1996.

———. "The Seventh National Congress." http://www.cpv.org. June 24–27, 1991.

Consultive Group Meeting for Vietnam. *Vietnam 2010: Entering the Twenty-first Century.* World Bank, Asian Development Bank and UNDP. World Bank, 2001.

Coutsoukis, Photius. "Vietnam Economy." http://www.photius.com. March 1, 1999.

"Destination ASEAN Vietnam: Positively Productive Transition." Pacific Basin Economic Council. http://www.pbec.org. 1995.

Embassy of Vietnam. "Economic Overview." http://www.vietnamembassy-usa.org. 2000.

Fforde, Adam. *The Agrarian Question in North Vietnam, 1974–1979.* Armonk, N.Y.: M. E. Sharpe,1989.

Le, Manh Hung. *Vietnam Socio-Economy: The Period 1996–1998 and Forecast for the Year 2000.* Hanoi: Statistical Publishing House, 1999.

Nguyen, Dung, and James Cassing. *Working Papers on Economic and Political Tension and Trends: China, Indonesia, Korea, and Vietnam.* Pittsburgh: University of Pittsburgh of International Business Center, 2000.

Raymond, Chad. "Rational Resistance to a Weak Authoritarian State: The Political Economy of Vietnamese Farmers from Collectivization to Doi Moi." Ph. D. Diss., University of Hawaii, 2000.

SRV Party Central Committee. "SRV Party Central Committee Political

Report." http://coombs.anu.edu. June 30, 1996.

"Statistical Data." Vietnam Economic Information Network. http://www.
vneconomy.com. July 2, 2001.

Than, Mya, and Joseph Tan, eds. *Vietnam's Dilemmas and Options: The
Challenges of Economic Transition in the 1990s.* Singapore: Institute of
Southeast Asian Studies, 1993.

Vo Nhan Tri. "Party Policies and Economic Performance: The Second and Third
Five-Year Plans Examined," ed. David G. Marr and Christine P. White.
Ithaca, N.Y.: Cornell University, 1993.

Vietnam Communist Party. "Press Communiqué from the Fourth and Last
Working Day of the Ninth National Party Congress." http://www.cpv.org.
2000.

Williams, Michael C. *Vietnam at the Crossroads.* New York: Royal Institute of
International Affairs, 1992.

CHAPTER THREE
Vietnamese Institutions

Tradition, codes, and values are threads that intertwine the fabric of society. With a history more than two thousand years old and a past century that witnessed numerous wars and ideological changes, deep-seated institutions have held Vietnam together. With an eye to the past, present, and future, this chapter examines four primary institutions that make up the pallet of Vietnamese society.

Politics and Government. The Vietnam Communist Party controls the state of Vietnam. The party is made up of various subsets of groups including the National People's Congress, the central committee, and the politburo. Vietnam currently operates under its fourth constitution. The first constitution, established after the 1945 founding of the Democratic Republic of Vietnam (DRV), emphasized human rights. The DRV leaders hoped that this would encourage non-Marxist countries to recognize this new state. In 1960, the DRV leaders wrote a new ideologically loaded constitution. In 1976, the DRV became known as the Socialist Republic of Vietnam (SRV). Four years later, Vietnam received its third constitution as its leaders made a conscious shift toward the pattern of the Soviet Union. Finally, in 1992, the year the SRV adopted its latest constitution, Vietnamese officials were confronted with a world where their main allies, the Soviet Union and East Germany, no longer existed. Their comrades had shifted toward an open-market economy. This 1992 document defends Marxist ideology while recognizing the need to give its citizens greater freedom.

Armed Forces. A quick survey of Vietnam's history convinces even the casual observer that it has remained united because of a strong military. Its wars with China, Mongols, Japan, France, the

United States, and the Cambodian Khmer Rouge regime are just a few examples of how the Vietnamese have struggled to remain independent and secure. However, in the twenty-first century, this once-proud institution of the SRV is now a liability. The SRV's inability to pay for basic maintenance of military equipment is just one of the many crises that its modern military machine faces.

Education. Education is synonymous with economic, social, and political advancement in traditional Vietnamese society. Based on Confucian philosophy, the scholars, not the soldiers, directed state affairs. The educated elite gathered around the emperor and served as the potentate's trusted advisers. In modern-day Vietnam, schooling remains a highly prized enterprise. Unfortunately, the government is not able to commit the needed resources to give students an adequate opportunity to advance through education. This chapter examines the current structure of Vietnam's primary, secondary, and higher education system.

Religion. From the first days of its existence, Vietnam has been a deeply religious society. Confucianism, Buddhism, and Daoism were transmitted to Vietnam from China. Catholicism, and more recently fundamentalist and Pentecostal Protestant sects, have also deeply affected the spiritual life of the Vietnamese—much to the consternation of SRV officials. Underneath these foreign doctrines, however, is an indigenous belief system that predates the arrival of outside organized religion. One section of this chapter explores the amalgamation of different faiths and how the SRV tries to control this aspect of society.

VIETNAMESE POLITICS AND GOVERNMENT

The Vietnamese Communist Party

Compared to past and present communist states, Vietnam ranks near the top in terms of political rigidity. One reason for the inflexibility in Vietnam's Communist Party (VCP) is due to its entrenched leadership. In fact, whereas communism's mission is to remove society's political and economic elite, leaders within the

VCP tenaciously cling to political, economic, and even cultural control. Historical events allowed the VCP to monopolize authority over every aspect of Vietnam. This section charts the evolution of the only viable political party in the SRV from its birth in 1930 to the present.

Founded in February 1930, the first name given to the organization was Vietnam's Communist Party (Dang Cong San Viet Nam). Eight months after its establishment, it was renamed the Indochinese Communist Party (Dong Duong Cong San Dang). In late 1945 it was formally disbanded due to the DRV's agreement with France (see Chapter 1). However, the party remained as a secret organization and reemerged in March 1951 under the name Vietnam Workers' Party (Dang Lao Dong Viet Nam). The Vietnam Workers' Party name was changed to the Vietnam Communist Party in late 1976.

The party was first organized in Hong Kong with just a handful of people in 1930. Ho Chi Minh, whose absence from Vietnam spanned the years 1911 to 1941, was already an acknowledged party leader. Although it was a fledgling organization, by 1945 it emerged as Vietnam's primary political party. How did it become so powerful in such a short time? The multifaceted answer begins with the political chaos Vietnam experienced during the first half of the twentieth century. One advantage that the VCP had in its first decade of existence was relatively limited competition. In the north, the only major rival to the VCP was the previously mentioned VNQDD. This nationalist party was essentially demolished following its failed 1930 military uprising. Other political entities were weak and were aligned with the colonial government, which was the very institution that the VCP sought to remove.

Human tragedy also bolstered the VCP's prestige among the rural inhabitants. In 1945 a severe famine enveloped the country. People were starving because of the war-centered agrarian policies imposed by Japan. Hundreds of thousands of peasants died. An opportunity presented itself for the VCP to demonstrate its compassion. Japanese army personnel, along with the Vietnamese families who collaborated with the foreign oppressors, enjoyed large stores of rice. The VCP raided these stockpiles and redistributed the plunder to the starving. These Robin Hood–type tactics created a somewhat mythical aura around the VCP and its leader, Ho Chi Minh. Thus, following the Vietnamese surrender, the political vacuum in North Vietnam was easily filled by the VCP. The foundation for the Vietnamese revolution was laid by helping the peasants survive the crises of war and starvation.

The absence of a major unifying ideology in Vietnam also facilitated the quick growth of the VCP. Compared to other Southeast Asian nations, such as the Philippines and Malaysia, where Catholicism and Islam dominated the religious, social, and political aspects of society, Vietnam's Buddhist institutions were so diverse that they did not dominate society. To be sure, there were millenarian figures among the Buddhists in Vietnam that wielded political power, but as shown previously, the geographical influence of these cultic figures was limited. Historically, Confucianism was the ideological foundation in Vietnam. However, by the end of World War II, it was clear that this ethical system had not prevented the exploitation of the Vietnamese by foreign powers; it also had not produced a society with political, social, or economic stability. Communism in general, and the VCP in particular, offered the defeated Vietnamese an alternative worldview—one that promised to limit exploitation and starvation.

Finally, the VCP gained legitimacy because it continued to fight against foreign-dominated politicians and political parties. France tried to reassert its hegemony over Vietnam after World War II through the institution of the emperor, but the Vietnamese viewed Bao Dai's government with much skepticism. Following the withdrawal of the French from Vietnam, the United States continued the failed policy of propping up a government that was identified with foreign money and alien influence. The Vietnamese were keenly aware of their land's history and its numerous foreign intrusions. It was easy for the VCP to present itself as the most viable political party that was truly indigenous.

Political scientists conclude that the VCP dominates the government in an unprecedented fashion, even when compared to

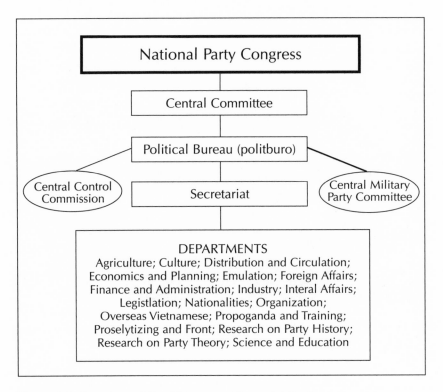

Figure 3.1: Structure of the Vietnamese Comunist Party

other communist states. Political careers in Vietnam are advanced and destroyed in the VCP, not in the government itself. Not surprisingly, then, those that have risen in the VCP have held on to power for several generations.

The Figure 3.1 outlines the structure of the VCP and gives a brief explanation.

National Party Congress

In theory the National Party Congress (NPC) is the party's highest authority. The NPC is a group of approximately one thousand delegates who represent the nation's communist members. It is supposed to meet every four or five years or in times of political crisis. Because of external threats, the first NPC meetings were sep-

Two Muong women sewing cloth. The Communist Party has never been strongly supported by the ethnic minorities in Vietnam. (Alison Wright/ CORBIS)

arated by more than five years. By the turn of the twenty-first century, the NPC had met nine times. A brief description of these nine meetings is noted below.

The first NPC was held outside of Vietnam because of the volatile domestic situation. Thus, in 1935 several Vietnamese party members gathered in the Portuguese colony of Macao, just across the bay from Hong Kong, to strategize the party's next steps.

This first NPC coincided with the seventh congress of the organization known as the International Communist, or Comintern. Held in Moscow, the directive from this congress was that communist movements in various regional countries should join with noncommunist nationalist organizations. This suggestion was extremely relevant to the Indochina Communist Party. In 1935 there were numerous nationalist movements throughout Vietnam that were not aligned with Marxist ideology.

The Socialist Republic of Vietnam has its hands full in trying to control an economy that includes floating markets like this one in Phung Hiep. (Steve Raymer/CORBIS)

Party members in Hanoi sought out noncommunist nationalist leaders and attempted to create a coalition to overthrow the colonial oppression.

Due to the interruption of World War II and the First Indochina War, it was sixteen years until Vietnam's second NPC. At this congress, held in 1951, party officials gathered in a remote region of the North Vietnam highlands, where the French were reluctant to fight. The war dominated the discussions. It was agreed that the party should continue to work primarily in rural areas. The party did not wholly abandon the French-dominated cities, but it did continue to encourage undercover activities in Hanoi and in other metropolitan areas. It was also decided that the new name for the Indochina Communist Party would be the Vietnam Workers' Party (VWP, Dang Lao Dong Viet Nam).

Another decade passed before the NPC met again. Meeting in

Hanoi, this was the first NPC where the party could look beyond an immediate crisis. The party's demographics was the prominent topic. Some officials were greatly disturbed by the party's imbalance of workers in relation to other groups. Statistics indicated that only 3.4 percent of the party was made up of workers. The definition of a "worker" was any individual who was directly involved in industrial production. The remaining members of the Workers' Party were peasants and individuals who had a position in Vietnam's economic, social, and education communities. Another major topic of discussion was the strategy to spread revolution to South Vietnam, where the anticommunist, pro-American Ngo Dinh Diem was in power. The NPC was resolved to support communist sympathizers in South Vietnam. This aid came in the form of weapons, propaganda, and a limited number of advisers.

The fourth congress, held in 1976, was the first NPC of a politically united Vietnam. It was a self-congratulatory gathering. Party officials basked in the glory of having defeated the United States and the Army of the Republic of Vietnam. Ho Chi Minh's goal of national unification was accomplished, though this was the first NPC without his presence. With the momentum of such a great victory, the VCP had an opportunity to positively reshape Vietnam. Unfortunately for the Vietnamese, congress members did not take stock of the major economic, social, and political crises facing their country, and the opportunity was lost.

The fifth NPC took place in 1982, and during the meeting the VCP confirmed Vietnam's alliance with the Soviet Union. This was merely a formality. It was also a clear signal to the outside world that Vietnam was consciously snubbing China. Vietnam's ties with China went beyond their shared communist ideology. History and geography also bound the two states. Yet, their relations through the centuries alternated between sweet and sour. Vietnam's 1982 alliance with China's enemy, the Soviet Union, indicated that Sino-Viet relations were at a low point.

At the fifth NPC there was also an unprecedented admission that the party had made mistakes. Vietnam's economy was a wreck, and just three years earlier its army had suffered setbacks from a surprised Chinese invasion. Vietnam's military forces were forced to defend their country's northern borders while sinking deeper into the quagmire of their Cambodia occupation.

Despite these problems, the top party leaders maintained their positions. However, there was a significant shift among several politburo members. General Vo Nguyen Giap, the chief architect of Vietnam's victories over France and the United States, retired, as did other middle-tier politburo members. There were whispers that these men had caused Vietnam's economic and military woes.

The year 1986 was a time of transition for Vietnam. It also was the year that the sixth NPC was held. Vietnam's economic crisis emboldened the liberal members of the party to press for some type of open-market system. Three of the party's highest members retired, including Premier Pham Van Dong, President Truong Chinh, and fourth-ranked politburo member, Le Duc Tho. Vietnam remained an international pariah because of its continued occupation of Cambodia. For this reason, there were lengthy discussions on foreign policy issues.

The seventh NPC was held in Hanoi from June 24 to June 27, 1991. More than a thousand delegates represented the nation's 2.1 million communist party members at this meeting. These representatives approved the Central Committee's ten-year economic proposal. The seventh NPC also insisted that the *doi moi* process continue in earnest.

Political stability has allowed the NPC to meet every five years ever since the 1980s. The eighth and ninth NPCs were held in 1996 and 2001. These meetings were broadcast over Vietnamese television and radio. Through the medium of the Internet, the summaries of these conferences are available on-line. Concerned mainly with the economy, the 1996 and 2001 NPC assemblies have projected a Vietnam that is fully industrialized by the year 2020. This desired modernization is still within the context of communist ideology. In his 2001 closing speech, the newly-elected party general secretary, Nong Duc Manh, spoke about the need for modernization, patriotism, and ideological goals to link into an unbreakable chain:

> Our nation's future is bright, however untold difficulties and trials are still ahead of our path. The success of our renewal process in a new stage depends on our abilities to realize and actively seize opportunities and overcome the dangers being encountered by our country, each branch, sector and area. Therefore, in his/her perception and action, each official, Party member and ordinary people must profoundly understand the line, viewpoints and policies laid down by the ninth national Party congress, and uphold national patriotism and self-reliance, as well as broaden external relations, strengthen political firmness and firmly seize opportunities, overcome dangers to ensure national stability and development. (Vietnam Communist Party 2000).

For the foreseeable future, the NPC will attempt to combine Vietnam's economic development with an orthodox Marxist ideology.

Central Committee

When the NPC is not in session, the Central Committee is the mouthpiece for the VCP. The Central Committee meets at least twice a year and directs Vietnam's domestic and foreign policy issues. It also creates party organizations to ensure that recommended policies are implemented. Approximately 150 people comprise the Central Committee, with about thirty alternates. Members are elected by the National Party Congress, and their terms span five years, though they are usually reelected with no term limits. Very much like the NPC, the Central Committee merely represents a much more influential group—the Political Bureau (politburo).

Politburo

The most dominant influence in Vietnam since World War II is not the VCP, but the politburo within that organization. Consisting of approximately fifteen members, it is estimated that between the years 1935 to 1991 only thirty individuals served on the politburo.

The slow turnover rate demonstrates political stability. It also has resulted in staleness. For most of its existence the main characters in the politburo were Ho Chi Minh, Le Duan, Truong Chinh, Le Duc Tho, Pham Van Dong, Vo Nguyen Giap, Pham Hung, Nguyen Van Linh, Van Tien Dung, and Mai Chi Tho. Following the economic chaos of the 1980s, most of the old politburo members were retired. However, the organization is still dominated by ultraconservative ideologues, which makes it difficult for the Vietnamese government to surpass outdated and irrelevant economic and political ideals. The politburo's continued conservative makeup also means that certain restrictions remain on the media, religion, and other aspects of society.

The three important committees directed by the politburo are the Secretariat, the Central Control Commission, and the Central Military Party Committee. Of the three, the Secretariat is the most significant. It manages the party and oversees the day-to-day execution of policies. There are thirteen members in the party Secretariat, five of those being politburo personnel. The second association that the politburo guides is the Central Control Commission. Usually under ten in number, this group investigates information related to party corruption. The Central Military Party Committee is the third group that answers directly to the politburo. Politburo personnel include high-ranking military officials, and the Military Party Committee likewise includes politburo members. In short, the blurred lines between political, military, and party personnel allow a handful of individuals to dominate the entire country.

Vietnam's Constitution

The Democratic Republic of Vietnam (DRV), known as the Socialist Republic of Vietnam (SRV) after 1976, has had four constitutions that correspond to the years 1946, 1960, 1980, and 1992. Each document was built on the preceding constitution.

The framers of the 1946 constitution were concerned that it would be acceptable to noncommunist governments. France still occupied much of Vietnam, and the DRV leaders hoped that promised freedoms of speech, the press, and assembly would demonstrate Vietnam's commitment to democracy. Indeed, these privileges were promised in the 1946 constitution.

In formulating the DRV's 1960 constitution, officials dropped the pretext of being ideologically neutral. In its preamble the framers wrote: "Our State is a people's democratic State based on the alliance between the workers and peasants and led by the working class." More than 50 percent of the 1960 preamble is dedicated to the past and present wars with imperialists and Vietnamese traitors—particularly southern collaborators.

It was not until the two Vietnams were reunited that another attempt was made to create a constitution. Five years following the reunification of Vietnam, the government set out to update its existing constitution. The tone of the 1980 constitution was a bit more practical than the 1960 version. For example, though the language in the 1980 preamble continued to glorify Vietnam's victories over imperialist nations, there was also an insistence that new revolutions were needed. These would be revolutions in production, science and technology, culture, and ideology. These sentiments mirror the transformations made in China following the 1976 death of Mao Zedong.

Another striking feature of the 1980 constitution was its proclamation of society's "collective mastery" over itself. This was a favorite expression of Le Duan, the party leader from 1960 to 1986. The 1980 constitution also promoted an extension of the VCP's authority over the legal system. Thus, Vietnam's entrenched leadership continued to extend its power through the constitution. An interesting aspect to the 1980 document was Article 67 from the fifth chapter on "Basic Rights and Obligations of Citizens." This section's language appeared quite radical as it came from the government's conservative leaders: "Citizens enjoy freedom of speech, freedom of the press, freedom of assembly, freedom of association, and freedom to demonstrate in accordance with the interests of socialism and of the people." The constitution also noted, however, an important qualification to these freedoms: "No one may misuse democratic freedoms to violate the interests of the state and the people." Party officials use this qualifying statement to justify their continued persecution of Vietnamese religious and journalist figures.

On April 15, 1992, Vietnam adopted its fourth constitution. World events, particularly the disintegration of communist states in Eastern Europe, forced the Vietnamese to reevaluate the ideology upon which the DRV was founded. This was particularly necessary as the Soviet Union had been Vietnam's closest ally, and in 1992 there no longer was a Soviet Union. The VCP tried its best to explain the breakup of the Soviet Union. Its leaders continued to blame the imperialist nations, particularly the United States, for spreading chaos and capitalist exploitation. Turning to the communists' faults, Vietnam's leaders also blamed corruption among high officials for the demise of communism throughout Eastern Europe.

With world events pointing to a definite shift toward a global open market, liberals within the SRV pressed for fundamental changes that would reflect the worldwide economic and political trends. Although the government recognized the need to begin the process of political reform, it adamantly rejected any suggestion that the VCP should have less power in directing government policies.

There were, however, major differences between the SRV's 1980 and 1992 constitutions. Even before the adoption of a new constitution, there were hints that Vietnamese officials wanted to soften the language of the 1980 constitution. Between 1980 and 1992 Vietnam's constitution was amended twice. In 1988, antagonistic references to China and the United States were toned down in its preamble. One year later, several minor articles were amended, while the National Assembly commissioned a committee to begin transforming the text. (The National Assembly is the legislative branch of the SRV. It is composed of about 400 individuals who are nationally elected to serve five-year terms.) Several drafts of the new constitution made their way through appropriate committees, until a final version was adopted in 1992.

Compared to how Vietnam's three previous constitutions were

simply adopted, a much greater amount of discussion surrounded the language used in the 1992 document. Four issues were heatedly debated. The first matter was how to limit the VCP's influence in the government and society. The source of the dispute was the wording of the 1980 constitution, which described the VCP as "the only force leading the state and society." Although VCP conservatives were happy with this statement, the more progressive elements in the National Assembly believed that organizations outside the VCP could also positively direct society. A compromise was reached, and the resulting statement is that the VCP is "the leading force of the state and society."

A second sensitive issue was moderates' desire to have a government that reflected the U.S. system where there existed a defined separation of powers between the executive, judicial, and legislative branches of government. The conservatives and the VCP did not wish to share power with judicial and executive officials. The moderates lost this battle as the 1992 constitution affirmed that the National Assembly "is the people's highest representative agency and the highest organ of state power of the Socialist Republic of Vietnam. It exercises its supreme right of supervision over all operations of the state." The message from this portion of Article 83 is that the executive and judicial branches are subordinate to the continued dominance of the legislative arm of the government.

The third controversial matter was the reworking of the executive element of the government. Up to this point in the SRV this wing of the government was administered by a group of politicians in an organization called the Council of Ministers (COM). No one disputed that the COM's collective leadership was ineffective and needed transformation. It was finally decided that the executive branch should be headed by an individual instead of a group. Moreover, the COM was replaced by a prime minister who would work with a cabinet-style government. The National Assembly now elects the prime minister, who in turn nominates ministers to the various cabinet-type posts. These nominations are subject to the approval of the National Assembly.

Vietnamese officials expressed concern that too much power in the hands of one person could change the entire system. They insinuated that Mikhail Gorbachev was solely responsible for the collapse of the Soviet Union and that this might happen in Vietnam if a moderate ever became prime minister. The framers of the 1992 constitution intended to check the powers of the prime minister by creating an office of a president who would be the head of state. Although a somewhat ceremonial position, the president is the chief of the armed forces and holds high positions within the National Assembly. Also elected by the National Assembly, the president has the authority to dismiss the prime minister and the nation's highest justice official.

A fourth topic of debate was the relationship between local and centralized authorities. Provincial authorities enjoyed a surprising amount of autonomy based on former constitutions. Prior to 1992, local governments were controlled by committees, which were in turn supervised by local party officials. This pattern of local government created a gap between the state and the local governments. In short, it was the local communist officials who managed the provincial governments.

Before the implementation of the 1992 constitution, Vietnam had forty-eight provinces. The constitutional reformers wanted to reduce the governmental authority of local party officials, so they broke up the larger provinces. The number of Vietnam's provinces increased to sixty-one. In addition to reducing the size of Vietnam's largest provinces, the new constitution increased the state's authority in provincial regions by giving the prime minister the right to appoint and dismiss local leaders.

VIETNAM'S ARMED FORCES

The Vietnam People's Army (VPA) is the third strand, along with the VCP and the National Assembly, in a cord that binds the SRV together. The three organizations are interlinked and at times even redundant. Because of the VPA's size and history, it is essential to understand its place within Vietnam's government and society.

A judo class at the South Vietnam Military Academy (Bettmann/CORBIS)

Southeast Asia's history is marked by local, regional, and international conflicts. Yet, even within this area, Vietnam stands apart from its neighbors in the amount of war it has experienced. War and armies are integral parts of Vietnam's history. A legend concerning the very founding of Vietnam includes a man of prowess coming out of the sea to defeat an invading northern king. The country's earliest heroes are men and women who fought against intruders. By the ninth century, Vietnam's navy was considered the largest in the world, and one hundred years later it was reported that Vietnam's army was one million strong. These statistics are astounding considering that at the time its entire population was two million.

Foreign intrusion into Vietnamese territory necessitated that Vietnam have a strong army. As discussed in Chapter 1, the Vietnamese had endured one thousand years of Chinese rule before they successfully repelled their northern neighbor. Following this, the Vietnamese resisted the invading Mongol armies. During the nineteenth and twentieth centuries Vietnam successfully pushed out occupying forces from China, Japan, France, and the United States. It is quite evident that Vietnam has had to rely on its army for survival.

Compared to Vietnam's past great military forces, its modern army had extremely humble beginnings. On December 22, 1944, with a total membership of thirty-one men and three women, the Vietnam People's Army was founded. Just decades later, however, it was considered the fourth-largest army on the planet. It grew, in part, because it was so active. From 1946 to 1954, it battled the French colonial forces. This was followed by a two-decade struggle between North and South Vietnam—with the South receiving economic, military, and personnel assistance from the United States. Just three years after the 1975 unification of Vietnam, the VPA found itself entangled in another foreign war, this time in Cambodia. From 1978 until September 1989 Vietnam struggled to keep the Cambodian Khmer Rouge forces from reestablishing control over all Cambodia. During this decade-long war it was estimated that there were more landmines in Cambodia than human beings. Adding to Vietnam's military woes was China's February 1979 invasion of Vietnam's northern provinces. Following a brief occupation of northern Vietnam, China withdrew its forces. However, China stationed a substantial military force just across from Vietnam's border. This forced Vietnam to post thousands of troops in its northern provinces. During the 1980s and 1990s, Vietnam and China each expressed their military resolve to "protect" the potentially oil-rich Parcel Islands, which both countries claimed as their territory.

It is estimated that during the 1980s more than five million Vietnamese served in some aspect of their country's military establishment. This represented 8 percent of the population. Vietnam supported this massive army at the same time that the country was suffering economically. Most governments would have recognized that one obvious problem in Vietnam's economy was that 8 percent of the population was not contributing to the means of production. Moreover, the only reason Vietnam was able to support such an army during the 1980s was due to massive loans from the Soviet Union. Because of the strong military presence in the all-powerful politburo, the SRV refused to reduce its armed forces.

From the outset, VPA leaders were also high-ranking officials in the VCP. Most of these men (there were no leading women military officials) had similar backgrounds beginning with their teenage years. From their youth, these future military leaders were heavily involved in anticolonial activities. The French imprisoned many of them, but they were undeterred. While in jail, these young men preached a nationalist message to their fellow prisoners. A good number of the DRV's future leaders were converted to Marxism and nationalism while in jail. Once released from captivity, this group created a more sophisticated three-tier military system.

At the most basic level of Vietnam's military machine were the militia and self-defense forces. These groups consisted of all able-bodied Vietnamese adults, though most of the militia were between the ages of 17 to 45. The primary responsibility of the militia was to protect local areas. Officers in the VPA believed that the Vietnamese people were so attached to their farms and ancestral lands that they would fight tooth and nail to drive back invading forces. Moreover, the local militia's effectiveness was due, in part, to its extensive knowledge of local terrain.

Those that excelled in the local militia were promoted to serve at the provincial level. These individuals left their local areas and served as full-time military personnel throughout their particular province. Their duties included regular military exercises as well as participation in political classes. Above the rigors of battle, training, and political education, these soldiers also assisted the farmers in the daily duties associated with an agrarian society.

At the highest level in the VPA was the main army. Personnel at this tier of the military came from the elite within the provincial armies. Those assigned to the main army were called to move outside their provinces and at times to move into foreign land, including Cambodia.

Generals in the VPA take their orders from the VCP, and more particularly from the politburo within that organization. This is not surprising given that the highest military officials were also members of the politburo. However, following the reunification of Vietnam and the subsequent invasion of Cambodia, it became clear that changes had to be made to the VPA structure, particularly with regard to its relation to the VCP. Consequently, unit commanders received more authority to make decisions apart from party committees. Also, prior to 1983 each military unit had a political officer—who was the most authoritative figure in that section of the armed forces. In 1983, the political officer position was eliminated from the army, giving military officers greater authority. Nonetheless, it remains a fact that the party continues to wield control over the armed forces. Every member of the VPA must accept the decisions of the party—even above the desires of their military commanders.

Two years, 1986 and 1989, proved pivotal for the VPA. Though not far apart, these two years represented substantial internal and external changes that shaped the VPA's future. In December 1986, Vietnam's sixth National Party Congress was convened. At the meeting it was decided that Vietnam needed to begin a process of widespread reform throughout its institutions. This reform, also known as *doi moi*, had a profound effect on the VPA. Still wedged in an increasingly unpopular campaign in Cambodia, the politburo met to hammer out a new policy for the army. Although the results of these meetings remain secret, a so-called Politburo Resolution No. 2 was passed with regard to the army. Several points of this document included a shift in Vietnam's defense policy. Foremost in its new strategic outlook was a slash in the army's budget. This could only take place if three changes were implemented. First, the enormous size of the army had to be cut. Internal documents indicate that up to 600,000 troops were discharged from the military following the implementation of doi moi programs. Second, Vietnam's occupation of Cambodia had to be resolved. Not only was this costing Vietnam economically, it was also crippling Vietnam's efforts to normalize relations with its neighbor, China.

Third, military personnel were to become more involved in the means of production throughout the economy. In 1989, the Vietnamese withdrew from Cambodia.

Although the VPA has certainly had a glorious past, the current situation in Vietnam has meant hard times for those in Vietnam's military services. Demobilization of close to a million troops is a logistical nightmare even in a moderately strong economy. In the early 1990s, the reduction of Vietnam's armed forces coincided with the party's decision to move away from a state-controlled, subsidy-based economy to one where individual units were responsible to earn profits. In this new business pattern, managers were careful to measure their output against the salaries they had to pay workers. Workers were laid off just as unemployed soldiers were flooding into the urban areas. Some urban areas experienced a 30 percent unemployment rate. Business managers were also unwilling to hire former military personnel. Despite the government order to give priority for soldiers in new hiring situations, businesses turned a deaf ear to the soldiers because they were usually the least educated and rumored to be more difficult to manage than those without a military background. This was particularly an acute problem in Ho Chi Minh City and the rest of southern Vietnam. Most of the soldiers who were sent to Cambodia, and subsequently returned, were from the southern provinces. Moreover, when they returned to Vietnam after serving in Cambodia, they were passed over for jobs by those who had evaded the draft.

Responding to this situation, the veterans united to create the Club of Former Resistance Fighters (CFRF). At its outset the CFRF assisted veterans and their families. However, as its ranks swelled, and the government proved ineffective in providing aid for the poverty-stricken unemployed veterans, the CFRF became a political organization. Its vocal nature became evident in 1990 as hundreds of CFRF members sent petitions to reinstate the reformist leader Nguyen Van Linh. Several newspapers were published by the veterans' group, and its overt attack on the government and some of its leaders proved too much for the VCP. In 1992 the most influential figures in the club were seized, and the government created a Vietnam War Veteran's Association (WVA) and instructed all the disgruntled veterans to join this new state-approved society. Members of the WVA were promised a role in selecting future leaders in the National Assembly.

For those that remain in the Vietnam's armed forces, there is the ever-present problem of budget cuts and subsequent salary cuts. The government is delinquent in paying soldiers' salaries. These basic economic inadequacies also mean that the SRV does not have the funds to conduct basic maintenance on most of its equipment. An oversized military coupled with severe economic recession and the disintegration of the Soviet Union, the main supplier of funds for Vietnam's armed forces during the 1980s, have crippled Vietnam's armed forces.

VIETNAM'S EDUCATIONAL SYSTEM

Confucianism profoundly affected the development of education in Vietnam. Scholars were expected to control Confucian societies. In fact, the idealized Confucian government was ruled by a benevolent emperor surrounded by virtuous scholars. Of the three East Asian Marxist countries—North Korea, China, and Vietnam—it is the latter that most closely followed the Confucian pattern of education. That is, Vietnamese boys who demonstrated a propensity for learning were directed to the institutions of learning. Students in these schools primarily studied the Chinese literary classics. State-sponsored exams were based on Confucian literature, and Chinese was the language used by the bureaucratic scholars.

Historically, education in Vietnam was valued for several reasons. First and foremost, education was the primary, if not only, means for an individual and family to rise above poverty and the daily rigors of an agrarian life. Social prestige was another motivating factor for the Vietnamese to seek advancement through scholarship. The most admired and respected individuals in a Confucian society were scholars. Though other countries, such as Korea and China, also esteemed education, it was particularly prized in Vietnam. In Korea the bureaucracy was filled by the favorites of

A university in Vietnam. Education has always been a priority for Vietnamese families. (Leonard de Selva/CORBIS)

the court rather than through an open examination system. In China, there were other avenues for economic advancement apart from passing the state exams. Chinese entrepreneurial families created a merchant class that rivaled even the scholars in wealth. In Vietnam, however, options for social and economic advancement did not usually include nepotism or private enterprise. Villages and clans placed their aspirations for a better financial and political future onto local relatives who attempted to gain admittance to the bureaucracy through scholarly prowess. Private academies for aspiring examination candidates became part of the village landscape. Most of these schools were led by the local individual who had the most educational experience.

Despite the obvious rewards for the state's top scholars, education was not solely for aspiring exam candidates. Organized

Vietnamese women are finding opportunities for advancement through education. These high school girls are on their way to school. (Owen Franken/ CORBIS)

In an effort to plug into the capitalist markets of the world's economy, Vietnam has partnered with U.S. universities, including Boise State University. Here, Dr. Daryl Jones, the provost of Boise State, hands MBA diplomas to Vietnamese students who earned their degrees by studying in Hanoi and Boise. (Courtesy of Daryl Jones)

schooling was even accessible to those who would never take the state exam. Parents taught their sons and daughters to read and write in order to refine their minds as they cultivated the fields. However, when the French colonized Vietnam they reformed the education system. Teachers were forced to follow a strict French-approved curriculum. Most of the subjects taught were merely to prepare young people to work for the French. The colonial government needed indigenous clerks to assist the French. Many of the local teachers refused to follow the Western-centered courses in the colonial education system. It is estimated that only 2 percent of the population received a rudimentary introduction to the French-based education system.

By the time Ho Chi Minh declared the founding of the Democratic Republic of Vietnam in 1945, it is estimated that only 10 percent of the population was literate. An immediate goal of the DRV leaders was to educate the populace because they assumed that literacy would lead to political liberation. People would supposedly learn through books and essays that exploitation accompanied colonialism and that only a socialist government could remove the scourge of poverty. Between 1945 and 1949, the country began the drive for universal literacy with the "guerrilla model" of school. During this period, the Vietnamese freedom fighters were on the run from the French. They used the long periods between their fighting engagements to set up small schools throughout northern Vietnam. It is estimated that close to three million individuals gained literacy during these four years.

Between 1950 and 1975 both North and South Vietnam opened more educational facilities despite the military crisis both governments faced. When the country was unified in 1975, a national educational policy was set in place. Over the past twenty-five years there have been major changes in this system. This next section examines contemporary Vietnamese education on three levels: the primary and secondary levels of education, higher education, and the role of private schools.

Primary and Secondary Schools

It is somewhat understandable that the first priority of the SRV leaders was that the curriculum used in the education system reflect the nation's ideology. Southern Vietnamese teachers were required to attend reeducation camps as the communist party attempted to root out capitalist ideas that these educators might have learned. Between 1975 and 1979 the government used the public schools to promote a socialist political view. A consequence of this was that very little attention was directed toward the practical need to learn subjects such as math and science. During the first five years following North Vietnam's victory, however, a declaration made it clear that fundamental reform was needed in Vietnam's education system:

> Quantitatively our socialist education has developed very quickly, but it still has many weaknesses in all areas with respect to quality. The

principle that theoretical studies are to be combined with practice, education with productive labor and the school with the society has not been carried out, either with respect to content or to pedagogical method. In many areas the school has fallen behind social development as well as developments in science and technology and does not meet the demands of the socialist revolution. (Rubin 1993, 46)

An educational reform was made by the party in 1979 and was scheduled for implementation beginning the 1981–1982 school year. Before this reform was announced, Vietnam's education system was characterized by a three-tiered approach. Initially children would enter school at a primary level lasting four years. This was followed by a three-year lower-level secondary school. From this point students entered a three-year upper-level secondary school. Under this system students entering primary school were expected to possess rudimentary reading and writing skills. As such, children attended "ABC" classes prior to their entrance to primary schools. The 1979 reforms made fundamental changes to this system. ABC schools were converted to the first grade of primary school. Preuniversity schools in Vietnam followed this system: primary school (grades 1–5), lower secondary school (grades 6–8), and higher secondary school (grades 9–11).

After experimenting with this arrangement, the government finalized its precollege education structure:

Primary School (Grades 1–5)
    Age level: 6 to 11
Lower Secondary (Grades 6–9)
    Age level: 11 to 15
Technical Secondary: Three-year training program
    Age level: 12 to 15
Upper Secondary (Grades 10–12)
    Age level: 15 to 18

Just as with the earlier pattern, there are two levels of secondary schools. Also, for those students who have no desire or propensity to pursue academics, there is an opportunity to enroll in a technical or vocational school at the age of twelve. Students complain that these schools only prepare them for low-level skills such as hotel maids, office clerks, waiters, and other service-oriented careers. Other countries that offer vocational training as an alternative educational path usually prepare students for careers in computers or other technical jobs. Yet, despite the service-oriented training in Vietnamese vocational schools, it is estimated that the average salary of these waiters, office clerks, and so on exceeds teachers' wages.

The grading system in secondary schools is on a scale of 1 to10, with 10 being the highest score. A passing mark is above 5; an average grade is anywhere from 5.00 to 6.99; 7 to 7.99 marks represent an above-average score; 8 to 8.99 is very good; and 9 to 10 is excellent.

Although Vietnam is proud of its high literacy rate of nearly 95 percent and the successes of its mass education programs, there are at least four glaring problems with preuniversity training. First and foremost is the teacher shortage crisis. In the mid-1990s, the SRV reported that it faced a deficit of 60,000 elementary teachers. There is a similar lack of qualified personnel for secondary schools. Salary inequity is the primary reason why it is difficult to place qualified personnel in teaching positions. In 1995 the average salary of teachers was 60,000 dong per month (U.S. $6.00). This was only half of what individuals earned in the private business sector. Most teachers must have a second job— they often sell beverages or food in a makeshift market stall during the early evening hours. Some have resorted to ignoring the prescribed curriculum during the daytime. These educators then use the evening hours for private sessions where parents must pay for their children to learn the needed information to proceed to the next grade level.

Closely linked to the first crisis in Vietnam's education system is the problem of illiteracy among Vietnam's highland ethnic minorities. Despite the government's policy to monetarily reward teachers who volunteer for these remote assignments, educators complain that work among the highlanders is socially isolating. There is also a double price to pay for highland parents who send their children to primary and secondary schools. Although schooling is supposed to be free, this is not the case. Parents must financially supplement their local schools by paying for their children's textbooks or the teachers' salaries. In the highland areas, where the economic situation is bleaker than the lowland region, parents do not have the extra income to pay for their children's education. Ethnic minorities also depend on the entire household to assist in the family's economic enterprise. A child in school means that there is one less laborer in the field.

Although these problems are more acutely felt in Vietnam's highlands, they also plague the country's population. It remains an economic hardship for Vietnam's rural farmers (Vietnam's population is still 80 percent rural) to send their children to school. In the urban areas, the shift toward a more market-driven economy has entrepreneurial families abandoning the normal pattern of sending their children to school. Instead, they employ their offspring in the latest family enterprise. Scrounging together the money to open a business also results in parents abandoning the relatively expensive endeavor of sending their children to school.

The third crisis is the recent curriculum shift away from the traditional emphasis on history and ideology to the subjects of foreign language, mathematics, and science. Although these changes result in students with a more sophisticated understanding of the modern world and technology, the implications of a worldly wise youth on a communist society are potentially perilous. For example, in a recent survey less than 60 percent of Vietnam's teenagers recognized the name of Hung-Vuong, the legendary founder of Vietnam. In the same survey, more than 85 percent of the same respondents recognized the pop stars Michael Jackson and Madonna. In a society where ancestors are revered, the inability of young people to identify the supposed founder of their country is surprising if not disturbing. The VCP is keenly aware of how quickly European Marxist countries turned to new ideologies, and the government is trying to provide a modern education for its youth without compromising its socialist ideology.

One final problem in Vietnam's modern education system is the lack of opportunities for secondary school graduates. Over 1.3 million graduates join the country's workforce every year. Most of these job seekers spend years searching for their first job. Given this situation, it is not surprising that most upper secondary school graduates try to continue their studies. Unfortunately, less than 30 percent of these graduates are admitted to Vietnam's public university system. Thus, most youths find themselves with a secondary degree, but without any employment opportunity. Consequently, most secondary graduates are in a worse economic position than those students who entered vocational school at an earlier age.

In rural districts, local governments are reluctant to hire secondary education graduates. In fact, there is a stigma attached to these students because they are reportedly more difficult to manage than those young people who have not learned "so much new information." With few options, many return to agricultural labor, though they complain that they are underemployed.

Higher Education in Vietnam

Higher education in Vietnam is patterned after Western models, offering bachelor, masters, and doctorate degrees. There are approximately 125 institutions of higher education throughout Vietnam, all under the authority of the Ministry of Education and Training (MOET).

Several changes in the higher education system occurred following the 1975 reunification of the country. Previous to this, most colleges in the north focused on one discipline, and students chose a university based on what subject they intended to master. These colleges have since been turned into multidisciplinary institutions. In the mid-1990s, the MOET also combined more than a dozen colleges and created two national universities in Hanoi and Ho Chi Minh City.

The same issues that challenge Vietnam's secondary and elementary schools are evident in the nation's colleges. Salaries are so low that college professors are also forced to find second jobs. Equipment for basic experiments and lab sessions is not provided by the government. Many professors also complain that their students are not motivated once they enter college. Reportedly, students who pass the very difficult exam to qualify for higher education are confident that the hardest aspect of their education is over. They mistakenly assume that entrance into college assures them that they will one day become professionals.

Higher education's primary hurdle is that it cannot accommodate the hundreds of thousands who wish to enter its world. Less than one-third of those that apply for college are accepted. Students who are not admitted have an opportunity to wait a year and retake the college entrance exam. Thousands of young men and women spend an entire year reviewing for the exam, but even this does not guarantee success. Scores of junior colleges have emerged for students who fail to gain access to colleges. In addition, many rural towns are now offering state-sanctioned college courses for anyone who wishes to attend. The pattern in these schools is that local officials will invite professors from the larger cities to visit their town and teach a two-week intensive course on their area of specialty. When students accumulate enough credits from these two-week courses, they are awarded a college degree. Although this helps alleviate the overcrowded universities, many in Vietnam pejoratively call these schools "instant noodle universities." The growth of these rural college courses and junior colleges demonstrates that Vietnamese students, like their ancestors, tenaciously strive after the most education they can achieve.

Private Education in Vietnam

Although there is a rich tradition of private education in Vietnam, the DRV closed all nonpublic forms of education after the 1975 reunification of the country. Communist officials believed that they had to keep a close watch on every aspect of their new society, especially education. They were paranoid and defensive because of the foreign influence in South Vietnam, particularly between the years 1955 to 1975. Thus, all organizations, including private religious schools and orphanages, were forced to close after 1975.

Major problems in Vietnam's education system, some of which were previously noted, forced the government to soften its stand on private education. Following renovation programs in the later 1980s, private schools were once again permitted to open their doors to the public.

In the 1990s, a blurring between the public and private education systems made it difficult to correctly categorize various schools. Today there are three types of schools in Vietnam. First, there is the ordinary public school, which is supposed to be completely financed and managed by the state. In truth, parents who send their children to these institutions must pay for basic necessities such as textbooks. It is an expensive enterprise for Vietnamese children to attend public school. Second, there are semipublic schools wherein government facilities are used, but parents are responsible for paying the teachers' salaries. Finally, there are private schools that are established and maintained by nongovernment organizations.

In the primary grades, almost all children (98 percent) attend public schools. Semipublic schools at the primary level number just over 200. They are more highly regarded than the basic public instruction. Children spend more time in the classroom in the semipublic primary schools than they do in their public counterparts. The SRV has also allowed Catholic nuns to establish private urban schools for children who live on the streets or whose parents are too poor to send them to public school. The Daughters of Charity, a Catholic organization, runs more than a half dozen such schools. The SRV allows these schools to function because of their social benefits.

At the secondary level, private schools have grown in popularity because the competition to enter higher education has prompted parents to send their children where the graduation and college entrance rates are highest. More than 5 percent of secondary students now attend some type of private school in Vietnam. Private school officials advertise that they can guarantee that disciplined students who enter their institutions will pass the college entrance exams. It is probable that private secondary schools will increase in number as long as it remains difficult to gain entrance into Vietnam's college system.

Finally, 96 percent of higher education students attend public colleges and universities. Students who attend private colleges typically pay double the tuition cost of a public school. It can be expected, however, that as the number of college-aged young people continue to increase, there will be more opportunities to establish private schools. At this point, the government cannot commit the funds necessary to properly educate its youth, and alternative schools continue to grow in number.

VIETNAMESE RELIGION

Although it identifies itself as a Buddhist state, the complex nature of religious affiliation in Vietnam is rooted in a long history of numerous indigenous and external faiths shaping the spiritual landscape of Vietnam. It has been said that the imported world religions in Southeast Asia are merely thin sacred coverings over the indigenous faiths. This is evident in the Philippines and Indonesia, where Catholicism and Islam have accommodated local folklore and heroes to fit into these foreign religions.

In Vietnam, the first inhabitants were deeply spiritual, despite the absence of any organized religion. The earliest deities for the Vietnamese were identified with nature, and the first forms of worship involved trying to appease animistic (nonphysical) spirits. This form of religion is called animism. Animists believe that the gulf between the dead and living worlds is minimal. Based on this doctrine, spirits of the dead inhabit the world of the living. As the pantheon of gods grew in Vietnam, so too did the people's conviction that these deities' spirits hovered around the world of the living. For the earliest inhabitants in Vietnam, these unseen spirits determined whether to bless or curse particular people and areas. A host of taboos and rituals emerged based on the belief that people could appease the angry spirits.

Vietnamese animists also constructed a theory wherein certain words, when spoken, had magical powers. Thus, if someone would just speak the name of a deity, that spirit would automatically become present. Because most spirits were harmful, their names were rarely mentioned. Similarly, the names of other entities that brought fear and destruction, such as tigers, elephants, typhoons, and floods, were only whispered during day-to-day conversations so as to keep these objects from suddenly appearing. The alarm of conjuring up evil spirits through the spoken word influenced how Vietnamese parents named their offspring. Children were usually not given the names of deceased relatives since speaking that name would disturb the rest of the departed. Consequently, children eventually became identified by numbers—according to their birth order. Southern Vietnamese parents were particularly fearful that the evil spirits would kidnap their most precious possession—their first sons. For this reason first sons were often named "Two." It was also not unusual for the first sons to be dressed in girls' clothes until they reached puberty. These were a few of the measures parents used to protect their first sons from the unseen world. Another custom of Vietnamese parents was to assign their children unflattering names that would reportedly make their children unattractive to the evil spirits. Children who safely reached adolescence were often given permanent, more pleasant, names.

Although profound mourning accompanies the death of a loved one, most Vietnamese continue to believe that there is little that separates the worlds of the living and dead. It is imperative, therefore, that a proper burial and continued veneration be provided for the deceased. This includes choosing the proper location for the gravesite. Geomancers now use helicopters to survey the land for proper burial sites—a telling example of ancient beliefs mixing with modern technology. For most Vietnamese farmers, burial grounds are adjacent to their villages or farmland. Their natural attachment to these graveyards is one reason for the failure of the U.S.-South Vietnam peasant relocation programs during the 1950s and 1960s.

Not every person lives a virtuous life, however, and not every individual has the privilege to be accorded a proper burial followed by years of veneration. Vietnamese believe that if a corpse is not given a proper burial or appropriate veneration, then the deceased's spirit will aimlessly roam the earth. Such wandering souls are reportedly a menace to the good spirits and to those still living. These so-called lost souls are honored every year on the full moon of the seventh lunar month. This festival is a time of cele-bration with gifts of food and money offered to the sorrowful departed spirits.

Although some may characterize these actions as supersti-tious, there remains an established belief in Vietnam that the world is ordered by spiritual forces. Particular days of the lunar month are still regarded as so ill-omened that one should avoid beginning any major project on such dates. Certainly one should not marry on these dates, and farmers do not begin the process of planting or harvesting on these days. It should also be noted that similar views are held throughout Southeast Asia. For example, farmers in the Philippines choose particular days to begin the harvest and refuse to transplant rice seedlings on certain days of the month—though they follow the Western calendar rather than the lunar months.

Chinese Religious Influence

Institutions that came to Vietnam from China include Daoism, Confucianism, and Buddhism. Confucianism and Buddhism are evident in Vietnam's past and present, but the impact of Daoism should not be underestimated. Daoism is based on the third-cen-tury compilation of sayings in the *Daodejing,* or *The Way and Integrity Classic.* Sketchy at best, this philosophy's origins are supposedly traced to a group that emphasized breathing regimens, particular diets, and intense meditation. The reported goal of the first Daoists was to extend life. Because most people want to live longer than they do, Daoist priests had little trouble attracting followers—including emperors, who had just about everything except the promise of a long life. Following the introduction of Confucianism, Daoist leaders used their tenet of embracing all of life to counteract the Confucian prescriptive rules on relationships. Although Daoism evolved into a philosophy where one is taught to enjoy life and welcome whatever fate brings, it did not lose its original emphasis on extending life through particular disciplines and alchemy. Daoist temples were built throughout Vietnam, housing the priests that spread the message of the *Daodijing*.

People argue whether Confucianism is primarily a religion or a philosophy. One issue that is clear is that Confucianism has had a profound impact on many Asian societies. Indeed, apart from the city-state of Singapore, Vietnam is the most Confucian-influenced society in Southeast Asia. This is evidenced by the centuries-long Confucian-centered bureaucratic system that held Vietnam together.

Born into a world of political chaos in northeast China during the middle of the sixth century B.C.E., Confucius based his teaching on the writings and traditions of China's sage kings who lived more than a millennia before Christ. Surveying the incessant civil war in China, Confucius believed that if society would follow his systematized doctrines, then peace would prevail. In short, Confucius taught that a man's (he was chauvinistic in his teaching) chief end was to become a virtuous gentleman through the means of proper ritual behavior and through the maintenance of hierarchical relationships. Thus, it was not enough for an individual to conduct a burial ceremony for a departed relative; it had to be done with correct etiquette and proper attitude. An example of a simple ritual in many modern societies is shaking hands. Although this is a common activity on a social level, a handshake can convey a host of different feelings and attitudes. It might be a signal that someone is happy to see you, is angry with you, is apathetic, and so on. Thus, it is not enough to know how to shake someone's hand; it must be done correctly.

Confucian scholars studied the wisdom literature of China's sage kings so they could teach the uneducated masses the correct protocols for the numerous rites that were part of Chinese society. These scholars were also paid to perform ceremonies, thus giving the people confidence that the proper etiquette had accompanied the formal procedure.

Confucius also taught that social harmony was based on hierarchical relationships. Chinese teachers insisted that people remain in their assigned social stations. There are five human relationships that Confucian scholars focused on: ruler-subject, father-son, husband-wife, older brother–younger brother, friend-friend. In the first four associations, there is a definite hierarchy wherein the second party was required to demonstrate obedience and deference to the individual above them.

Mencius, a later disciple of Confucius, elaborated on the ruler-subject connection. He claimed that a ruler reigned based on a mandate from heaven. Chinese were advised to obey their emperor because heaven had placed him on the throne. Disobedience against the sovereign was tantamount to questioning the wisdom and authority of heaven. At the same time, rulers were ordered to conduct themselves in a manner worthy of their position. If through decadence and moral recklessness emperors abused their position, then heaven would withdraw its blessing. Natural disasters such as famine, flood, and disease indicated heaven's displeasure with a particular ruler or dynasty. Mencius taught that if such catastrophes occur, it was the people's responsibility to replace the emperor. Vietnamese used this doctrine to justify their periodic rebellions against corrupt regimes.

Mencius also placed a high value on education. In his estimation, every human being (male) was born with equal abilities. However, only a very few develop their intellectual capabilities while others are content to work with their hands—whether as farmers or ditch-diggers. Based on this doctrine, a scholarly elite class emerged both in Vietnam and China, as previously discussed.

Of the numerous aspects of Confucianism adopted in Vietnamese society, the two most apparent facets were the bureaucratic system and the emphasis on veneration of parents. From the tenth century until the second half of the twentieth century, Vietnam was ruled by emperors who surrounded themselves with scholars. Confucianism also matched Vietnam's preexisting concept of ancestor worship.

Yet, while the Vietnamese were ready to follow Confucian direction with regard to parent-child relationships, they would not fully embrace the deeply chauvinistic aspects of the foreign philosophy. Vietnamese women continued to hold a higher position in family and society than their counterparts in China.

Buddhism in China

Vietnam enjoyed a cosmopolitan atmosphere from the outset of its existence. Situated at the crossroads between the great civilizations of China and India, Vietnamese ports were inhabited by East, South, and Southeast Asia merchants. Foreign Buddhist missionaries made their way into Vietnam by following northern and southern trade routes. By the second century A.D. the region surrounding modern-day Hanoi was designated a center of Buddhist studies. Eventually, this religion became so pervasive that Vietnam is identified as a Buddhist state.

Myanmar (Burma), Thailand, Laos, and Cambodia are other Southeast Asian countries that are also considered Buddhist states. However, the branch of Buddhism practiced in Vietnam differs from the form followed in these other countries. The two main divisions of this religion are the Theravada and Mahayana schools. Theravada Buddhism is the more orthodox and conservative arm of this world religion. It is the primary form practiced among most Southeast Asian Buddhists. Mahayana Buddhism, the religion of Vietnam, is more elastic in its doctrines. The Mahayana branch of Buddhism is sometimes referred to as the "greater vehicle" because it is characterized as a cart of salvation that is so large and accessible that it can carry an innumerable number of people to nirvana, the Buddhist heaven. The notion of a heaven where joy, peace, and pleasure reign is not advocated among orthodox Buddhists. Nevertheless, the focus on eternal life for the Vietnamese Buddhists created an amalgamation of Daoism and magic incantations to facilitate one's salvation.

A Cao Dai temple in Vietnam. One of the branches of Buddhism in Vietnam is the Cao Dai sect. (Corel)

A type of folk-religion emerged from the syncretism of Buddhism, Daoism, and animism. Although Buddhism remained the title of the religion, it was in essence a conglomeration of indigenous, Chinese, and other foreign beliefs.

Buddhist monks were one of the two scholarly groups on which Vietnamese leaders relied to provide advice on domestic and foreign matters. The other learned assembly of scholars was Confucian intellectuals. Although the Vietnamese emperors employed members from both groups, they were hesitant to rely too much on the Confucian literati because of their ties with China. Confucian intellectuals were steeped in China's philosophy, which advocated the supremacy of China over all other states. In contrast, Buddhist monks were not tied to any particular family or ethnic group—their loyalties supposedly transcended the earthly world.

As the centuries passed, Vietnamese Buddhist monks and monasteries grew in number and influence. By the eleventh cen-

The monks scattered throughout Vietnam try to remain free of politics, but they are closely monitored by the Vietnamese government. (Steve Raymer/ CORBIS)

tury the Buddhist sangha (church) was so influential that it was able to install Ly Cong Uan, an orphan that had been raised by Buddhist monks, as emperor. Imperial favor on the Buddhist sangha legitimized this foreign religion for Vietnam's mostly rural population.

One example of Vietnamese regal support for Buddhism was the eleventh-century command that a Buddhist temple be built in every Vietnamese village. Close to one thousand structures were constructed in response to the emperor's decree. Vietnamese leaders also had Buddhist structures erected on the periphery of Vietnam's boundaries as well as in the highland areas. These buildings were also used to demonstrate Vietnamese supremacy in the state's remote regions.

One dilemma for Buddhist clergy was that their emphasis on the transitory nature of human existence clashed with their involvement in the very earthly matter of politics. Their expanding influence at the imperial court was justified through the Mahayana doctrine of the bodhisattva. This is the notion that there are people who achieve full enlightenment in this life. However, because of their compassion, these enlightened beings remain in the world to work for humanity's salvation. There is a Buddhist text wherein bodhisattvas are instructed to assist political powers. They are told to advise governors, kings, and emperors so that these leaders will follow the way of compassion. Vietnamese Buddhist monks used this text to justify their intrusion into the political realm.

However, Buddhism and politics in Vietnam have occasionally been at odds with each other. For example, during the nineteenth and twentieth centuries there were three Buddhist movements that resulted in political chaos. In the first two, the religious zeal, while labeled Buddhism, was actually a product of popular folk religion mixed with various Buddhist doctrines. This amalgamation was possible because of the inclusive nature of Mahayana sects.

The first noted clash occurred at the midpoint of the nineteenth century. At this point in history, Vietnam was in the throes of internal decay and also faced external threats from a colony-hungry France. These hard times reinforced the Vietnamese Buddhist understanding of the cyclical nature of history. This theory claims that the cosmos experiences phases of richness, decay, and destruction. When this cycle is completed, then a natural disaster, such as a flood or earthquake, cleanses the earth. This is immediately followed by a cosmic renewal. Most in the Mahayana vein hold that the present age is ruled by Siddhartha Gautama, the Indian prince who achieved enlightenment and became the Buddha. Many Vietnamese in the 1850s believed that the age of Gautama was ending and the universe was on the brink of complete chaos. Monks preached that a new age would soon be ushered in by the appearing of Maitreya, the new Buddha. Maitreya, a semi-Messiah figure, is an extremely popular figure in Vietnamese history, and numerous temples are dedicated to the anticipated savior who will lead the universe into a new age of peace and prosperity. Around 1850, monks asserted that they knew the exact site where the new Buddha would descend to earth. The supposed locale was a hilly region in southwest Vietnam that bordered Cambodia. The area was named the Buu Son Ky Huong or Strange Fragrance from the Precious Mountain. The Maitreya was supposed to appear on a mountain, and his teachings were likened to a pleasant aroma (Strange Fragrance). Buddhist leaders instructed those that wanted to view this revelation to move to this region and purify themselves through meditation. Despite the inhospitable weather, scores of families congregated to the Vietnam-Cambodian border. A disparate group of religious zealots, including numerous Daoist priests, created a community of believers at the Buu Sun Ky Huong.

At the outset, the Buu Son Ky Huong community steered clear of politics. It was less interested in the present than the anticipated future. However, as French intrusion increased in southern Vietnam, members of the Buu Son Ky Huong became involved in anticolonial activities. They justified this political/military action by asserting that since the end of the age was so near, violence against the French was the final push that would usher in the new era. The French responded to this social/religious upheaval by proclaiming the community illegal. There did, however, remain an underground remnant of this sect that would emerge during the first half of the twentieth century.

During 1939, the twenty-year-old Huynh Phu So revived the teachings of the Buu Son Ky Huong and founded the Hoa Hao Buddhist sect. Originally from southwest Vietnam, the Hoa Hao founder grew up surrounded by the legends of earlier apocalyptic leaders. As a young man, Huynh Phu So claimed that he was the reincarnation of a Buu Son Ky Huong leader. According to Huynh Phu So, the cosmos was on a downward spiral due to humanity's selfishness. To counteract this negative energy, he taught that people needed to move away from meaningless religious rituals that governed so much of their spiritual lives. In place of these hollow acts of piety, Huynh Phu So stressed the necessity of positive outward action toward one's neighbor. Salvation was also expressed in terms of a communal event rather than something centered on the individual. This doctrine spilled over into political action. In some sense it had to, as members of the Hoa Hao tried to prevent the colonial government's exploitation of society's poor and disenfranchised citizens.

The year 1939 was an opportune moment for Huynh Phu Su to launch his sect of Buddhism. Vietnam immediately felt the effects of World War II and from 1939 to 1945 its citizens were buffeted economically, socially, and politically by French and Japanese soldiers. Japanese and French soldiers had little regard for the Vietnamese people's welfare. This resulted in widespread famine and a thousand other sorrows for the Vietnamese. Surely these trials demonstrated that the world was in such a degenerate state that the Hoa Hao's reported new age was imminent. Millions of southern Vietnamese people joined the Hoa Hao sect. An underground Hoa Hao political network labored to relieve the suffering of the poor farmers. It also sought to destabilize the oppressive political system in and around Saigon.

Japan's sudden surrender created a political vacuum in southern Vietnam. A host of competing organizations rushed in to fill the void. Members of the Hoa Hao sect were the strongest indigenous political presence in 1945 southwestern Vietnam. Once again, Buddhism mixed with politics. The result was fatal. As Ho Chi Minh's northern Vietminh soldiers spread the message that a Democratic Republic of Vietnam was the country's new independent government, many southern Vietnamese were unwilling to pledge allegiance to this new political organization. Leaders of the Hoa Hao rejected the northern-based DRV. Vietminh agents responded by finding the whereabouts of Huynh Phu So, assassinating him, and persecuting disciples of the Hoa Hao sect. Consequently, many Hoa Hao members became ardent opponents of the communist regime in the north and, in fact, turned to the French and then the United States for political guidance.

During the 1960s the political situation in South Vietnam created the third major Buddhist-government crisis. After the 1954 division of Vietnam, based on the Geneva Accords, the United States supported Ngo Dinh Diem's presidency in the south. Diem, from Hue, was a devout Catholic, and his brother Ngo Dinh Thuc was the archbishop of Hue. As mentioned earlier, President Diem experienced political pressure on numerous fronts during his tenure as South Vietnam's leader. The main issue that caused his domestic and foreign allies to forsake him, however, was his alleged discriminatory treatment of the Buddhist church. A couple of incidents escalated the poor relations between the Buddhist leaders and Diem's government. Paradoxically, the first of these crises took place in Diem's hometown of Hue. On May 8, 1963, a rally was held in Hue at which several speeches were made denouncing the government's oppression of Buddhism. At the heart of these allegations was the government's order that religious flags could not be publicly displayed. The government's rationale for this proclamation was that a sense of national pride needed to be fostered among its citizens; thus, the state's flag should be the only emblem allowed in public places. Diem's officials stated that this policy was not exclusively directed toward Buddhist organizations because Catholic parishes also had to comply with these orders; they were prohibited from displaying the Vatican flag in public.

Officials regarded the May 8 speeches as an all-out protest against the Diem regime. That day troops were called in and eight protestors were killed. Two days later, the Buddhist clergy issued a five-point proposal for better government-Buddhist relations. The first proposal was that the government cancel its prohibition against the public display of religious flags. They also insisted that Buddhists be accorded the same legal rights as Catholics, that the government cease their arbitrary arrests of Buddhist leaders, that the families of the eight killed on May 8 be compensated, and that those responsible for the deaths be punished.

Diem laughed off these requests because he believed that the Buddhist influence in South Vietnam was insufficient to create a political crisis. He was wrong. At noon on June 11, 1963, the venerable Thich Quang Duc, a seventy-three-year-old Buddhist monk, was brought to a busy intersection of Saigon where he sat down while his companions poured gasoline over him, soaking his saffron robe. A moment later the monk struck a match and remained in place while his body was destroyed by the flames. Malcolm Browne, an Associated Press correspondent, was on the scene and took photographs of the dramatic event. His images were on the front pages of newspapers throughout the world the following day. Diem's sister-in-law referred to the incident as a barbecue. The peaceful protest of a Buddhist monk brought so much criticism on the Diem regime that it was just a matter of months until a U.S.-approved military coup pushed him out of power.

Religion and the SRV

During 1947, Ho Chi Minh wrote a letter to Vietnam's Buddhist Association in which he noted that "Buddhism can develop only in an independent Vietnam. The French colonialists had wanted to rob us of our country. They burned down Buddhist temples and statues of Buddhas, they persecuted the monks and nuns, and massacred Buddhist followers, all in the aim of destroying Buddhism [in Vietnam]. Buddha is compassion itself, succor to those in suffering and misery. To succor people from such a state, he sacrificed himself in the struggle to fight the demons and devils of this world" (Do 2000). Despite these kind words from Vietnam's foremost communist leader, the DRV persecuted many Buddhist religious figures. Because of this harassment, many Buddhist leaders, like their Catholic counterparts, relocated to South Vietnam in the 1950s. Throughout the Vietnam-U.S. War, the southern Buddhist Church served as a voice of conscience for the poor. It was also instrumental in making the world aware of social and political conditions in South Vietnam.

Immediately following the DRV's 1975 victory over South Vietnam, religious organizations were required to cooperate with the Hanoi-based government. In 1977 Prime Minister Pham Van Dong issued Resolution 297, which spelled out the limits of religious freedoms. It also proclaimed that the government had the authority to confiscate Buddhist church properties. This was not an idle decree. Various Buddhist-run orphanages were seized in an effort to demonstrate that society's ills would be cured through a communist enlightened society, not by religious institutions.

The foremost organization of the Buddhist religion in Vietnam is the United Buddhist Church of Vietnam (UBCV). In 1975 this organization had more than 30,000 monks that served in monasteries across the country. When the DRV united Vietnam the top three leaders of the UBCV in hierarchical order were Thich Don Hau, Thich Huyen Quang, and Thich Quang Do. Each of these men continued to speak out against social injustices, and all were arrested. In 1981 the government replaced the UBCV by a new "patriotic" Vietnam Buddhist Church. This new organization, which is controlled by the government, is not sanctioned by the UBCV leaders. Despite the UBCV's peaceful protest, the SRV has been quite successful in quieting the religious voices of dissent. Of the three above-noted leaders of the UBCV, only Thich Quang Do remains a free voice of opposition against the SRV and the state-run Buddhist Church.

In 1992 Thich Don Hau died and the UBCV mantle of leadership fell on Thich Huyen Quang—who was exiled to the Hoi Phuoc Pagoda in Quang Ngai province. Thich Quang Do, now in his seventies, has also been in and out of detention. Yet the more he is mistreated, the greater his influence grows in Vietnam and around the world. He is not afraid to speak up against the government's attempt to control the Buddhist church. In a 1999 letter addressed to CPV and SRV officials—as well as the international community—Do made three requests of his government: to reduce taxes so that the people would have enough money to buy basic necessities, to allow the Unified Buddhist Church of Vietnam to once again be a legal organization, and for the SRV to do away with the death penalty. Although the SRV did not honor Do's requests, its leaders did not punish him for sending the letter to the government. Human-rights activists believe that the SRV allows Do to speak openly because it realizes that the outlawed UBCV is led by old men. Once these senior monks pass from the scene, the SRV assumes that the dissenting UBCV will join the government-approved Vietnam Buddhist Church.

Since 1975, the Vietnamese government's relationship with Christian churches has followed two tracks. First, with regard to the Catholic Church, SRV officials have allowed indigenous clergy to maintain relations with the Vatican. Catholic bishops are free to travel to Rome, and Catholic nuns are permitted to manage private schools and orphanages for the cities' poor children. Nevertheless, the government continues to maintain strict control over the training, ordination, and placing of Vietnamese Catholic priests. This has created a major shortage of Christian ministers in Vietnam. Many priests, especially in the north, must serve more than a half-dozen parishes. During 1992, the SRV only permitted twenty of the forty-three men who completed their course at the Ho Chi Minh City seminary to be ordained. The arbitrariness of this decision is evident in that six years earlier the government approved all forty-three men to begin their careers as novices at the seminary.

Catholic priests, like the rest of the Vietnamese, are limited in their free speech. In 1990, the Catholic priest Chan Tin was placed under house arrest for preaching three sermons wherein he called on the SRV to repent for its past sins. He pointed to the example of the Soviet Union as a country that was rightly changing from the inside-out. The government also rejected the Vatican's request that Nguyen Van Thuan, a nephew of President Ngo Dinh Diem, be allowed to return to Vietnam and take a post in the Vietnamese Catholic Church. Finally, the SRV encourages Vietnamese priests to serve in the National Assembly. The Vatican continues to disagree with the SRV on this matter. The Catholic Church fears that if priests join the National Assembly, the SRV will gain control over them and split the church, just as it has done with the Buddhist Church.

The SRV's relationship with the Vietnamese Protestant churches is even more volatile than with the Catholic Church. In fact, it is the rapid growth of Protestant groups throughout Vietnam that has the SRV government deeply concerned. The Christian organizations gaining the most converts in Vietnam are the fundamentalists and the Pentecostals. The doctrines of these Protestant churches make them both attractive to the Vietnamese people and cause grave concern for SRV leaders.

A major tenet of Protestant fundamentalist theology is that Christians must not become entangled in popular society and culture. This means that Vietnamese fundamentalists do not participate in animistic-based rituals, non-Christian religious celebrations, or any social gathering that does not have conservative Christian overtones. In Vietnam—where Buddhism is the dominant religion—the implications of Christian fundamentalist separatism affect every area of social interaction. Consequently, Vietnamese fundamentalists refuse to participate in community celebrations such as a town's annual festival celebrating the municipality's patron god.

Vietnamese communities are noted for their intense kinship loyalty and the emphasis placed on group behavior. Yet, Protestant fundamentalism stresses spiritual individualism and a personal relationship with Jesus Christ. It is with some astonishment, then, that one finds thousands of fundamentalist congregations throughout Vietnam. What motivates the Vietnamese to make such a radical departure from tradition and culture? The answer to this question is multifaceted, but it is certainly rooted in three aspects of fundamentalist doctrine, that is, the explanation for current suffering, the guarantee of a glorious future, and the personal aspect of this conservative community.

As an antiintellectual movement, fundamentalism in Vietnam does not attract the professional elite. Demographically, it is the economic lower class that fills the conservative Christian congregations. A dominant theme in fundamentalist sermons is that the Christians' poverty and persecution in this life are due to the wickedness of this world and the rule of the devil on this earth. Moreover, fundamentalism claims that Christ's return to earth is about to happen, and Christians are encouraged to patiently wait for this event.

Another motivation for Vietnamese conversion to fundamentalism is the biblical promise that in the end, the last will be first and the first will be last. Fundamentalists proudly hold to the literal translation of the Bible; therefore, they promise that every believer will receive a mansion and walk on streets of gold when they get to heaven. It only takes a prayer to be guaranteed that one will be rich for eternity. Vietnamese pastors tell their followers that though every true believer must wear the badge of an antisocial religious fanatic, this brief humiliation will result in eternal rewards.

Finally, in a region where monks, priests, and nuns must minister to millions of people, there often arises a sense of impersonal leadership. Many Vietnamese claim that their spiritual needs are not met because of the sheer number of people to whom their religious leaders must minister. Fundamentalists, in contrast, emphasize the duty of pastors to make weekly visitations to all their church members. Fundamentalist churches also foster a community where accountability, emotional and financial support, and a close-knit subculture are nurtured.

Protestant charismatic groups in Vietnam are increasing for the same reasons that the fundamentalists congregations are. Much to the chagrin of the SRV, these conservative Christian churches are growing rapidly among the highland ethnic minorities. The government cites the power of the radio for these successes. Religious radio programs are broadcast to these regions from outside Vietnam—mainly from the Philippines. The religious zeal of charismatic and fundamentalist Protestant groups is such that they broadcast Bible programs in the various Vietnamese dialects and languages, and then make sure that the ethnic minorities have a radio set and are able to listen to the programs in their particular language.

In a 1998 document from the SRV's Bureau of Minority and Religious Affairs in Lao Cai province, the government insinuated that this Protestant religious revival is a calculated plot of the old imperialist nations: "The U.S. imperialists still manoeuvre various foreign Protestant denominations to provide financial aid for their related churches to multiply believers and expand their area of influence. . . .The Americans hope that some day there will be a conflict between the local government authorities and the new followers of the evangelical faith" (Hiebert 2000). Despite the government's contention that this religious proselytizing is imperialism in a different guise, it cannot seem to curb its growth among the poor and ethnic minorities throughout Vietnam.

References

Baker, G. "Small but Perfectly Formed with Vietnam's Economy Bucking the Asian Trend by Exhibiting Decent Growth, Foreign Investors Are Beginning to Look Seriously at What the Country Has to Offer." *Euromoney,* February 2001: 68–71.

Cheng, Allen T. "From Our Correspondent: A Tale of Two Countries." *AsiaWeek,* mail@web.asiaweek.com, http://www.asiaweek.com. January 8, 2001.

Chifos, Carla Marie. *Southeast Asian Urban Environments: Structured and Spontaneous.* Tempe, Ariz.: Arizona State University Press, 2000.

Communist Party of Vietnam. "The Seventh National Congress." http://www.cpv.org. June 24–27, 1991.

Dinh, Quan Xuan. "The Political Economy of Vietnam's Transformation Process." *Contemporary Southeast Asia* 22, no. 2 (2000): 360–381.

Do, Thich Quang. "Amnesty Plea from Thich Quang Do." Radio Free Asia. http://www.vinsight.org. March 31, 2000.

Drummund, L. B. W. "Street Scenes: Practices of Public and Private Space in Urban Vietnam." *Urban Studies* 37, no. 12 (2000): 2377–2391.

Duong, L. B., and W. J. Morgan. "The Contribution of Vocational Education and Training to the Integration of Refugee Returnees in Vietnam." *Compare* 31, no. 1 (2001): 93–112.

"Ethnic Uproar: Vietnam's Press and Legislators Pursue the Corrupt in a Government Scandal." *Far Eastern Economic Review* 164, no. 3 (2001): 28.

Glewwe, Paul, and Harry Anthony Patrinos. "The Role of the Private Sector in Education in Vietnam: Evidence from the Vietnam Living Standards Survey." *World Development* 27, no. 5 (1999): 887–901.

Gluckman, Ron. "Stops and Starts: A Journey Through Vietnam Finds That as Pumped as Its Baby Boomers Are, Change Is a Fitful Process." *AsiaWeek,* mail@web.asiaweek.com. http://www.asiaweek.com. April 14, 2000.

Hang, Nguyen Thi Lien. "The Double Diaspora of Vietnam's Catholics." *Orbis* 39, no. 4 (1995): 491.

Henin, Bernard Henry. "Transformation of Vietnam's Upland Societies under Market Reform." Ph. D. thesis. University of Victoria, Canada, 1999.

Hiebert, Murray. "The Drop-out Factor." *Far Eastern Economic Review* 153, no. 38 (September 19, 1991): 20–21.

———. "No Jobs for the Boys." *Far Eastern Economic Review* 153, no. 38 (September 19, 1991): 21–22.

———. "Secrets of Repression: 'Top Secret' Documents Offer a Rare Glimpse of Official Views on the Need to Control the Spread of Religion." *Far Eastern Economic Review.* http://www.feer.com. November 16, 2000.

Izumida, Y., and P. B. Duong. "Measuring the Progress of Rural Finance in Vietnam." *Savings and Development* 25, no. 2 (2001): 139–166.

Kabeer, Naila, and Thi Van Anh Tran. *Leaving the Rice Fields but not the Countryside: Gender, Livelihood Diversification and Pro-Poor Growth in Rural Viet Nam.* Geneva: United Nations Research Institute for Social Development, 2000.

Kelly, David, and Anthony Reid. *Asian Freedoms: The Idea of Freedom in East and Southeast Asia.* New York: Cambridge University Press, 1998.

Kent, Stephen A. *From Slogans to Mantras: Social Protest and Religious Conversion in the Late Vietnam War Era.* Syracuse, N.Y.: Syracuse University Press, 2001.

Kerkvliet, Benedict, and Doug Porter, eds. *Vietnam's Rural Transformation.* Transitions: Asia and Asian America. Boulder, Colo.: Westview Press, 1995.

Khanh, Huynh Kim. *Vietnamese Communism 1925–1945.* Ithaca: Cornell University Press, 1982.

Koichiro, Toyama. *Young Vietnam: Doi Moi's Children.* Singapore: Think Centre, 1999.

Kolko, Gabriel. *Vietnam: Anatomy of Peace.* New York: Routledge, 1997.

Marr, David G. "Tertiary Education, Research, and the Information Sciences in Vietnam." Pp. 15–44 in *Postwar Vietnam: Dilemmas in Socialist Development,* edited by David G. Marr and Christine P. White. Ithaca: Southeast Asia Program, Cornell University, 1993.

McLeod, Mark W. "Nationalism and Religion in Vietnam: Phan Boi Chau and the Catholic Question." *The International History Review* 14, no. 4 (1992): 661–680.

Nguyen, Thai Thu. *History of Buddhism in Vietnam.* Washington, D.C.: Council for Research in Values and Philosophy, 1997.

On the Cruel Edges of the World: The Untold Story of the Persecution of the Church among Vietnam's Minority Peoples. Bangkok: Religious Liberty Commission, 1999.

Pettus, Ashley S. "Vietnam's Learning Curve: Dwindling Subsidies Squeeze Teachers and Parents." *Far Eastern Economic Review* 157, no. 33 (August 18, 1994): 36–37.

Porter, Gareth. *Vietnam: The Politics of Bureaucratic Socialism.* Politics and International Relations of Southeast Asia. Ithaca: Cornell University Press, 1993.

Raymond, C. "The Power of the Strong: Rural Resistance and Reform in China and Vietnam." *China Information* 14, no. 2 (2001): 1–30.

Roper, C. T. "Sino-Vietnamese Relations and the Economy of Vietnam's Border Region." *Asian Survey* 40, no. 6 (2000): 1019–1041.

Rubin, Susanne. "Learning for Life? Glimpses from a Vietnamese School." Pp. 45–60 in *Postwar Vietnam: Dilemmas in Socialist Development,* edited by David G. Marr and Christine P. White.. Ithaca: Southeast Asia Program, Cornell University, 1993.

Stier, Ken. "Keeper of the Flame: Thich Quang Do Is the Conscience of Buddhism in Vietnam—and a Nobel Prize Prospect." *AsiaWeek* 29, no. 25 (June 30, 2000). mail@web.asiaweek.com. http://asiaweek.com.

Tai, Hue-Tam Ho. "Religion in Vietnam: A World of Gods and Spirits." Pp. 22–39 in *Vietnam: Essays on History, Culture, and Society,* edited by David Elliott and Sara Robertson. New York: Asia Society, 1985.

Thu, Nguyen Xuan. "Higher Education in Vietnam: Key Areas Need Assistance." *Higher Education Policy* 10, no. 2 (1997): 137–143.

Tri, Vo Nhan. "Party Policies and Economic Performance: The Second and Third Five-Year Plans Examined." Pp. 77–89 in *Postwar Vietnam: Dilemmas in Socialist Development,* edited by David G. Marr and Christine P. White. Ithaca: Southeast Asia Program, Cornell University, 1993.

Turk, Carrie. *Vietnam, Voices of the Poor: Synthesis of Participatory Poverty Assessments.* Hanoi: World Bank in Vietnam, 1999.

Turner, Robert F. *Vietnamese Communism: Its Origins and Development.* Hoover Institution on War, Revolution, and Peace 143. Stanford: Leland Stanford Junior University, 1975.

Turner, Sarah, and Andrew Hardy. *Migration, Markets and Social Change in the Highlands of Vietnam.* New York: Oxford, 2000.

Vietnam Communist Party. "Press Communiqué from the Fourth and Last Working Day of the Ninth National Party Congress." http://www.cpv.org.. 2000.

"Vietnam Discontent: Hanoi's Bid to Arbitrate in Rural Disputes May Only Cause More Trouble." *Far Eastern Economic Review* 163, no. 49 (2000): 32–34.

"Vietnam—Education System." International Association of Universities/UNESCO; International Centre of Higher Education. http://www.usc.edu. 2000.

"Vietnam Government 2000." http://www.geographic.org. http://www.photius.com. 2000.

Woodside, Alexander. "The Triumphs and Failures of Mass Education in Vietnam." *Pacific Affairs* 56, no. 3 (fall 1983): 401–427.

CHAPTER FOUR

Vietnamese Society and Contemporary Issues

Vietnam is undergoing rapid change in its social, political, and economic spheres. The breathtaking speed at which these transformations are occurring makes it difficult to identify what is a passing, versus lasting, phenomenon. Certain aspects to Vietnam, such as language, remain intact through the winds of social change. Nevertheless, there are very few things in Vietnamese society and culture that are not changing. It seems that the people continue to grow disillusioned by an increasingly corrupt political system and an economy that is sometimes based on ideology and at other times on whatever officials think will work to make the nation rich. In a sense, the two aspects of this chapter's title, Vietnamese Society and Contemporary Issues, are more closely related than they appear. These topics are interrelated because change is what drives Vietnam's culture and present-day concerns.

It is a bit paradoxical that Vietnam, a country so rich in tradition, is now characterized by an unprecedented transformation. This chapter examines five aspects of modern Vietnam that are in a state of flux: rural Vietnam, women and their roles in society, the growing problem of AIDS and drugs in Vietnam's cities, the generation gap caused by modernization, and the plight of overseas Vietnamese.

RURAL VIETNAM

The rural farmer is Vietnam's foundation. Since the first people came to inhabit this country, its social and economic stability were directly related to what the soil would yield. During the twentieth century, the Communist Party recognized that if it was to succeed, it would have to gain the support of the farmers. In the 1940s and 1950s Vietnam did not have a large urban working class, which some orthodox communists believed was necessary to create a new social system. Ho Chi Minh did not agree with this theory. Rather, he sought the aid of the peasants to fight and die for the dream of an exploitation-free economic structure. Vietnamese farmers fought and died for other people's dreams as well as for the promise of a better future for themselves. Thus, despite the enormous debt that Vietnam's government owes to its country folk, it is this segment of Vietnamese that is currently under the greatest amount of stress. Although the government claims that the present crises are due to conditions beyond its control, many rural citizens blame the contradictory policies coming out of Hanoi for their desperate plight.

A brief background provides context for the current social and economic crises among the Vietnamese farmers. During the 1950s the North Vietnamese government required farmers to join cooperatives. The cooperatives were agricultural teams where land, labor, and tools were pooled to increase production. Poorer farmers were more excited about this new system than were the wealthier peasants, who had much to lose in giving up their larger, well-irrigated farmlands. Following the 1975 unification of Vietnam, the government placed this cooperative pattern on the rural lands in South Vietnam and in the rich Mekong Delta area. In short, all private farms were abolished and the land belonged to the government. The low-level communist members, also known as cadres, managed the cooperatives; the government provided seed, fertilizer, and other items to assist the farmers. This gave the farmers what some call an "iron rice bowl." Although no one would get rich by this system, there was a promise that every person would be cared for by the government. The iron rice bowl metaphor was an illustration of a system where no one would fall through the cracks. Cooperatives also assisted over five million soldiers who had finished their service and returned to their homes in the country. Thus, the cooperative farming system was intricately linked with the army and the government. By the mid 1980s, however, Vietnam faced economic disaster. Prices of grain were fixed by the government, and farmers were forced to sell their products to the government. This regulated system hindered any entrepreneurial spirit that farmers might have had. The entire economy suffered because of the tight government control of farming activities. In 1986, officials responded to this downturn by radically transforming the structure of the countryside. New land laws allowed farmers to privately work certain portions of land, and they were permitted to claim these lands for up to twenty years. Inheritance and transfer laws accompanied the new land system. By 1993 farmers were given permission to privately farm land for fifty years, with the additional freedom to lease their land to others. Land that was part of the cooperatives was divided and transferred to individual families. In short, the government created a land market.

In a country where agriculture plays a primary social, economic, and historical role, the overnight shift from one system to another can throw the society into chaos. This is what has happened in Vietnam. Old rivalries between families were inflamed by the winds of arbitrary land reform laws. Tension between the "haves" and "have nots" was not considered by Vietnam's government. In fact, officials believed that the new land laws would level the playing field between the rich and poor farmers. This belief was based on the idea that those who work hard would prosper while the lazy people would have to change their ways in order to survive. They assumed that this free-market idea is the only factor that made capitalist countries so rich. The Vietnamese government decided that similar economic policies would pull the country out of its economic slump.

Certain things were not taken into account when the Vietnamese government abruptly gave the responsibility of land management to households. For example, though the new distribution of land was supposed to be fair, only households that could muster enough money and labor were able to stake claims to land. Because farmers need to buy fertilizer and seed at the *beginning* of each planting season, before they realize any profit from their crops, poorer farmers—who lacked money for these essentials—

were at a severe disadvantage. As stated earlier, the government had provided these necessities to farmers during the years of communal farming through loans at the beginning of each planting season. Because the government's interest on these loans was reasonable, and because the government made exception on repayment for those farmers who fell ill or those whose crops were destroyed by natural disasters, farmers rarely fell into debt. However, under the new system of private farming, there is no safety net for farmers who experience unforeseen calamity. Because the poorer farmers have no capital to buy seed and fertilizer, they must borrow money to purchase these supplies. With no real property such as houses to put up for security, the poor peasants must rely on nongovernment sources—mainly their richer neighbors—to acquire funds for their farms. It is estimated that more than half of the available government loans go to 10 percent of the farmers—the richest group among the rural population—while the remaining 90 percent of farmers borrow from their richer neighbors and must pay three times more than the government-sanctioned interest rate. The cycle that this creates is similar to what happened during the French occupation of Vietnam. A pattern of increased indebtedness results in the poor farmers losing the small portion of land that they had to begin with, while the rich landowners increase in wealth. Although the government might think that it is promoting the development of a rural middle class, the reality is that a small group is increasing in wealth while the vast majority of farmers are now at the mercy of the land-rich minority.

During the first half of the 1990s more than 200,000 written complaints on land-use rights were sent to the government. Thousands of violent confrontations between peasant groups demonstrated an obvious breakdown of social order in Vietnam's rural areas. This social chaos tends to be exacerbated by the role of the cadres in country municipalities. During the earlier communal stage of land use, communist cadres were deployed throughout the countryside to serve as managers of the group farms. These outside supervisors were often resented by the local community because they were unfamiliar with local customs and the nutrient distinctions of the soils and crops in the region. Nonetheless, the cadres were obeyed because they carried with them the authority of the Communist Party.

When the government decided to deregulate land use, there were approximately one million cadres in the countryside. The party relied on these managers to democratically redistribute the land. The results were mixed at best. By the time the government changed the land use from cooperatives to private ownership, the cadres had become fixtures in the rural areas and held inordinate influence in the villages. They allocated land to the most influential families. Their unfairness did not end there. The cadres took the most excellent farmland for themselves. Poor farmers had little say in these developments. The cadres' duplicity served to destroy the legitimacy of the government and the Communist Party in the eyes of the average peasant. It is the party officials themselves that cheated the masses. Vietnam's so-called middle class that is emerging from the privatization of farmland is a small minority of farmers, and their privileged status is rooted in bribery, nepotism, and exploitation—the same economic and social problems that the Communist Party promised to eliminate. It is a sad paradox that the class of people that the communists relied on to bring about a revolution is now ignored by the government.

WOMEN IN VIETNAMESE SOCIETY

During the 1990s Vietnam created legislation providing equal rights for women. For example, the 1994 Labor Code guarantees affirmative action for women in job recruitment, and the new laws supply preferential policies for women, especially pregnant women and breastfeeding mothers. In addition, by June 1998 every province and major city had established committees for the advancement of women. More than twenty "action agencies" for women have been established, as well as two state institutions that conduct research on women's and gender issues. Despite these efforts, there is a clear gap between current legislation and the pre-

Vietnamese women prepare for Tet celebrations (Leonard de Selva/CORBIS)

vailing social views concerning women. Discrimination against women still exists in Vietnamese society. Even though there are supposed guarantees for women's equal rights, it is hard for real change to happen on this issue because there is limited education on the evils of chauvinism. Much of the blame for gender discrimination is placed on the deep-rooted Confucian tradition in Vietnamese society. Confucian values are present both in the workplace and in homes. This philosophy accords women a subordinate position in society to men, as women are responsible first to their fathers, then to their husbands; if they outlive their husbands, they are to submit to their sons. Two popular Confucian proverbs that directly deal with male/female relations are "One hundred women are not worth a single son," and "Even though you sleep intimately on the same bed and use the same cover with him, you must treat your husband as if he were your king or your father."

Unemployment is high among women in the city. Seventeen percent of women who live in cities cannot find a job. This compares to 12 percent for men. However, a greater difficulty that women face is not a lack of work but *too much* work. Studies show that women are expected to equal men in overall economic production activities, but women must also carry the majority of childcare duties. It is not uncommon for women, at specific times of the year, to work sixteen hours a day. In their childcare responsibilities, women are minimally assisted by older children, grandparents, and other relatives. Combined, these groups contribute less than 4 percent of the total time involved in caring for young children. A husband's assistance with housework is determined by the strength of his relationship with his wife and his perception of how the community sees such involvement.

Recent economic changes (see Chapter 2) have widened the gender gap, as the increased demand for agricultural production has to be met by women. It is estimated that over 70 percent of agricultural labor in Vietnam is performed by women. This is because men are more likely to leave the farm and try to earn a living in larger cities. Lack of access to education because of familial obligations makes it difficult for many women to do much more than plant rice.

Women are also limited in their ability to provide economic stability for their families because they traditionally do not hold land titles, have limited access to financial services such as accountants, and often have less education than their male counterparts. These factors severely limit women in their ability to earn money, which, in turn, increases their dependence on their husbands and fathers. Nevertheless, many wives are responsible for managing their family's income. This time-consuming and emotionally draining responsibility is often given to women because they are less likely than their husbands to frivolously spend money on alcohol, tobacco, and entertainment.

Women comprise more than half of Vietnam's workforce, with approximately 71 percent of women between the ages of thirteen and fifty-five employed in one capacity or another. Though they make up more than half the country's workers, women are paid just 70 percent of the salary that their male counterparts receive.

This is attributed to the fact that women are underrepresented in every sector of the business culture except for the lowest levels in the workforce.

The recent emergence of a wide range of light industries has created numerous employment opportunities for women. Some of these opportunities are in foreign-owned city factories. Clothing and shoemaking companies are attracted to Vietnam because of the number of individuals who will work for low wages, even in difficult conditions. As Vietnam seeks to become an industrialized country, its manufacturing companies recruit young rural women as a cheap domestic labor source that will not complain about squalid conditions. Indeed, Vietnamese women are easily exploited—given unsafe work environments and inadequate salaries—because they need the work and whatever income they can find.

In the early 1990s, it was estimated that close to two million Vietnamese young adults could not read or write. Of this number, 70 percent were women. This statistic can be partially attributed to the fact that the number of females who go on to secondary schools is much lower than that of males. In general, boys complete more years of education than girls. Vietnamese women are at a disadvantage early in life because they do not attain the same level of education as boys do. Until this changes, women will continue to remain behind men in terms of knowledge and opportunity.

After 1975, Vietnamese couples were told to seek government approval before they could marry. This practice has since been discarded. Arranged marriages are also declining in Vietnam, which means that young women rely on friends, relatives, and social gatherings to meet their future husbands. Surveys indicate that Vietnamese women think husbands should be five years older than wives so that the relationship can be dominated by the man. Vietnamese women also noted that they prefer their husbands to be like older brothers so that they can rely on them to protect, nourish, and guide them. Although the legal age for women to marry in Vietnam is eighteen years old, the average age for women to marry is twenty-one. The institution of marriage in Vietnam is predominantly built on Confucian values, wherein women are subservient to their spouses. Some young Vietnamese women are attempting to cast off this tradition. These more independent-minded women tend to have been exposed to values promoted in television shows and movies, live in the larger cities, and are more educated than their peers. Vietnam's large cities allow more opportunities for exposure to non-Confucian values, and there are also more options for employment in the city. Rural work, in contrast, is centered on agriculture and perpetuates the notion that a woman's role is to support her husband and family. But observers believe education is the driving force behind the current challenge to male domination. The more education Vietnamese girls receive, the more they will be able to make their own decisions as they get older.

Due to increased government efforts, the representation of women in government is slowly increasing. Current state-established goals set target representation for women in elected bodies at 25 percent, and the government hopes women representatives at all levels of administration will reach 30 percent by 2010. Between 1989 and 1999 the number of women in the provincial People's Council increased from 12 to 20 percent. At the district level, however, the rate of female membership dropped from 16 to 14 percent. Finally, the percentage of female deputies in the National Association grew from 17 to 26 percent, giving Vietnam the ninth-highest female membership rating out of 135 member states in the International Parliamentarians Union, and making Vietnam second in the entire Asia-Pacific region.

Despite the numerous wars Vietnam endured during the second half of the twentieth century, at the turn of the twenty-first century Vietnam is the thirteenth most populous country in the world. In 1979 Vietnam was estimated to have a birth rate of 2.6 percent a year—a growth that the economy could not keep up with. Like its neighbor China, Vietnam instituted policies to control the country's population. Its leaders put in place a two-child guiding principle. Couples exceeding this limit risk incurring penalties such as an increase cost in housing, health care, and a reduction of salaries. The growth rate remains high, at 2.1 percent in 2000. The birth rate is lower within Vietnam's cities, as there is greater access to contraceptives and abortion. The average age for marriage is also higher in the urban areas.

For every 100,000 births in Vietnam there are 130 infant deaths. Poor nutrition factors heavily into this high number of deaths. It is estimated that more than 40 percent of Vietnamese women with children under the age of five are chronically tired and that 60 percent of pregnant women are anemic during their last trimester. These problems are directly related to the hard work that women are expected to do, even when they are heavy with child.

Vietnam has the highest number of abortions to live births of any country in the world. A conservative estimate is that 40 percent of pregnancies are terminated by abortion, though foreign observers believe that more than half of pregnancies do not come to term. These statistics mean that a typical Vietnamese woman undergoes at least two, and usually three, abortions in her life. Current family planning programs provide money for abortions, sterilization, and limited forms of birth control. Withdrawal and the rhythm method are the most popular forms of birth control, but they are not reliable. The intrauterine device (IUD) is advocated by the Communist Party, and being fitted for an IUD, as well as agreeing to an abortion, often results in rewards for women who undergo these procedures. These rewards include money, vacation from work, and food. Medical personnel claim that inadequate supplies and insufficient medical expertise have caused injuries and serious complications in many Vietnamese women. One out of four women who wear the IUD contract some type of infection from this contraceptive tool. With such obvious flaws in birth control, abortion can be considered the result of inefficient family planning methods rather than a procedure that women undergo for reasons of convenience. It is also the impetus for a new moral standard that is causing problems for women of childbearing age.

AIDS AND DRUGS IN VIETNAM

If the Cold War was about a capitalist economic system versus a state-controlled one, it appears that capitalism was victorious. Russia, Eastern bloc countries, and the People's Republic of China have all softened the once-strict regulations of their economies. Yet in nations like China, leaders seek to open certain portions of the system while leaving other sectors under lock and key. For example, the Internet has transformed the way people communicate, collect information, and transact business. Chinese leaders wish to utilize this communication tool, but they do not want their citizens to have access to what they consider the darker side of the Internet, such as pornographic or antigovernment websites. The question to be answered is whether a government can give its citizens economic freedom while it attempts to control other parts of society. Vietnam's leadership is trying to stop the moral decay that they believe accompanies a more open system. Since the adoption of doi moi (see Chapter 2), the country has witnessed an unparalleled breakdown in society. This section explores the current unpleasant consequences of globalization on Vietnam's society.

During October 1992, the Vietnamese government officially recognized the growing problem of AIDS in the country, and a committee was created to address the spread of this disease. By February 2000 it was reported that 17,596 people living in Vietnam had tested positive for HIV. Although this number is relatively low, it only represents the reported cases. The government actually conservatively estimates that more than 100,000 Vietnamese are HIV-positive. Nongovernment agencies believe that close to half a million Vietnamese carry the virus and attribute approximately 8,000 deaths annually to AIDS-related illnesses.

Compared to other Southeast Asian countries, Vietnam had some time to prepare for the outbreak of AIDS. In the early 1990s more than 93 percent of Vietnamese were aware of the worldwide problem of AIDS. Officials also followed the strategies that various governments were implementing to stop the spread of the disease. In particular, Vietnam's western neighbor Thailand

The Vietnamese government believes that children must be taught about the danger of AIDS at an early age. (Corel)

was frantically trying to bring AIDS to a manageable level. Vietnam was not immediately hit by the devastation of AIDS because the population had limited contact with the outside world. In fact, the first reported case of HIV in Vietnam was from a woman who had worked in Germany and then returned home. Other initial cases were of Thai fishermen who were in Vietnamese jails due to their having trespassed in Vietnamese waters. Based on these reports, Vietnamese mistakenly assumed that HIV was a foreign disease. Thus, though there was knowledge of this illness, it was perceived as something that the local population could avoid by not associating with outsiders.

HIV also has spread throughout Vietnam through increased drug use. Heroin use throughout Vietnam has spread faster than anyone could have imagined. One reason for this is that Myanmar (Burma), which in the 1990s was second only to Afghanistan in the production of heroin/opium, exports this drug to Laos, where local warlords have established poppy farms. In the 1990s, Chris Beyrer, a research team leader of the Johns Hopkins School of Hygiene and Public Health, reported that new HIV outbreaks occurred along the Vietnam-Laos border. However, more than half of Vietnam's heroin users live in Ho Chi Minh City. Increased urbanization and the new farm policies have forced young people and middle-aged poor farmers to move to the cities to search for employment. With a bulging population of more than seven million, Ho Chi Minh City is the most popular destination for the unemployed rural folk. Away from home and facing an uncertain future, members of this roving populace find comfort and solidarity in the underworld drug culture. A Western AIDS consultant noted in the late 1990s that up to 80 percent of the city's intravenous drug users are infected with HIV. In some backrooms, the same needle is used to inject a score of addicts.

The early government response to drug use was to start a needle exchange program. However, during the mid-1990s, officials backed down from this policy, stating that providing needles to drug addicts was the same thing as approving of their habit. Two years later, the government reversed its stance on a needle exchange program. These reversals demonstrate a hard-line Marxist government's reluctance to take into account the portion of its society that is disillusioned and turning to drugs as an answer. At the turn of the twenty-first century in Vietnam, the opiate of the masses is not religion, but opium.

In Vietnam, AIDS is now spreading to heterosexual nondrug users faster than to any other segment of the population. Sexual transmission of HIV is increasing in Vietnam due to social attitudes, official reaction to the sex industry, and misconceptions about how the virus is spread.

More than 100,000 prostitutes were sent to reeducation camps in 1975 after the fall of Saigon. North Vietnamese officials were intent on removing prostitution from the country. At the turn of the twenty-first century, however, there were more than 100,000 sex workers in Ho Chi Minh City alone. Although the government claims that this industry's growth is due to an increase in foreigners, the sex trade in Vietnam caters primarily to the local clientele. Prostitution does not have the stigma in Vietnam that it does in the West. A 1998 poll among Vietnamese youth indicated that less than 20 percent see prostitution as a social evil or as wrong. Male sexual promiscuity is extremely high, and part of adolescence for many Vietnamese young men includes visits to prostitutes. Indeed, it is common for men to visit brothels in groups. Fidelity among married men is low in Vietnam's urban areas. The rural farmers who migrate to the city for employment opportunities usually leave their families on the farm. The physical separation between husband and wife often results in the husband engaging in sex with urban prostitutes. Unprotected sex with prostitutes is spreading HIV throughout Vietnam.

Education about the need for protected sex is a tough sell in Vietnam. High school teachers do not feel comfortable speaking on this subject. The government believes that distributing condoms and providing seminars on safe sex only encourages illicit activity. In late 1995, officials responded to the growing sex trade by issuing decrees known as 87/CP and 88/CP. Although Prime Minister Vo Van Kiet ordered these decrees, it is believed party conservatives pressured him to carry out these reforms. In Hanoi alone, the campaign's immediate results included the raid of 14 music stores, 144 video shops, and 253 karaoke bars. Tons of pornographic materials were confiscated. In Ho Chi Minh City expensive store signs were painted over if the English words were larger than the Vietnamese writing. Street-walking prostitutes were arrested, and neon lights were turned off. According to the sex workers, this temporary crackdown only led to increased unprotected sex. Transactions were made with greater secrecy and more hurriedly, which meant that there was no time for the partners to protect themselves against a sexually transmitted disease.

Finally, as alluded to earlier, the women who are moving into prostitution are, for the most part, forced into this trade because of poverty. One authority reports that more than 70 percent of Vietnamese prostitutes take up this employment because of poverty. Just as the rural farmers move to the city for work, so too do their daughters. The tight job market combined with the socially acceptable status of sex-for-pay encourages desperate young women to help their families and themselves through the selling of their bodies.

A NEW GENERATION

Vietnam is a young country. Close to 50 percent of the population is under the age of twenty. Vietnamese idealize the teenage years of life because it is a time when one's obligations are limited to family duties. Yet, there is a growing complaint by the Vietnamese youth that too much is expected of them. The government continually reminds young people that it was their parents and grandparents who fought to bring about a communist revolution. Therefore, the Communist Party expects the new generation to follow this pattern and devote their energies to building a strong socialist country by joining the party. At the same time, parents insist that their children assist them in the new free-market economic system. The rural household responsibility system means that farmers must use all their resources, including their children, to develop their lands. The increase in entrepreneurial activity also has placed pressure on children to work in fledgling family businesses.

In addition to these pressures, young people are told that a bright future is rooted in a good education. Children are sent to school and expected to excel for their own future as well as for the development of their family and country. Vietnamese young people are pulled in many directions by their Confucian familial obligations, a new economic system, and a government that is depending on the upcoming generation. These duties would be enough to keep any generation busy, but the greatest competition for the attention of the Vietnamese young people is popular culture. The icons of Vietnam's younger generation are not party leaders or folk heroes but music and movie stars, both foreign and domestic. Western grunge bands and the hundreds of Vietnamese bands that attempt to copy this music and culture are more popular among

The future of Vietnam is bright as an increasing number of Vietnamese are receiving higher education. (Steve Raymer/CORBIS)

the Ho Chi Minh and Hanoi young people than are traditional forms of Vietnamese culture. Even the events and heroes of the Vietnam-American War are not as important as the modern culture exported from the West. An entire generation has emerged with no direct involvement in the Vietnam War. Turning away from the past, the common sentiment by Vietnamese youth is that "the war was the war." The ideologies that once divided North and South Vietnam are irrelevant to a group seeking an identity that transcends a place and a time. Millions of Vietnamese desire to throw off the shackles of societal norms and government expectations. Rather than devoting themselves to ideological pursuits, the youth claim that they want to fall in love, have fun, play video games, listen to rap music, and live without traditional constraints.

Although Western parents may view youthful antisocial behavior as part of the maturation process, the independent spirit exhibited by today's teenagers in Vietnam is unprecedented in that country. Parents and grandparents claim that these rebellious children are "losing roots" (*mat goc*). However, what needs to be explored from an analytical standpoint is the nature of these transformations. Wearing grunge clothes, dying hair orange and blue, and body piercing are changes on the surface. The question is whether these outward stylistic changes are temporary or are manifestations of an internal psychological/cultural transformation. Observers note that compared to Western young people, socially rebellious Vietnamese youth prefer to avoid confrontation with their parents. Thus, rather than bringing something into the home that might be offensive, such as rap music or videos, children stay away from home to engage in activity frowned on by their parents. This demonstrates a type of continued respect for authority, particularly toward parents, and indicates that below the façade of a "modern" Vietnamese teenager lie Confucian core values. Nonetheless, the new generation is trying to fit traditional moral codes into a very different world. Daily newspapers publish letters from college and high school students that express a new attitude toward life and identity. The following is a representative letter from a twenty-first century female medical student in Ho Chi Minh City:

> I love and respect my entire family, but I cannot be their shadow. I must assert a place in life for myself. If anyone asks "who are you?" I will reply: "I am myself, a twenty-year old university student who knows how to master her own thoughts and actions."

In the mid-1990s, the term "speed culture" (*van hoa toc do*) became the label for the new approach to living in Vietnam. Young people are characterized by zooming around on Honda motorcycles—the status of "cool" in the urban setting. Fast music, frivolous romantic relationships that are entered and exited with little trouble, and a race to make as much money as possible characterize lives of an entire generation in Vietnam. The government responded to the growing gap between party objectives and the somewhat disillusioned youth by conducting a survey of young people and the general population. The results indicate that the primary goal of the younger generation is to become wealthy, whereas only a quarter of the general population indicated that this was a priority in their lives.

SEX AND THE NEW GENERATION

Through most of Vietnam's past, strict moral codes governed interaction between boys and girls. From the onset of puberty, it was common practice to keep interaction between young men and young women to a minimum. On certain occasions where the entire community joined in a festival or other group activity, young women were provided adult chaperones. The emphasis on female chastity (*trinh*) was a major part of morality in traditional Vietnam. The same emphasis on male virginity did not exist. During the 1930s, critics of the feudal past rejected the discriminate notion of chastity. Following World War II, it became impractical to keep young people separate as war, mixed education, and the disappearance of the imperial system transformed society. Following the 1975 reunification of Vietnam, an attempt was made to impose on society the importance of female chastity and reassert strict prohibitions against social interaction between male and female adolescents. Older people insisted that the primary utility of marriage was for procreation. Arranged marriages continued through much of society.

These traditional views of marriage and sex in Vietnam were antithetical to the popular material coming into the country during the late 1980s. Explicit music videos, information about the personal lives of movie stars, television programs, and movies provided other moral standards such as the acceptance of premarital sex, extramarital affairs, and homosexuality—which is against the law in Vietnam—and served as a catalyst for the Vietnamese to reject the past and embrace a more permissible approach to sexual activities.

Newspaper columns devoted to the subjects of sex, love, and marriage began appearing in urban newspapers. Women, in particular, wrote to express their rejection of a double standard between male and female chastity and fidelity. Billboards with pictures of bikini-clad Vietnamese women selling products was further proof of a new approach to morality and modesty. During the 1990s, beauty contests sprang up throughout Vietnam; these include a swimsuit segment where the contestants were judged on their physique.

This new openness has achieved mixed results. As discussed, HIV is on the rise throughout Vietnam, and women between the ages of fifteen and nineteen are now most heavily affected. Teenage unwanted pregnancies are higher than ever previously recorded. In a 1993 survey a question was posed as to what an unmarried seventeen-year-old woman should do with an unwanted pregnancy. More than 50 percent of the respondents noted that the best recourse would be an abortion. In fact, it is estimated that more than half of pregnancies in the country are terminated before the fifth month of the fetus's development. A mid-1990s survey in Vietnam indicated that 80 percent of young men and 29 percent of young women had recently viewed pornography. Safe sex and the benefits of monogamous relationships are not usually promoted in this media. Though government leaders and members of the older generation complain about the growth of pornography and more permissive attitudes of the Vietnamese youth, it might prove helpful for officials to be more direct in their approach to educating the youth about sex.

THE *VIET KIEU*

A growing economic and social influence in Vietnam is the *Viet Kieu* (*kieu* means "living abroad"). This is the title given to the almost three million Vietnamese who live outside of Vietnam. Three-quarters of this population live in the United States, France, and Canada. Orange County, California, houses the largest Vietnamese community outside of Vietnam. The reintegration of Viet Kieu into Vietnamese society has been a difficult process for the government, the general population, and especially for those trying to reestablish ties with their homeland.

For the Viet Kieu, returning to Vietnam is somewhat bitter-sweet because of the manner by which they departed. Most first-generation overseas Vietnamese left their country as refugees after North Vietnam's victory and reunification. Many escaped illegally by purchasing tickets on boats and throwing their fortune to the unpredictable waves and shady underworld pilots (see Chapter 1). Stories are told about boats drifting for weeks with no fuel and no fresh water or food for the passengers. Some boats beached on atolls in the South China Sea. Stuck on the island, the famished passengers survived by eating uncooked birds and raw fish until the marooned people were spotted and rescued. Even if these so-called boat people found a safe harbor where they could disembark, most countries were reluctant to accept these refugees. In the United States, where many of the boat people settled, a 1979 Gallup poll reported that more than 60 percent of Americans opposed the admission of Vietnamese. Many Viet Kieu experienced a cool reception in the global community. It is in this context that overseas Vietnamese have worked to establish vibrant communities around the world.

During the 1990s, Viet Kieu watched with interest as the Vietnamese government relaxed its control of the state's economy. Party officials began to encourage foreign investment into Vietnam. The more open economy, along with restored diplomatic ties between the United States and Vietnam, has spurred many Vietnamese to return to what they consider their home. However, their return trip is usually limited to a brief visit. Few Viet Kieu go to Vietnam with an aim to reestablish residency. One Viet Kieu woman frankly confessed that she had grown too accustomed to the relative luxury in the West and does not desire to live with the inconveniences in a poorer, less technologically developed society. Yet even for the overseas Vietnamese that return for a short visit, there are stigmas attached to their return home. For example, Steve Lee made his first return visit to Vietnam in 1992. He reported that when he traveled back to southern California he and his family were labeled communist-lovers by the surrounding Vietnamese community. The bitterness that many Viet Kieu have toward a government that destroyed their former homes, lives, and businesses is deeply rooted and has not diminished over time. Viet Kieu who visit Vietnam also face their community's accusation that they approve of a communist-led government. This division in an otherwise tight-knit community will probably diminish as the staunchly anticommunist first-generation Viet Kieu is replaced by a younger group whose past is not scarred by war and political suffering.

The Vietnamese government's official policy toward Viet Kieu is one of reconciliation. Vietnam needs the money that overseas Vietnamese inject into the economy in the form of remittances that families receive from their geographically-distant relatives. In 1999 Viet Kieu sent more than $1 billion into Vietnam through official channels. This represented almost 4 percent of Vietnam's 1999 total economic output. Each year the amount of cash making its way into Vietnam through Viet Kieu drastically increases. The government claims that Viet Kieu are an integral part of Vietnam, but it also insists that returning Vietnamese are expected to support the government and not criticize the political system.

Close to 300,000 Viet Kieu visited Vietnam in 1999. This was more than triple the 87,000 that returned during 1992. In 2000, more than 125,000 overseas Vietnamese returned to their homeland to celebrate Vietnam's New Year. A common sentiment among these returning Vietnamese is that the most prejudice they encounter is from Vietnam's general population. Viet Kieu are stereotyped as traitors who abandoned their country during a time of great need. They are perceived as wealthy (after all, they are able to regularly send money to their Vietnamese relatives) and consequently are charged double the standard prices at hotels, restaurants, and other businesses. Many Viet Kieu send pictures of their new cars, large homes, and business establishments to their relatives in Vietnam, often exaggerating their success; for example, a waiter might have his picture taken outside his place of employment and claim that he owns the business. Motives for exaggeration and duplicity are obvious: After experiencing past humiliation, loss, and suffering, the Viet Kieu wish to portray themselves as people who have not only overcome adversity but have also flourished in their new setting. "Local boy/girl makes good" is a headline that most people who have left their home want written about them. Likewise, Viet Kieu want their old neighborhoods and towns to know that they "have made the big time" in New York, Paris, or Los Angeles. The catch to this ruse is that when these Viet Kieu return to visit their relatives and hometowns they are expected to have suitcases full of expensive gifts such as designer clothes, the latest technological hand-held devices, and costly jewelry. It is common for Viet Kieu to borrow large sums of money before making the trip so that they can distribute luxurious gifts to family and friends. This perpetuates the stereotype that all the refugees that escaped after 1975 are rich and prospering in their new suburban homes.

Viet Kieu claim that the Vietnamese government must do more to demonstrate its genuine interest in welcoming them back. In particular, Vietnamese-Americans are skeptical about the invitation from the Vietnamese government to place their investments in Vietnam's new open-market economy. Between 1988 and 1996 the SRV government reported that Viet Kieu had invested about $127 million in various local projects. Of this amount, only $6.3 million came from Viet Kieu residing in the United States. This is a bit surprising considering that more than half of overseas Vietnamese live in the United States. The Viet Kieu's reluctance to invest in their former country is illustrated in the fact that less than 1 percent of foreign investment comes from Vietnamese living abroad. Their hesitancy is a result of ever-changing government policies, some of which are noted below.

During the mid-1990s Vietnam was desperately seeking sources of capital to prop up its weak economy. One source of funds that it began to notice was the remittances that Viet Kieu were sending to their relatives via bank transactions. This cash totaled more than $600 million annually. In 1996, the government placed a tax on all remittances. The Viet Kieu saw this as a penalty for assisting relatives who were in financial need. Predictably, these kinds of bank transactions dwindled as Viet Kieu found unofficial means to transfer money to their relatives. The government responded to this revenue loss by accusing foreign governments of racist policies that hindered Vietnamese from fairly competing in their adopted countries. Vietnamese officials reasoned that discriminatory business practices, especially in the United States, kept Viet Kieu from making money. This accusation failed to account for the millions of dollars that the overseas Vietnamese sent home prior to the government's tax policy on remittances. The Viet Kieu found it ironic that Vietnam blamed foreign governments for economic discrimination when it was its own tax laws that discouraged overseas Vietnamese from sending money home. The SRV reversed its position on taxing remittances several years after it was implemented, providing further proof of instability in Vietnam's economic policies.

Vietnam has also tried to attract Viet Kieu investment by offering a 20 percent reduction on business tax and a flat 5 percent tax on profits. Viet Kieu are also given the same rights as domestic businesses in terms of leasing property and hiring employees. These privileges are not extended to foreign companies in Vietnam. In response to this overture, Viet Kieu also want their former homes and property returned to them. Many of the overseas Vietnamese had substantial possessions that were left behind when they fled their homeland. Because many departed quickly, they were unable to take much more than the clothing on their backs. In practical terms, they could not carry their homes and ancestral lands on the boats and airplanes on their way out of Vietnam. Most of this abandoned property was confiscated by the government or distributed among families. The issue of who owns this property is another hurdle to good Viet Kieu—SRV relations.

One final complaint that the Viet Kieu have with SRV policies is the problem of dual citizenship. Vietnam does not recognize dual citizenship. Consequently, if a Viet Kieu finds himself/herself in trouble with the Vietnamese government and this person appeals to his/her adopted home consulate for assistance, the request is dismissed as invalid by the SRV. Vietnamese-Americans who have not previously renounced their Vietnamese citizenship are considered by the SRV to be Vietnamese citizens, not American citizens, even though they may hold a U.S. passport. In this respect, the Vietnamese government treats Viet Kieu not as foreigners but as citizens of the SRV. At the same time, Viet Kieu complain that when they enter the country they are harassed by certain customs officials who take delight in intimidating the understandably nervous Viet Kieu. Once these travelers are past the country's entry ports, they are confronted by a public and business community that charges double rates for these outsiders. Thus, the Viet Kieu must labor under a double standard: When it is convenient, they are treated as Vietnamese, and when inconvenient, they are regarded as foreigners.

Away from their homeland, Viet Kieu have had various success rates in establishing a stable existence in foreign countries. There were three different waves of Vietnamese migration. The first large group of Vietnamese that fled their country did so in 1975. Most in this group had some exposure to Western culture prior to leaving Vietnam, and many could speak a Western language. More than 180,000 from this group came to the United States. This mass exodus, also referred to as the "brain drain," included many of Vietnam's social and intellectual elite. In the United States there was a somewhat ambivalent feeling toward these Viet Kieu as they set out to make a new life in America. President Richard Nixon's resignation, a society divided over the Vietnam War, a national recession, and the humiliating departure of U.S. personnel from the roof of the U.S. Embassy in Saigon led many Americans to try to put Vietnam behind them. The 1975 Vietnamese refugees were accepted as part of the closure of this chapter in U.S. history.

The second wave of departures from Vietnam, the aforementioned boat people, left their country between 1976 and 1980. Their exit was much more harrowing than that of the first group. If the boat people were able to successfully escape Vietnam, months and years in detention camps awaited them. When these refugees were finally accepted in host countries, the postwar ambivalence toward Viet Kieu had turned into animosity. Largely unwelcomed and lacking the education and ties that the previous Viet Kieu had, the boat people were shuffled from one place to another, with many landing in the West's big city ghettoes.

Finally, during the 1990s a group of Vietnamese, mostly northern fishermen and their families, fled their economically depressed homeland and sought relief in any country that would accept them. These individuals were even less affluent and did not, for the most part, have as much education as did the boat people. Many from this final group found their way to Hong Kong and various Southeast Asian countries. Illegal immigration to Western countries was also an option that many followed.

Once the Viet Kieu settled in host countries, the process of acculturation created at least three unanticipated difficulties. First, in many families there was a new tension regarding gender relations. Vietnamese wives became important, if not primary, wage earners for Viet Kieu in Australia, Europe, and North America. Economic empowerment, along with a differing views of gender equality, created tension in Viet Kieu marriages that has spilled over to domestic violence, clinical depression, and a relatively higher divorce rate among Viet Kieu. A related difficulty that the Viet Kieu face is the seduction of opportunity. Having left their possessions in Vietnam, they have started over in countries where opportunities exist for honest workers willing to earn minimum wage. This has prompted industrious Vietnamese to work more than twice the number of hours of a conventional workweek. It is because Viet Kieu are willing to work so many hours that they are able to send remittances to their relatives. This heavy work schedule adds to other pressures in Viet Kieu homes. Although they might be able to afford new cars and large houses, many overseas Vietnamese claim they have lost their identity because there is no time to develop important relationships or nurture their spiritual lives.

The third problem that Viet Kieu must confront is the growing cultural divide between generations. The stereotype of Vietnamese students in American high schools is that they study diligently and excel in math and science. Viet Kieu parents do pressure their children to succeed through education. However, there is a darker side to Viet Kieu youth. Abandoned by parents who work twelve to sixteen hours a day, many young Vietnamese have found solidarity in gangs and illegal activities.

These problems that Viet Kieu face are rarely acknowledged in Vietnam. Moreover, they are rarely discussed even in the overseas Vietnamese communities. One individual who has sought to confront the difficulties and stereotypes of Viet Kieu is Hong Le. As a nine-year-old, Le joined his parents as they fled Vietnam in 1975. After days adrift at sea, they were eventually picked up and sent to Guam. From there Le's family moved to Australia. During the mid-1990s Le began breaking down racial barriers and Viet Kieu stereotypes through satire and comedy. A gifted violinist, Le combines his musical talents with a stand-up comedy routine where he answers his own questions such as, "How can you tell when your house has been robbed by a Vietnamese person? Your children's homework is done and your pet dog is missing." Confronting caricatures through comedy has provided an opportunity for members of the Viet Kieu to speak more openly about the particular difficulties of overseas Vietnamese.

CONCLUSION

Vietnam is changing. Whether one studies its social, political, economic, or popular culture, the one theme running through all of the country is change. Globalization and a generation that has been able to grow up in a relatively peaceful country have combined to force the country's leaders to make adjustments in their national goals. Communist Party officials have also acknowledged that the rhetoric of Marxism has not produced an economically vibrant state in Vietnam. The SRV is attempting to implement positive social and economic changes while endeavoring to maintain traditional and ideological values. From what we see in this chapter, the results of such efforts are not promising for SRV officials.

Vietnam continues to join regional and world trade organizations. As it does this, Vietnamese officials have a greater responsibility to provide an economy and society that is more open. Businesses want to know if it is safe to invest in this Southeast Asian

A negative outcome of Vietnam's growing free-market system is that many parents send their children to work in the streets rather than attend school. (Courtesy of Daryl Jones)

country. More important, however, is the government's responsibility to its own people. There is a growing disillusionment that women, rural farmers, and young people have with a government whose policies appear vague at best and contradictory at worst. An opportunity is open for the SRV, but it must come to terms with a new generation and globalization.

References

Abdul-Quader, A. S., V. M. Quan, and K. O'Reilly. "A Tale of Two Cities: HIV Risk Behaviors Among Injecting Drug Users in Hanoi and Ho Chi Minh City, Vietnam." *Drugs and Alcohol Review* 18, no. 4 (December 1999): 401–407.

Bao Duong, P., and Y. Izumida. "Rural Development Finance in Vietnam: A Microeconometric Analysis of Household Surveys." *World Development* 30, no. 2 (February 2002): 319–335.

Biers, Dan, and Margot Cohen. "Return of the Prodigal Sons." *Far Eastern Economic Review* 163, no. 38 (September 21, 2000): 45–48.

Bui, H. N., and M. Morash. "Domestic Violence in the Vietnamese Immigrant Community: An Exploratory Study." *Violence against Women* 5, no. 7 (July 1999): 769–795.

Cohen, Margot. "Vietnam Transfusion: The Communist Party Seeks Fresh Blood as It Struggles to Rejuvenate Itself." *Far Eastern Economic Review* 163, no. 34 (August 24, 2000): 26–29.

Dahm, Bernhard, and Vincent J. Houben, eds. *Vietnamese Villages in Transition.* Germany: Passau University, 1999.

Du', Phu'o'c Long., and Laura Richard. *The Dream Shattered: Vietnamese Gangs in America.* Boston: Northeastern University Press, 1996.

Elliott, Duong Van Mai. *The Sacred Willow: Four Generations in the Life of a Vietnamese Family.* New York: Oxford University Press, 1999.

English, T. J. *Born to Kill: America's Most Notorious Vietnamese Gang, and the Changing Face of Organized Crime.* New York: William Morrow, 1995.

Epstein, Michael. *Vietnam: A Book of Changes.* New York: W. W. Norton, 1996.

Fforde, Adam, and Stefan de Vylder. *From Plan to Market: The Economic Transition in Vietnam.* Boulder, Colo.: Westview Press, 1996.

Flanagan, Maureen. "A Changed and Changing Vietnam." *Far Eastern Economic Review* 163, no. 39 (September 28, 2000): 31.

Freeman, James. *Hearts of Sorrow: Vietnamese American Lives.* Stanford: Stanford University Press, 1989.

Giang L. T., et al. "Evaluation of STD/HIV Prevention Needs of Low- and Middle-Income Female Sex Workers in Ho Chi Minh City, Vietnam." *AIDS and Behavior* 4, no. 1 (March 2000): 83–91.

Gluckman, Ron. "Hung Up Down Under." <http://www.gluckman.com. 1997.

———. "Stops and Starts: A Journey through Vietnam Finds that as Pumped as Its Babyboomers Are, Change Is a Fitful Process." *Asiaweek* 26, no. 14 (April 14, 2000): 52–58.

Hayslip, Le Ly, and Jay Wurts. *When Heaven and Earth Changed Places : A Vietnamese Woman's Journey from War to Peace.* New York: Plume, 1989.

Hiebert, Murray. *Vietnam Notebook.* Hong Kong: Review Publishing, 1994.

Hien N. T., et al. "The Social Context of HIV Risk Behavior by Drug Injectors in Ho Chi Minh City, Vietnam." *AIDS Care* 12, no. 4 (August 2000): 483–495.

Luong, Hy V. *Revolution in the Village: Tradition and Transformation in North Vietnam, 1925–1988.* Honolulu: University of Hawaii Press, 1992.

Marr, David G. *Vietnamese Youth in the 1990s.* Sydney: Macquarie University, 1996.

Mazumdar, S, F. Docuyanan, and C. Mclaughlin. "Creating a Sense of Place: The Vietnamese-Americans and Little Saigon." *Journal of Environmental Psychology* 20, no. 4 (December 2000): 319–333.

Nguyen, Qui Duc. *Where the Ashes Are: The Odyssey of a Vietnamese Family.* New York: Addison Wesley, 1994.

Pike, Douglas Eugene. *Viet Kieu in the United States: Political and Economic Activity.* Lubbock, Tex.: Texas Tech University, 1998.

Rutledge, Paul James. *The Vietnamese Experience in America.* Bloomington: Indiana University Press, 1992.

Rydstrøm, H. "'Like a White Piece of Paper.' Embodiment and the Moral Upbringing of Vietnamese Children." *Ethnos* 66, no. 3 (November 2001): 394–413.

Sikor, T. "Agrarian Differentiation in Post-Socialist Societies: Evidence from Three Upland Villages in North Western Vietnam." *Development and Change* 32, no. 5 (November 2001): 923–949.

Springstubb, Tricia. *The Vietnamese Americans.* San Diego: Lucent Books, 2002.

Tana, Li. *Peasants on the Move: Rural-Urban Migration in the Hanoi Region.* Singapore: Institute of Southeast Asian Studies, 1996.

Templer, Robert. *Shadows and Wind: A View of Modern Vietnam.* New York: Penguin Putnam, 1998.

Tran, Tini. "Business Opportunities Draw Viet Kieu Back to Vietnam." *AsianWeek* 21, no. 36 (May 4, 2000): 14–16.

Tran, Tri Vu. *Lost Years: My 1,632 Days in Vietnamese Reeducation Camps.* Berkeley: University of California Press, 1988.

UNICEF. *Viet Nam Children and Women: A Situation Analysis.* Hanoi: UNICEF, 2000.

Vu, Ngu Chieu. *The Other Side of the Vietnamese Revolution.* Houston: Van Hoa, 1996.

Wilson D., and P. Cawthorne. "'Face up to the Truth': Helping Gay Men in Vietnam Protect Themselves from AIDS." *International Journal of STD & AIDS* 10, no. 1 (January 1999): 63–66.

PART TWO
REFERENCE MATERIALS

Key Events in Vietnamese History

VIETNAM BEFORE CHINESE DOMINATION

2879–258 B.C.E.   Vietnamese legend ascribes the founding of the country to Lac Long Quan, whose offspring founded the Hung dynasty

700 B.C.E.–42 C.E.   Increased sophistication in farming and the establishment of Lac rice fields

THE CHINESE MILLENNIUM

111 B.C.E.   China defeats Vietnam (Nan Yueh) and incorporates it into the Han empire

40 C.E.   Trung Trac, the wife of a Lac lord, leads a revolt against the Chinese rulers. The rebellion is crushed two years later.

543   Ly Bi rebels against Chinese rule

544–602   Early Ly dynasty

907   The dissolution of China's Tang dynasty

VIETNAM'S TRANSITION TO INDEPENDENCE

938   In the Battle of Bach-dang River, Ngo Quyen defeats the Chinese navy, thus ending the Han invasion

965–979   Dinh Bo Linh establishes the short-lived Dinh dynasty

1009   Ly Con Van establishes the Ly dynasty (1009–1225)

1078   Three Cham provinces are ceded to Vietnam

1225–1400	Tran dynasty
1257, 1284, and 1287	Mongol forces make three unsuccessful attempts to invade and defeat Vietnam
1400–1407	Ho dynasty
1407–1427	China invades and occupies Vietnam

LE DYNASTY (1428–1788)

1428	Le Loi claims the throne and renames the country Dai Viet
1460–1497	Le Thanh Tong brings the Le dynasty to its zenith
1470	The Champa kingdom is defeated and ceases to exist
1483	The Hong Duc Code systematizes Vietnam's civil and criminal laws
1527–1592	The Mac clan usurps the throne for almost a century
1558–1772	Trinh and Nguyen clans support rival Le emperors; a national division takes place, with the Trinh dominating the north and the Nguyen ruling in the south
1627	The Jesuit priest Alexander de Rhodes arrives in Vietnam
1771	Tay Son rebellion
1783	Nguyen Anh makes an alliance with the French priest Pigneau de Béhaine wherein Pigneau agrees to support Nguyen Anh's aspirations to unite Vietnam and become its sole emperor

NGUYEN DYNASTY (1802–1954)

1802	Nguyen Anh defeats his final rival and establishes the Nguyen dynasty. He designates the central citadel of Hue as the capital and changes his name to Gia Long.

1820–1841	Minh Mang continues the policies of isolation set in place by his father
1825	Minh Mang makes it illegal for foreign priests to live in Vietnam
1841–1847	Thieu Tri rules as the Nguyen dynasty's third emperor
1847	French warships bombard Da Nang to pressure the Vietnamese into submission
1847–1883	Emperor Tu Duc capitulates to French military pressure
1862	Tu Duc signs the Treaty of Saigon, giving the French Gia Dinh and its three surrounding provinces
1873	The French receive sovereign status over Cochin China
1883	Tonkin and Annam become France's protectorate states
1887	The Indochinese Union (ICU) is created
1890	Ho Chi Minh is born in the central Vietnamese province of Nghe An
1903	Phan Boi Chau establishes the Restoration Society
1912	The Restoration Society is renamed the Modernization Society
1927	Nguyen Thai Hoc organizes the Viet Nam Quoc Dan Dang (VNQDD, the Vietnamese Nationalist Party)
1930	With Ho Chi Minh presiding at the organizing assembly, the Indochinese Communist Party (ICP) is founded. After gaining a foothold in Nghe An province, the party is dealt a serious blow by French troops. Minh is arrested by the British in Hong Kong.
September 1940	Japanese troops occupy northern Vietnam
February 1941	Ho Chi Minh returns to Vietnam after a three-decade absence

March 1945	Japan abolishes the 1885 French-Vietnam treaty and declares that Vietnam is independent under the Nguyen emperor, Bao Dai
September 2, 1945	Ho Chi Minh declares the founding of the Democratic Republic of Vietnam (DRV)
March 1946	The French and the DRV secure a temporary political agreement
November 1946	French ships bombard the port town of Haiphong
1946–1954	First Indochina War
May 7, 1954	France surrenders to Vietnamese forces at Dien Bien Phu

NORTH AND SOUTH VIETNAM

1954	During one of several Geneva conferences, an agreement is made to divide Vietnam at the seventeenth parallel with a nationwide plebiscite to be held within two years' time
October 26, 1955	The Republic of Vietnam, widely know as South Vietnam, is founded with Ngo Dinh Diem as its first president. This pro–United States government is a fierce enemy of the Democratic Republic of Vietnam, or North Vietnam.
December 20, 1960	The National Liberation Front (NLF) is organized in South Vietnam by Vietminh supporters. Diem's advisers pejoratively term the Southerners who join the NLF "Vietcong."
November 1, 1963	Diem is overthrown in a military coup that is supported by the United States
August 7, 1964	The U.S. Congress passes the Gulf of Tonkin Resolution, which authorizes the U.S. president to do all within his power to protect U.S. interests in Vietnam

March 1965   First U.S. ground combat troops land in
                    Vietnam
January 30–31,   The Tet Offensive is launched by the
  1968   Vietcong and Vietminh
September 2, 1969   Ho Chi Minh dies. Le Duan subsequently
                    takes over power of North Vietnam.
January 27, 1973   An agreement is reached to end the
                    Vietnam War
April 30, 1975   South Vietnam is overrun by North
                    Vietnamese forces

SOCIALIST REPUBLIC OF VIETNAM

1976   Vietnamese officials change the name of
                    their country to the Socialist Republic of
                    Vietnam, and change the name of Saigon
                    to Ho Chi Minh City
December 25, 1978   Vietnam invades Cambodia to drive out
                    the pro-Chinese Khmer Rouge regime
February 1979   China invades Vietnam to punish its south-
                    ern neighbor for invading Cambodia
1986   Vietnam launches a "renovation" of its
                    economy with the *doi moi* campaign
1989   Vietnamese troops withdraw from
                    Cambodia
July 11, 1995   Vietnam and the United States normalize
                    relations
July 2000   Vietnam opens its first stock market
April 19, 2001   Vietnam holds the Ninth Party Congress of
                    the Vietnamese Communist Party
July 24, 2001   U.S. Secretary of State Colin Powell visits
                    Vietnam to assure Vietnamese leaders of
                    continued U.S. support of reforms
                    throughout Asia
March 3, 2002   U.S. and Vietnamese scientists meet in
                    Hanoi to discuss the effects of Agent

	Orange on the Vietnamese. This herbicide was used by the United States to defoliate trees throughout Vietnam during the U.S.–Vietnam War.
May 31, 2002	The Vietnamese government accuses former U.S. Senator Bob Kerry of killing civilian Vietnamese when he led a Navy Seal team into a village during the Vietnam War. According to the Vietnamese government, more than a dozen unarmed civilians were killed during this raid.
September 25, 2002	Pham Thi Mai Phuong is crowned Miss Vietnam in the communist nation's first government-sanctioned beauty pageant

Significant People, Places, and Events

Army of the Republic of Vietnam (ARVN) The Army of the Republic of Vietnam was the successor to the anti-Vietminh, pro-French, Vietnamese National Army. Following the 1954 Geneva Conference, the United States organized the ARVN with the help of 342 American personnel, who were given the title of Military Assistance Advisor Group (MAAG). The MAAG trained the inexperienced Vietnamese Army and recruited hundreds of thousands of young Vietnamese men to join the ARVN. Some estimate that up to one million Vietnamese joined the ARVN during the U.S.–Vietnam War. During the war, the primary duty of the ARVN was to suppress antigovernment activities in South Vietnam. While U.S. troops engaged in search-and-destroy missions against the more sophisticated soldiers of the People's Army of Vietnam, ARVN soldiers suffered much higher casualty rates fighting against local antigovernment elements. In January 1973, the United States forces departed from Vietnam as was stipulated by the 1973 Paris Agreement, leaving the ARVN to defend itself against external and internal enemies. ARVN troops were poorly equipped because of U.S. monetary cutbacks and corruption among some of the ARVN generals. Its leadership suffered from an inability to strategically redeploy its forces. These obstacles made it difficult for the ARVN to hold off the highly trained, well-equipped North Vietnamese forces. In spring 1975, Hanoi launched the Ho Chi Minh Offensive with the goal of gaining territory in Vietnam's central highlands. The ARVN's ineffective response to this offensive allowed the North Vietnamese to continue to move south. On April 30, 1975, the ARVN collapsed and South Vietnam was defeated by North Vietnam.

Bao Dai (1913–1997) Bao Dai served as the last emperor of the

Nguyen dynasty (1802–1954) and as the chief of state of the Associated State of Vietnam from 1949 to 1955. He was born in 1913 as Prince Vinh Thuy and succeeded his father, Emperor Khai Dinh (r. 1916–1925). As a child, Bao Dai studied in France while his government was handled by regents in Hue. In 1932 he returned to Vietnam to engage in the limited duties that the French colonial government mapped out for him. When the Japanese declared the abolition of the 1885 Vietnam-French Treaty and gave the Vietnamese limited independence during World War II, Bao Dai was authorized to appoint his own prime minister. Upon Japan's subsequent surrender, Bao Dai was forced to abdicate his throne and accept the position of supreme adviser to Ho Chi Minh's Democratic Republic of Vietnam (DRV). Realizing the limits of this position, he moved to Hong Kong. In 1947 he accepted the position of chief of state to a Vietnamese government that was working with the French to overthrow Ho Chi Mihn's DRV. His concessions to the French and his reputation as being irresponsible gained him little support during the few years that this government existed. After the 1954 Geneva Accords divided Vietnam into two states, Bao Dai remained, for one year, the chief of state in South Vietnam. In 1956 Ngo Dinh Diem was elected president of the Republic of Vietnam and Bao Dai left for Paris, never to deal in Vietnamese politics again.

Battles of Bach-dang River This river, which flows into the Gulf of Tonkin, played a significant role in Vietnam's independence from Chinese rule. The first major Bach-dang battle was led by Ngo Quyen in the tenth century. He believed that China would use its navy to recapture Vietnam, so he directed his troops to sink poles in the riverbed at the mouth of the river. These posts were hidden under the surface of the water at high tide. When China's naval vessels entered the mouth of Bach-dang, the sunken stakes served to trap the ships. This allowed Quyen to attack and defeat the invading army, giving the Vietnamese their first independence from Chinese rule after 1,000 years. Three centuries later, the Vietnamese general Tran Hung Dao defeated a Mongolian invasion at the river by using the same tactics. The invaders were destroyed, and Vietnam enjoyed independence throughout the Yuan dynasty.

Pigneau de Behaine (1744–1799) The eldest of nineteen children, Pigneau de Behaine joined the priesthood against the wishes of his father. At the age of twenty-two he was sent by the French Society of Foreign Missions to a seminary for Asians on the island of Phu Quoc in the Gulf of Siam. In 1768 he was forced to flee to Malacca due to official persecution. Pope Clement XIV subsequently assigned him to India as the bishop of Adran. He was able to return to Phu Quoc in 1775 and there met Nguyen Anh. Pigneau agreed to act as Nguyen's emissary to the court of Louis XIV, and took Nguyen's son with him on the trip as a security measure. In Paris, de Behaine told the French court that Nguyen Anh agreed to cede the island of Poulo Condore and part of the port of Da Nang to the French if they helped Nguyen defeat his enemies. Louis XIV reluctantly agreed but then betrayed de Behaine and did not provide the promised support. Undeterred, the bishop raised the funds himself and obtained two ships, ammunition, and French mercenaries to help fight for Nguyen Anh. He returned to Vietnam in 1789. Suffering from dysentery, he died in 1799 at the siege of Qui Nhon.

Boat People Following the creation of the Socialist Republic of Vietnam (SRV) in 1975, many South Vietnamese entrepreneurs were forced to surrender their businesses and other property to the communist state. The social and economic humiliation of losing their property and being required to enter reeducation camps drove many southern Vietnamese, in particular ethnic Chinese, to leave Vietnam. Because Vietnamese were not allowed to leave their country without government approval, which very few Vietnamese received, the most common means of escape was to buy a ticket on a boat that would secretly slip out of Vietnamese waters and sail toward Malaysia, Hong Kong, the Philippines, Thailand, or other such ports. The desperate plight of the so-called boat people was worsened by pirates that intercepted many of the boats, robbing and abusing the escaping Vietnamese. International press reports about Vietnam's desperate escapees served to further alienate the SRV government from many world relief organizations.

Bui Quang Chieu (1872–1945) Bui Quang Chieu was born into a scholar-gentry family in the Mekong Delta's Ben Tre province. He attended the National Institute of Agronomy in Paris and returned to Vietnam, publishing a French-language newspaper, *La Tribune Indigene,* beginning in 1917. Supported by Governor General Albert Sarraut, the newspaper was a mouth-piece for the pro-French reformists living in Cochin China. Bui established the Constitutional Party (CP) with the goal of reforming the Colonial Council of Cochin China (CCC), which was the bureaucratic organization that ruled Cochin China. The CP's first appeal was for the CCC to be more liberal in its governing policies and to create more seats for Vietnamese men on the CCC. The CP requested that Vietnamese officials receive higher salaries, remove some of the traditional scholar-officials in favor of a modern bureaucracy, and give leniency in the naturalization laws that were designed to keep Vietnamese from obtaining French citizenship. Disturbed by the violent actions that accompanied the Yen Bay and the Nghe Tinh soviets in 1930, Bui aligned himself more closely with the colonial government. The CP eventually split because its members could not decide on the level of resistance they should give to French rule. The Vietminh assassinated Bui Quang Chieu at the end of World War II.

Can Vuong Can Vuong literally means "save the king" in Vietnamese, and it was an organization established for that very purpose. When Emperor Ham Nghi (r. 1884–1885) fled from his capital in Hue during July 1885, he and his regent, Ton That Thuyet, issued an appeal entitled "Can vuong." The Vietnamese leaders asked their constituents to support a rebellion to defeat the French and restore Vietnamese independence. Vietnamese from all walks of life rallied behind the emperor. This rebellion suffered a setback when the French captured the emperor and sent him to Algeria in 1888. This movement reached its zenith in the early 1890s. Led by Phan Dihn Phung, an imperial official living in his native province of Ha Tinh, the rebellion spread to many provinces surrounding Ha Tinh but quickly collapsed when Phan died of dysentery in 1895.

Cao Dai Cao Dai was a religion formed in southern Vietnam in 1919 by Ngo Van Chieu. By the end of World War II, it was the fastest growing religion in Vietnam. Syncretic in its doctrine, the Cao Dai belief system was based on tenets found in Buddhism, Confucianism, Islam, Christianity, and Daoism. Several hundred thousand Cao Dai adherents in Cochin China supported French colonial authority. Various Cao Dai leaders cooperated with the Japanese during World War II. Under Pope Pham Cong Tac, Cao Dai members supported the French in postwar Vietnam. Following the 1954 Geneva Accords, the Cao Dai leaders resisted Ngo Dinh Diem's attempt to control South Vietnam. Following the assassination of Diem, the Cao Dai cooperated with the Saigon regime during the Vietnam War. After 1975, Cao Dai was allowed to exist in the Socialist Republic of Vietnam, though the SRV has removed Cao Dai leaders who are hostile to the communist regime.

Champa Originally known as Lin Yi, and founded in 192 C.E. by rebels living in the south of Vietnam, this kingdom came into constant conflict with its neighbors. At first, it was controlled by the Chinese, but by the fourth century, Indian influence from the south created a distinct Cham kingdom. The traditional area of Cham territory ran from the Hoanh Son Spur to the present-day city of Da Nang. By the tenth century the kingdom had become a bitter rival of Vietnam. The Ly dynasty's steady encroachment on Cham territory forced the Cham rulers to relocate their capital further south, to present-day Binh Dinh province. In 1471 the Vietnamese took this capital as well and claimed Champa as a dependency of Vietnam; its land and people were officially absorbed into Vietnam during the nineteenth century. The Cham people are darker skinned, ethnically tied to the Malays, and primarily survived through fishing and commerce. Today between thirty thousand and fifty thousand ethnic Chams live in Vietnam and Cambodia. They perpetuate Cham culture through their Islamic religion and distinctive music, architecture, and cuisine.

Dien Bien Phu Dien Bien Phu is a district capital on the northwestern edge of Vietnam on the Vietnam-Laos border. It was established by the Vietnamese to keep Lao rebels out of Vietnam. In November 1953, French troops entered the valley and captured the town in an effort to keep the Vietminh from uniting with their Laotian counterparts across the border. General Vo Nguyen Giap engaged the French, who were hoping that the Vietminh would fight a conventional battle where 15,000 French soldiers could prove their military superiority. Giap ordered his troops to occupy the hills surrounding the valley. They carried heavy cannons up the mountain trails and enveloped the French with heavy artillery. The French commander, Henri Navarre, believed that French aircraft would be decisive in winning this battle, but dense jungle, fog, and consistent rainfall made it impossible for his planes to drop supplies to his troops. All the French troops at Dien Bien Phu were either killed or captured during the course of the battle; the Vietminh suffered 25,000 casualties.

Dinh Bo Linh (r. 965–979) Dinh Bo Linh was the illegitimate son of a provincial governor during the Ngo dynasty (939–965). He had humble beginnings as the leader of the buffalo-watching children in his village of Hoa Lu. As a young man, Dinh became a local military leader. With the support of his village's elders, he was able to seize power following the death of the last Ngo king in 963. He immediately moved the capital away from the heavily Chinese-influenced Red River delta and reestablished it in Hoa Lu, on the periphery of the delta. This location was easier to defend, and he combined that advantage with an army of 100,000 men that he amassed after taking power. China's Song dynasty (907–1276) was established during this same period, and Dinh sought political recognition from the Song rulers. After securing legitimacy from the Song officials, he set about creating a large militia that would remain a Vietnamese institution long after his death. He and his eldest son were assassinated in their sleep in 979, and political instability caused the decay of this dynasty within thirty years of its founding.

Don Dien *Don Dien* was the term used for military or agricultural settlements set up by the Vietnamese government to bring recently conquered lands under its control. This originally began during the later Le dynasty (1428–1788) when northerners colonized the land taken from the Champa kingdom. The military erected stations and relocated farmers and landless peasants to cultivate the surrounding area until there was no longer a threat from outside enemies. The soldiers would then move on to build a new fort and leave the don dien as an independent village. In the eighteenth century the Nguyen court used these stations to open new areas in the Mekong Delta, using labor from volunteers and prisoners who obtained their freedom after serving an allotted term in a don dien. The government usually provided the supplies to start a don dien and often granted tax relief to those who volunteered to stay on the land. Vietnam's current government has used similar settlements to make use of uncultivated land. Those settlements, started in the 1970s, are generally referred to as New Economic Zones.

Paul Doumer (1857–1932) Paul Doumer was one of the most influential social engineers of French Indochina at the end of the nineteenth century. He was a member of the Radical Party and had served as the minister of finance in France. Like many of his contemporaries, he believed that European colonies should not only pay for themselves but also support their European rulers. Doumer was instrumental in creating the Indochinese Union

(ICU) by designing how it would be able to pay for itself. Revenue for the ICU came from state tax monopolies on items such as salt, alcohol, and opium. In 1897 he was appointed governor-general of the ICU, a position he retained through the agency's formative years. He consolidated French authority in Vietnam by creating central administrative offices that would control agriculture, civil affairs, post and telegraph communications, and public works. He resigned in 1902 and returned to France, where he was elected president of the republic in 1931. He was assassinated by a Russian émigré in 1932.

Duy Tan (r. 1907–1916) Duy Tan was a rather controversial emperor who served between 1907 and 1916 under the French protectorate. He was the son of Emperor Thanh Thai (r. 1889–1907), who had resented French colonial power over Vietnam and was exiled to Reunion Island in 1907 on suspicion of conspiracy. Duy Tan took over when his father was deposed. He often complained about his lack of authority, and in May 1916 he fled his palace to support a rebellion led by Tran Cao Van. The French captured him two days later and sent him to join his father in exile on Reunion Island. He later served as a commandant in the French Army during World War II and was supposedly considered as a replacement for Emperor Bao Dai (r. 1926–1945) at the end of World War II.

Francis Garnier (1839–1873) Francis Garnier was a French naval officer who was promoted to the office of Inspector of Indigenous Affairs in the French-created colony of Cochin China in southern Vietnam. He was a product of his time, believing that the European powers had a mission to civilize and spread the gifts of free trade and Christianity throughout Asia. In June 1866 he joined a two-year expedition to learn if the Mekong River's route would allow the French to ship goods in and out of southern China. After this exploratory trip, he wrote a two-volume book entitled *Voyage d'Exploration,* which described the benefits of the Mekong and Red Rivers and ultimately attracted French commercial interests into the area. In 1873 he led a French military force that attacked Hanoi and forced Emperor Tu Duc (r. 1847–1883) to sign a treaty giving France protectorate status over Cochin China and access to the Red River. Garnier's motive was to allow French adventurers to run guns and other supplies up the Red River and open trade routes to southern China. This provided the French greater trade opportunities in southern China. In 1873 Garnier was killed and beheaded by members of the Black Flag, pirates who not only stole from villagers and merchants in northern Vietnam but were also instrumental in the earlier death of Henry Riviere. His head was paraded through the nearby villages.

Gulf of Tonkin Resolution The Gulf of Tonkin, or Tonkin Gulf, lies off the coast of North Vietnam. Its waters have long been the subject of territorial dispute between China and Vietnam. During the U.S.-Vietnam War, two clashes took place between U.S. naval vessels and North Vietnamese boats in the Tonkin Gulf. Two U.S. destroyers, the *Maddox* and *C. Turner Joy,* were patrolling off the North Vietnamese coast in August 1964. U.S. naval personnel reported that several small vessels from the Democratic Republic of Vietnam (DRV) engaged the destroyers and opened fire on the ships. The destroyers responded by sinking the DRV patrol boats. The *Maddox* and *C. Turner Joy* left the area, but several days later U.S. ships were again patrolling the Tonkin Gulf area when radar operators reported that DRV vessels were attacking the U.S. ships. Although this assault was never verified, President Lyndon Johnson used these alleged incidents to ask Congress for executive power to become more involved in Vietnam. Within a few days, Congress passed the Gulf of Tonkin Resolution, which gave the president the authority to use any means necessary to protect U.S. personnel in Vietnam. Johnson used this resolution to justify U.S. bombing raids on North Vietnam.

Ho Chi Minh (1890–1969) The founder of the Vietnamese

Communist Party was born in Nghe An province in central Vietnam. His father named him Nguyen Tat Thanh and sent him to be educated at the National Academy at Hue. He left Vietnam in 1911 and traveled around the world, eventually settling in France. While in Paris, he changed his name to Nguyen Ai Quoc (Nguyen the Patriot) and was a founding member of the French Communist Party. He caught the attention of various communist party leaders and was called to Moscow in 1923 to be trained as an agent of the Communist International organization. He next traveled to southern China, where he organized a Marxist Vietnamese movement that in 1930 became the Indochinese Communist Party (ICP). He was arrested the following year in Hong Kong for his antiimperialist activities. Through the graces of high-placed friends, he was released in 1933 and reportedly moved to Moscow to recover from tuberculosis. In 1941 he returned to northern Vietnam and continued to build up the antiimperialist, nationalist forces in Vietnam. In September 1945, now using the name Ho Chi Minh, he declared the founding of the Democratic Republic of Vietnam. He traveled to France and worked out an agreement so that the old colonial power would recognize the independence of the DRV. The settlement quickly broke down, however, and Ho and his followers fought an eight-year war against the French.

Throughout Ho Chi Minh's absences from Vietnam, and during the battle against the French, his reputation as a simple, nationalistic, affable man earned him the title "Uncle Ho." Vietnam's victory over the French further increased his status throughout Vietnam. At the 1954 Geneva Accords, the Vietnamese communists were promised that a nationwide plebiscite would occur before the end of 1956. It was believed by all that Ho would easily be chosen Vietnam's leader. The promised elections never occurred, and Ho Chi Minh and the North Vietnamese again took up arms to unite all of Vietnam. During the 1960s, Ho's frail health made it difficult for him to guide the day-to-day machinations of the party and war effort. He remained the bridge between various factions in North Vietnam and was also a key figure in keeping China as a main ally of North Vietnam. He died on September 2, 1969, and is considered a great hero among the North Vietnamese. Saigon, the principal city of former South Vietnam, has since been renamed Ho Chi Minh City in his honor.

Ho Chi Minh City. *See* **Saigon.**

Ho Chi Minh Trail The Ho Chi Minh Trail was first used by the DRV in 1959 to transport equipment, supplies, personnel, and information to communists stationed in South Vietnam. The trail began as a simple system of paths running from the DRV's southern provinces into South Vietnam but evolved into a complicated system of paths, roads, waterways, and trails that moved through the Truong Son mountain range in southern Laos and eastern Cambodia. During the U.S.-Vietnam War, the U.S. and South Vietnam governments suspected that North Vietnam was illegally moving material south via the Ho Chi Minh Trail, which was forbidden according to the 1954 Geneva agreement. At the height of the war, the trail helped to supply several hundred thousand pro-Hanoi troops fighting in the South. The United States did all it could to destroy this supply route by bombing it and spraying Agent Orange to deplete the tropical vegetation that provided cover for troops, but the trail continued to be an asset for the DRV's cause.

Ho Dynasty (1400–1407) The instrumental figure in this short-lived dynasty was Ho Quy Ly, a prominent figure in the Tran court who used his powerful position to further his own goal of usurping the throne. He served as a general during the Cham invasions at the end of the Tran dynasty and encouraged a Tran royal adviser to put his own adolescent son into power as emperor. Once this occurred, he forced the boy to abdicate in 1398 and then established the Ho dynasty. Within a year Ho Quy Ly turned power over to his son though he remained very influential as a royal adviser. One of the Ho dynasty's policies was to reduce the power of feudal lords by confiscating any land that was in excess of new imperial-established limits. This proved to be the Ho dynasty's downfall because Vietnam's alienated aristocrats requested the Ming Chinese government (1368–1644) to come save them from the Ho tyrants. In 1407 the Chinese arrived and quickly defeated Ho's forces. The Chinese exiled the Ho family to China and made them serve in the Ming imperial army while China took control of Vietnam.

Hoa Hao Hoa Hao is a reform Buddhist sect founded in 1939 by a young Vietnamese mystic named Huynh Phu So. As a belief system, Hoa Hao was a synthesis of Buddhism, folk religions indigenous to South Vietnam, and popular social ideas. This new religion attracted a large rural peasant following during the 1940s and 1950s because it provided spiritual and sociopolitical guidance. During World War II the Hoa Hao cooperated with the Japanese. When the war ended, Huynh opposed the Vietminh's attempts to control South Vietnam. He was assassinated by the Vietminh in 1947. Members of the Hoa Hao allied with the French following Huynh's assassination. The main political focus of the group during both Indochina wars was to retain as much religious autonomy as possible. During the 1970s, the Socialist Republic of Vietnam arrested many of Hoa Hao's leaders, but the group continues to exist with more than one million adherents.

Hue The city of Hue played an important role in Vietnam's history. Originally known as Phu Xuan, it is located in central Vietnam on the Song Huong River, known in English as the River of Perfume. Hue rose in importance when it was established as the Vietnamese imperial capital by Emperor Gia Long (1761–1820). It remained the imperial capital until Emperor Bao Dai abdicated the throne in August 1945. Hue's great imperial palace, surrounded by battlements and gates, was patterned after the architecture of a seventeenth-century French architect named Bauban. Many buildings within the old imperial city were damaged when communist troops occupied the city during the

1968 Tet Offensive. Hue remains the capital of present-day Binh Tri Thien province.

Indochinese Union (ICU) The Indochinese Union was the French bureaucratic organization that controlled France's colonial possessions in Southeast Asia. This administrative body evolved out of the office of the governor-general, which had governed Cochin China under France's Ministry of Colonies. The ICU was responsible for the administration of Cochin China, Annam, Tonkin, Cambodia, and Laos. Vietnam's emperors asserted minimal authority in local matters, and the emperor's advisers were replaced by a French resident superior who controlled the government. Rather than providing a representative democracy, the ICU left the imperial bureaucracy in place so that it could control most of the decisionmaking through that institution. Paul Doumer (1857–1932) was a French governor-general of the ICU who believed, like many others, that the colony should support itself as well as the five thousand French administrators stationed in Vietnam. Consequently, the ICU controlled the taxation of salt, alcohol, and opium in Vietnam and imported many French colonial settlers, who established large plantations in the Mekong Delta. The ICU weathered several revolts and peasant uprisings and managed to keep control of Vietnam until the end of World War II and subsequent creation of the Associate States of Vietnam, Laos, and Cambodia.

Lac Long Quan This mythological figure supposedly emerged out of the sea to defend the first inhabitants in Vietnam. Lac Long Quan was reportedly summoned by the Vietnamese people in the Red River delta to help them defeat evil spirits, but he also introduced them to advanced agrarian methods in the production of rice before returning to the sea. Years later he allegedly returned to help the Vietnamese repulse a northern invasion. He was victorious, capturing the invader's queen, whom he married. Their union is said to have produced over one hundred sons, who would later rule Vietnam's first kingdom, Van Lang.

He returned to the sea while his descendents, known as the Hung kings, remained on land. This mythological story of Vietnam's early civilization signifies a lasting relationship between the agrarian society on land and the various peoples of the sea. Lac Long Quan's defeat of the northerners and marriage to their queen is also symbolic because it shows the sweet and sour relationship that the Vietnamese people have had with China.

Le Duan (1908–1986) Between 1960 and 1986, Le Duan was the general secretary of Vietnam's Communist Party. This prestigious position contrasted Le Duan's humble beginnings as the son of a rail clerk in Quang Tri province. A founding member of the Indochinese Communist Party, he was arrested in 1931 for sedition and spent the next five years in prison. Upon his release, he rapidly rose in the party bureaucracy, and by 1939 he was a member of the Central Committee. He spent most of World War II in prison. After the war, he worked in Ho Chi Minh's new government and was sent south, becoming secretary of the Communist Party's leading office in South Vietnam. He remained an outspoken leader against the Saigon regime for several years after the 1954 Geneva conference. He was recalled to Hanoi in 1957 where he became a member of the politburo. In 1960 he became general party secretary, and upon Ho Chi Minh's enfeeblement, he assumed the reigns of power. Over the next fifteen years he worked to unite the Democratic Republic of Vietnam (DRV) and insisted that the DRV in turn focus on uniting Vietnam. Le Duan was a skilled politician who played the USSR and China off of one another in order to receive aid from both countries. After the fall of Saigon in 1975, Le Duan and the Communist Party faced the task of establishing and maintaining social, economic, and political order in a united Vietnam. Le and his aging colleagues at the top of the party hierarchy faced intense criticism during the mid-1980s. Upon his death in 1986, Le Duan was replaced by Truong Chinh, his longtime rival.

Le Loi (1385–1433) Le Loi grew up in a wealthy family during the end of the Tran dynasty (1225–1400) and became a civil servant during the Ho dynasty (1400–1407). When Vietnam came under Chinese rule in 1407 Le Loi returned to his native village and organized a resistance movement in the hopes of overthrowing the Chinese and regaining Vietnamese independence. Many people joined his movement due to the harsh policies handed down by the Chinese, and by the 1420s the group had retaken most of southern Vietnam. In 1426 Le, who had renamed himself the "Pacification King," won a major battle against the Chinese outside of Hanoi, and two years later the Chinese left Vietnam altogether. Although he had been fighting in the name of the former Tran empire, Le Loi changed his name to Le Thai To and took the throne himself in 1428. This was the beginning of the later Le dynasty, which would last until 1788. Believing in the Confucian ideal of a benevolent ruler, he created a compassionate administration that included returning to the "equal fields" system that had been championed by several previous dynasties. This land distribution scheme divided many of the large land holdings and returned great portions of farmland to the peasants.

Le Thanh (1441–1497) Often thought to be the greatest emperor of the later Le dynasty, Le Thanh took the throne at age nineteen in 1428 as the dynasty's fourth emperor. His thirty-seven-year reign included numerous bureaucratic changes highlighted by the formalizing of duties for the six ministries (rites, war, justice, interior, public works, and finance). He wrested power from the aristocrats by strengthening the role of the provincial governments and ordered a national census to ensure that proper taxation transpired. Confucianism took a leading role over Buddhism in the bureaucratic sphere. Le Thanh sponsored the *Hong Duc,* which was a penal code based on Confucian ethics. This document consisted of 721 articles. Significantly, the *Hong Duc* code broke from traditional ideology in that Vietnamese women were given the right to divorce their husbands, own property, and inherit family property. The lack of arable land created economic hardships for the peasants, so Le Thanh ordered the construction of new dykes and the cultivation of new fields, and he penalized any nobles who tried to seize communal property. He also expanded his empire south, defeating Champa in 1471 and setting up military colonies (don dien) for the landless peasants.

Ly Bi Ly Bi, an ethnic Chinese inhabitant in Vietnam, grew up in a military household during Vietnam's Liang dynasty. After serving as a bureaucrat in the Liang court, Ly became frustrated by the court's policies, and in 542 he began a rebellion against the local Chinese administration. Even with Champa causing problems for Ly in the south, he was able to overthrow the Chinese by 544. He set himself up as emperor of a new Nam Viet, harking back to the Trieu Da dynasty, and set up his capital at Gia Ninh near his family home, northwest of Hanoi on the edge of the Red River delta. For three years he was moderately successful at uniting the Vietnamese; however, the Chinese returned in 547 and quickly captured Gia Ninh. Ly Bi's army faced the Chinese a few miles south of Gia Ninh, and he was able to escape only to be killed by upland tribesmen. Ly Bi's kingdom disappeared despite various efforts made by his followers to resist Chinese rule.

Ly Cong Uan (974–1028) Ly Cong Uan was reportedly raised as an orphan in a Buddhist temple until he left the Bac Ninh province and joined the palace guard during the Dinh dynasty (968–980). He served as a general under Dinh Bo Linh's army and seized power shortly after the death of Le Long Dinh in 1010. After his ascension to the throne, Ly Cong Uan changed his name to Ly Thai To and moved his capital back into the heart of the Red River delta, to the former capital of Thang-Long. These actions demonstrated Ly's confidence in an independent Vietnam. His state was blessed with fertile soil and a large population, and he instituted numerous social changes during his reign. He rearranged the government bureaucracy so as to be ruled by his family members, divided the nation into new provinces, and built many Buddhist temples. His overt support of the Buddhist Church provided a spiritual foundation for his dynasty. He built dykes and improved agrarian practices in his realm while changing the tax base so that merchants and traders would take the burden off of the farmers. His political, social, and economic successes provided an opportunity for Vietnam to invade and conquer several Cham and Cambodian kingdoms to the south. The Ly dynasty lasted for more than two hundred years.

Ly Phat Ma (r. 1028–1054) Born in 1000, Ly Phat Ma was the eldest son of Ly Cong Van (974–1028), the founder of the Ly dynasty. Ly Phat Ma ascended to the throne after fighting off three of his brothers who wished to usurp his power. He continued many of his father's policies, especially those dealing with spiritual and imperial matters. The Ly dynasty was at its zenith during Ly Phat Ma's reign. Once in power, he changed his name to Ly Thai Tong and removed bureaucratic family members who threatened to unite against him. He also raised a conscripted army that he used to further Vietnam's northern and southern boundaries. His closest advisers were Zen Buddhist monks and Confucian scholars. Ever concerned to pacify heaven and his subjects, Ly changed the name of his reign six times and went to great lengths to build roads and a postal system that helped to speed up communications. He died at the age of fifty-four and was peacefully succeeded by his son Ly Thanh Tong (r. 1054–1072).

Mac Dang Dung (r. 1527–1530) Mac Dang Dung served as a dominant character at the end of the later Le dynasty (1428–1788). In 1516 Tran Lao engineered a rebellion in which he managed to seize the capital and murder the reigning Le emperor. Mac Dang Dung helped the Le rulers oust the Tran family and regain their throne, but in 1527 he claimed the throne for himself and inaugurated the Mac dynasty. He established a strong power base in Thang Long and received official recognition from the Ming emperor in Peking. In 1530 he gave the throne to his son, though he retained power as a royal adviser until his death in 1540. Even father and son together were unable to contain internal dissent, for two families supported the deposed Le dynasty and fought to reinstate the Le court during the entire Mac dynasty. The Nguyen family, led by Nguyen Kim, helped Le Trong Tang regain considerable territory in the central and southern portion of Vietnam. Finally in 1591 Le loyalists led to an uprising that captured Thang Long and deposed the Mac emperor.

Minh Mang (1791–1841) The second emperor of the Nguyen dynasty (1802–1954) and the second son of Gia Long, Minh Mang ascended to the throne when his father died in 1820. Once on the throne, he outlawed Christianity in his realm. Paradoxically, he encouraged the growth of commerce with the West but refused to open a foreign affairs department in his government. Thus, he had a strained relation with European governments. With regard to his anti-Christian sentiments, Minh went so far as to outlaw the presence of Catholic priests in Vietnam. This decision was made at a time when a religious revival was sweeping through Catholic France. Realizing that it was in his interest to explain his actions to France, he sent two mandarin scholars to negotiate with the French. The French government refused to recognize them because its militant church leaders were allying with France's navy. Minh Mang did take some positive steps to relieve his people of economic pressures placed on them by an inept and self-absorbed imperial court; for example, he established large-scale irrigation projects to help relieve the distress felt by many farmers who could not produce enough rice to feed themselves. Minh Mang died in 1841, and his son Thieu Tri served as the next Nguyen emperor.

Ngo Dinh Diem (1901–1963) Ngo Dinh Diem was born into a scholarly Catholic family that had substantial connections to the imperial court. He earned a law degree at the University of Hanoi and was both devoutly Catholic and anticommunist. Following World War II, he was asked to become prime minister of the Associated State of Vietnam, which he refused. In 1955 he orchestrated an electoral fix in which he placed himself as the new prime minister of the U.S.-backed Republic of Vietnam. He saw himself as a sage-ruler whose policies and piety would uplift his subjects. His brother, Ngo

Dinh Nhu, served as minister of the interior and together with his wife, Madame Nhu, they were considered to be the worst aspects of Ngo Dinh Diem's government. His land reform policies alienated many of his constituents. His devout Catholic background in a predominantly Buddhist state caused many Buddhist leaders to claim that he was actively persecuting Vietnam's Buddhist Church. He also disappointed U.S. advisers as he refused to be a political puppet of the United States. With the tacit approval of U.S. personnel in Saigon, his own generals plotted a military coup against his government and overthrew Diem and his brother, Nhu, on November 1, 1963. Diem and Nhu were captured and executed during the coup.

Nguyen Anh (1761–1820) Nguyen Anh was born a nephew to the Nguyen lord in 1761 and was among the few members of the Nguyen family to survive the Tay Son rebellion in 1778. He escaped to the Mekong Delta, where he proclaimed himself king and gathered troops in order to respond with a counterattack. Saigon (Gia Dinh) subsequently changed hands many times during the 1780s, until in 1783 Nguyen's navy was destroyed and the Tay Son contingent controlled southern Vietnam. Nguyen and his troops fled to Phu Quoc, an island in the Siam Gulf that was home to a Roman Catholic seminary. The leader of this school, Pigneau de Behaine, became instrumental in uniting French and Vietnamese interests. Although de Behaine died in 1799 before Nguyen Anh's final victory over the Tay Son kings, the fighting went on until Nguyen defeated the Tay Son emperor in 1802. He then changed his name to Gia Long, which combined the names of the capitals of North and South Vietnam, and he established Vietnam's final dynasty, the Nguyen dynasty (1802–1954). For the first time in its history Vietnam was ruled by one court and stretched from the Chinese border to the Gulf of Siam. Gia Long established his capital at Hue and removed himself from the people by residing in a forbidden city built in the fashion of a Chinese capital. A rigorous Confucian system was put into place, which lowered the status of women, raised taxes to pre–Tay Son levels, and required farmers to put in sixty days of corvée labor each year.

Nguyen Family. *See* Nguyen Kim.

Nguyen Kim (1467–1545). Nguyen Kim was a court adviser during the reign of the Le emperors, and he remained loyal to the Le emperors after Mac Dang Dung (r. 1527–1530) usurped the Le throne in 1527. Nguyen Kim was related to the Le family through marriage, and he stood by the side of Le Trang Tong, who in 1533 claimed to be the legitimate ruler of Vietnam even though he lived in exile in Laos. Together with the Trinh family, the Nguyen clan removed the Mac emperor and placed a Le descendent on the throne. Subsequent rivalry between the Nguyen and Trinh families divided Vietnam. The southern-based Nguyen clan fared better against superior numbers due to several factors, including superior military weapons, which were provided to the Nguyens by Europeans, and the fertile soil of the Mekong Delta, which attracted large numbers of immigrant Chinese families.

Nguyen Van Thieu (1923–2001) Nguyen Van Theiu was born into a central Vietnamese peasant family in 1923. During World War II, he served in the Vietminh forces. Following the war, he joined the French-led Vietnamese National Army. After the First Indochina War, he became the superintendent of the National Military Academy. Eventually, he assumed command of the fifth division of the Army of the Republic of Vietnam. Following the 1963 coup, which ousted President Ngo Dinh Diem, Thieu became intricately involved in South Vietnam's bureaucracy. In 1967, he received 37 percent of the vote in a national election. This was sufficient support to earn the presidency of the Republic of Vietnam (RVN). He remained the RVN's president until 1975. He tried to bring stability to South Vietnam by weeding out procommunist personnel in rural areas and sought to redistribute land so the peasants could own their own farms. His second term as president would prove disastrous. He bitterly opposed the Paris Treaty despite U.S. president Richard Nixon's assurances that the United States would stand by the RVN. With

the withdrawal of U.S. troops and Nixon's ignominious resigna-
tion, the U.S. Congress was reluctant to prop up Nguyen Van
Thieu's government. Saigon was overrun in April 1975, and
Thieu fled to Taiwan. He lived in exile there until resettling in
the United States. He died in Boston, Massachusetts, on
September 29, 2001.

Pham Van Dong (1906–2000) Born into a family of scholars in Vietnam's central area, Pham Van Dong was educated at the National
Academy in Hue. At the age of twenty he moved to the southern
China city of Canton, where he joined the Revolutionary Youth
League. He quickly gained prominence in this proindependence
organization. Because of his antigovernment activities, he was
arrested, and between 1931 and 1937 he was imprisoned on the
island of Paulo Condore, just off the coast of Vietnam. During World
War II he became a trusted aid to Ho Chi Minh. In 1946 he was
appointed as minister of finance for the newly created Democratic Republic of Vietnam. Five years later he was elected to join the
elite group in the politburo of the Vietnamese Communist Party.
He became the minister of foreign affairs in 1954 and one year later
became the RVN's prime minister. He remained in that position
until 1987. His long tenure as prime minister was due to his political savvy, his revolutionary background, and his ties with the other
reigning leaders in the Communist Party.

Phan Boi Chau (1867–1940) Phan Boi Chau was born into a
family of scholars in 1867. He was en route to a promising career
after passing several civil service examinations when he decided
to establish a revolutionary organization. In 1903 he helped to create the Vietnamese Restoration Society, which supported the
restoration of one of Gia Long's ancestors to the throne. In 1906 Phan
moved to Japan where he organized several hundred Japanese-based
Vietnamese students into a group known as Viet Nam Cong Hien
Hoi. France pressured the Japanese government to deport Phan.
In 1908 he left for China, where he looked to China's nationalist
leader, Dr. Sun Yat-sen, for revolutionary inspiration. Phan changed

the name and direction of his organization, giving it the new title of Viet Nam Quang Phuc Hoi (Vietnamese Restoration Society). This proved to be a disastrous miscalculation which angered many of his supporters, and he subsequently spent time in a Chinese prison. After his release he wrote a pamphlet suggesting that the Vietnamese should somehow reconcile their differences with French authorities. In 1925 he was seized by the French while passing through the international district in Shanghai and returned to Hanoi, where he was placed under house arrest until his death in 1940.

Phan Chu Trin (1872–1926) Phan Chu Trin was born into a military family in 1872 in central Vietnam's Quang Nam province. His father was a supporter of the Vietnamese independence movement and was assassinated by a colleague who suspected him of treason. Phan was well-educated and began his political life as a minor employee in the Ministry of Rites. He was not interested in restoring the monarchy or throwing out the French, but he believed that Vietnam was a backwards country in need of outside guidance. He wrote a letter to the French governor-general, Paul Beau, in which he requested the French to live up to their mission of civilizing and modernizing Vietnam so it could independently mirror its colonial mother. His writings and participation in a peasant demonstration popularly known as "the revolt of the long hairs" landed him in jail. He was later exiled to France, where he took a job as a photographer and wrote occasional letters on contemporary issues. In 1925, one year before his death, he was allowed to return to Vietnam. His funeral was an occasion for fervent protests by Vietnamese nationalists.

Alexander de Rhodes (1591–1660) Born in 1591 in the French city of Avignon, Alexander de Rhodes joined the Society of Jesus, a Catholic religious order, as an adolescent. In 1627 he was sent by the Jesuit order to Vietnam to help convert the Vietnamese population. His initial success at gaining Christian converts among mandarins and court aristocrats was offset by the Confucian scholars' growing suspicion of Christian doctrines; they had him expelled from the country in 1630. Rhodes's main talent was his ability to master various Asian languages, including Vietnamese, Chinese, Japanese, Hindustani, and Persian. He was instrumental in romanizing the Vietnamese spoken language, and he also authored a Portuguese-Latin-Vietnamese dictionary. After being expelled from the north, Rhodes attempted to move to the Nguyen-controlled portion of southern Vietnam, but he discovered that he was also unwelcome there. He settled on the Portuguese-controlled island of Macau but remained determined to convert the Vietnamese people to Christianity. He established a clandestine seminary for training indigenous believers for the priesthood. In 1645 he was caught by the authorities and sentenced to death, but unlike many of his companions, he was released and returned to Macao. Rhodes traveled to Rome hoping that he could persuade authorities of the Catholic Church to replace the Portuguese as the principal missionaries in Southeast Asia; his ideas were rejected. Rhodes next traveled to France, where he successfully lobbied the French court to extend its commercial and religious activities in Vietnam. He died in 1660 while on a mission to Persia.

Henri Riviere (d. 1883) Henri Riviere was a prominent military commander in Vietnam during the 1880s. In 1882 he was ordered by Ly Myre de Vilers, the French governor of Cochin China, to enlarge the area of French political influence in North Vietnam. He gathered six hundred troops and journeyed up the Red River delta to Hanoi, where he stormed the citadel and claimed authority over the city. Within a year he was killed in a skirmish between his troops and Vietnamese bandits known as the Black Flag, led by a Chinese secret society leader named Luu Binh Phuc. When the Black Flag paraded Henri Riviere's head throughout the local villages, the outraged French authorities decided to teach the rebels a lesson. This ended in the French surrounding the imperial capital at Hue, and within a year France held a protectorate status over all of Vietnam.

Saigon Now known as Ho Chi Minh City, Saigon has been the social, economic, and cultural center of South Vietnam since the eighteenth century. Prior to Vietnamese incursions into South Vietnam, Saigon was a trading post. During the 1700s, Vietnamese farmers and Chinese merchants migrated into the Mekong Delta and settled in Saigon. The Nguyen leaders built a fort in Saigon. Its importance as a cultural, political, and economic center increased when the French created the colony of Cochin China and made Saigon its capital. After World War II, Saigon's political importance increased as both the French and the United States supported an independent South Vietnam state. French and American soldiers, entrepreneurs, and advisers were fixtures in Saigon's economic and social landscapes during the two Indochina wars. During the second war, Saigon's economy became heavily service-oriented. Prostitution, black markets, and other entertainment/customer service businesses flourished in Saigon during the U.S.-Vietnam War. The withdrawal of U.S. personnel and aid devastated Saigon's economy. The city fell to the communists in April 1975. Many of Saigon's residents were targeted for political rehabilitation by the Communist Party. In the early years of the twentieth century, Ho Chi Minh City has recovered its position as the leading economic center of Vietnam.

Socialist Republic of Vietnam In 1946 Ho Chi Minh declared the founding of the Democratic Republic of Vietnam (DRV). The DRV was unsuccessful in uniting all of Vietnam until 1975. More than a year after Vietnam's unification, the government changed the name of the country from the Democratic Republic of Vietnam to the Socialist Republic of Vietnam (SRV).

Tay Son Rebellion The Tay Son rebellion emerged out of modern-day Nghia Binh province in 1771. It was led by three brothers from the village of Tay Son. A primary motive for this rebellion was the inordinate taxation of farmers to support military campaigns and wealthy scholars. Massive flooding, famine, and the disrepair of irrigation projects encouraged people to rebel. The Tay Son brothers attacked Nguyen lords and stormed Saigon, killing every Nguyen family member they could find. Tay Son forces also murdered up to ten thousand Chinese merchants in and around Saigon. The Tay Son army distributed the booty to the poor and landless peasants. Soon people from all walks of life had joined the rebellion, and by 1778 the rebels controlled all of southern Vietnam. In 1786 the Tay Son rebels overthrew the Trinh family in the north. Although they claimed the Le emperor as final authority, the Tay Son brothers proclaimed themselves kings of all of Vietnam. This lasted until 1788, when the Le emperor called on the Chinese to assist him in driving out the Tay Son faction. Nguyen Hue (1753–1792) successfully defeated the Chinese, drove the Le emperor out of Vietnam, and declared himself emperor Quang Trung of a new Tay Son dynasty.

Thieu Tri (1810–1847) The third Nguyen emperor came to the throne at possibly the worst moment in the Nguyen dynasty's (1802–1954) history. French military incursions into Vietnam placed Thieu Tri's administration in a very difficult position. Though he tried his best to steer Vietnam through strained foreign relations, he could do little to alter Vietnam's worldview, which was xenophobic and inward-looking in nature. In 1843 the French Navy received governmental approval to intervene in Vietnam with the aim of freeing imprisoned missionaries, interpreting its assignment as permission to invade Vietnam. In 1847 the French began bombarding the port of Tourane (Da Nang). They did this in the name of freeing a Jesuit priest who had been released several weeks previously. Thieu Tri did his best to rally his troops against the French but died within a few weeks of the bombing.

Tran Dynasty (1225–1400) The Tran clan enjoyed considerable political power and wealth during the Ly dynasty (1009–1225). Tran Thu Do, an influential adviser in the Ly dynasty, placed a member of his family into the power vacuum that was created when the Ly dynasty crumbled. The Tran court instituted a policy requiring Tran emperors to abdicate when the next generation of emperor was old enough to reign; this would prevent the hoarding of power by one person and would allow for a smooth transition of power. The Tran court conducted bureaucratic reforms to strengthen the state while confiscating land in the Red River delta in order to lessen the influence of competing clans. Although the Tran emperors sought the advice of Buddhist monks, bureaucratic leadership was given a boost through learning the Confucian values of morality and virtue. Moreover, an elite group of secular scholars emerged to lead the state. Perhaps the most impressive Tran accomplishment was their victory over invading Mongol forces. The Tran court rejected the Mongols' demand that Vietnam become a tributary state of Yuan China (1276–1368). The Yuan court responded by sending a huge army that captured the Tran capital of Thang Long. The Vietnamese general Tran Hung Dao initiated a guerrilla war that ended in a counterattack that liberated Thang Long. Despite these successes, the Tran dynasty suffered a major setback in 1371 when it was unable to repel Cham invaders from the south.

Treaty of Protectorate (1884) This treaty, signed between the French and Vietnam's court officials, allowed France to rule Vietnam for the next seventy years. In 1883 the imperial court signed an initial treaty recognizing France as a protectorate over Tonkin and Annam and conceding that Cochin China was still part of the French empire. The 1884 treaty furthered France's authority in Vietnam, for it gave France suzerainty over all of Vietnam. The primary negotiators of the treaty were the Vietnamese court official Nguyen Van Tuong and the French diplomat Jules Patenotre. This treaty lasted until 1945, when Emperor Bao Dai officially renounced it and declared Vietnam an independent country.

Trinh Family. *See* **Trinh Kiem.**

Trinh Kiem (d. 1570). Trinh Kiem was the first of what came to be known as the Trinh lords during the sixteenth through eighteenth centuries. He was from the province of Thanh Hoa and married the daughter of Nguyen Kim (1467–1545), a powerful mandarin who fought to support the Le dynasty after it was deposed by Mac Dang Dung (r. 1527–1530). When Nguyen Kim died, Trinh stepped up as the strongest leader in the movement to put Le Trang Tong back into power in the capital of Thang Long. With assistance from his brother-in-law, Nguyen Hoang, Trinh established a large resistance movement in Thanh Hoa province. Much like his successors, Trinh Kiem ruled the Le court from behind the scenes until his death in 1570, and his family continued to manipulate the reins of power until the Le dynasty ended in 1788. The Trinh clan was never able to control southern Vietnam because of the powerful Nguyen clan. Civil war was constant between the two families, with the Trinh lords commanding an army of 100,000 troops, 500 elephants, and 500 naval junks. This rivalry continued until the 1780s when the Tay Son Rebellion overthrew both the southern and northern authorities.

Trung Trac The daughter of a Lac lord from Tay Vu, Trung Trac in 39 C.E. led a rebellion against the Chinese with the help of her sister, Trung Nhi. Women at that time were held in much higher regard in Vietnam than in China, and when Trung's husband was executed by a Chinese prefect for complaining about high taxes, the Trung sisters led a popular rebellion. With the help of both peasants and aristocrats, Trung Trac was able to remove the Chinese from Vietnam and was set up as queen in the Au Lac capital of Me Linh. The Chinese returned in 41 C.E. to reestablish Chinese rule, and Trung Trac found herself abandoned by the Lac lords who had supported her earlier. She was dethroned, captured, and executed alongside her sister by the Chinese. Differing accounts claim that she committed suicide or was exiled to China. Trung Trac's courage and her love of freedom are celebrated in popular Vietnamese lore.

Tu Duc (r. 1847–1883) Tu Duc was the last emperor of an independent Vietnam. A sickly man, he was rather fatalistic in his view of Vietnam's future. Court intrigue put Tu Duc into power;

his older brother, the rightful heir to the throne, had been pushed aside and died in prison after trying to claim the throne. Tu Duc instituted wide-scale persecution of Catholic priests and their converts, further alienating the French and drawing the ire of Emperor Napoleon III. The French captured the port of Da Nang and then, in 1858, occupied Gia Dinh. After facing some formidable setbacks, the French sent reinforcements and seventy ships, which constrained Tu Duc to sign the Treaty of 1862, ceding three provinces of southern Vietnam to the French. In 1873 France invaded Hanoi and forced Tu Duc to sign another treaty that opened up the Red River to French commerce. Tu Duc died in 1883 shortly before the French took his capital at Hue. They captured Hue as a form of revenge for the death of several French explorers who had been beheaded by the local populace. Shortly after his death chaos ensued at the imperial court. Within a year of his death, three emperors had been enthroned and deposed while the French used the vacuum of power to take control of Vietnam.

Van Lang This bronze-aged kingdom, which was founded by the Lac people, is also referred to as the Dong Son civilization due to the archeological site found in that village in 1925. Located in the Red River Valley, Van Lang was supposedly created by Lac Long Quan in the first millennium B.C.E. and was ruled over by eighteen of his descendents, known as the Hung kings, until Thuc Phan destroyed it in the third century B.C.E. Until historians found the Dong Son archaeological site, they believed that stories of this kingdom had been invented by the Vietnamese to mirror the birth of Chinese civilization at the same time. Little is actually known about the people of Van Lang. Historians speculate that the name itself refers to a mythological bird used as a totem by the Hung kings. The society was agrarian, patterned after a feudal system that made use of both bronze and iron implements. Detailed myths (including a god of water) were created by these people to help explain the yearly monsoons that flooded their lands. The military leader who eventually overthrew the Hung kings in the third century was the first person to unite the lowland people of Lac Viet with the upland inhabitants of Au Viet.

Viet Cong Viet Cong was the pejorative term coined by Ngo Dinh Diem for elements in South Vietnam that opposed Diem's policies. Ideologically opposed to foreign influence in their country, members of the Viet Cong organized into the People's Liberation Armed Forces (PLAF) in early 1961. Ties between the communist government in Hanoi and the PLAF eventually placed the PLAF in subordination to Hanoi. During the 1968 Tet Offensive, the PLAF bore the brunt of battle casualties; it never fully recovered its pre-1968 strength. When North Vietnam defeated South Vietnam, PLAF personnel were offended by many of the policies of their comrades in the north. In short, the PLAF believed that their contributions to North Vietnam's victory were underappreciated by the Communist Party.

Vietminh This organization was founded by the Indochinese Communist Party (ICP) during World War II and was officially known as the League for the Independence of Vietnam. Ho Chi Minh suggested that this group attempt to attract popular support for economic and social reforms as well as to join like-minded Vietnamese to fight for independence. The Vietminh enlisted thousands of rural and urban workers. It organized associations for every niche in society, whether it be workers, students, women, writers, religious organizations, or peasants. During the Japanese occupation of Vietnam (1941–1945), the Vietminh waged guerrilla warfare to both harass the Japanese and confiscate food to distribute to the many Vietnamese on the brink of starvation. Following the Japanese surrender, the Vietminh seized power in the north, and Ho Chi Minh declared the founding of the Democratic Republic of Vietnam (DRV) on September 2, 1945. Shortly after this, the Chinese Army invaded North Vietnam. Ho Chi Minh was constrained to invite France back into the region. The French agreed to discuss these matters with the DRV, and an agreement was made between the French and the DRV. Unfortunately, some French personnel in the DRV reverted to their old colonial mentalities, and in December 1946, the First Indochina War (1946–1954) commenced. The Vietminh used all its contacts in the war effort, but by 1951 it openly acknowledged its alliance with the Indochinese Communist Party and became known as the Lien Viet Front.

Vo Nguyen Giap (b. 1910) This military leader of communist Vietnam was born into a peasant family. During the 1920s, Giap joined a growing Vietnamese independence movement. In 1930 he joined the Indochinese Communist Party, and two years later he earned a law degree from the University of Hanoi. He took a job as a history teacher at the Thang Long school in Hanoi, where he studied and taught military history. Giap married Ngyen Thi Minh Giang, the sister of Nguyen Thi Minh Khai, who was the rumored wife of Ho Chi Minh. During World War II, Giap went to assist Ho Chi Minh on the China-Vietnam border. While away from Hanoi, the French imprisoned Giap's wife and daughter. They both perished while in custody, which served to intensify Giap's hatred of French imperialism. Giap established a literacy program so that the rank-and-file Vietminh could better understand the cause for which they were fighting. During the First Indochina War, Giap's troops constantly harassed the French through guerrilla warfare. He planted spies in Hanoi to monitor French bureaucrats and to report on foreign military movements. One of Giap's greatest accomplishments was the Vietminh's victory at the Battle of Dien Bien Phu, wherein Giap lured the French into a valley on the border of Laos and northwest Vietnam and surrounded them, forcing their surrender. Giap served as a high-ranking member of the Communist Party during the U.S.-Vietnam War but lost most of his political power in the years following the war.

Vietnamese Language, Food, Etiquette, and Holidays

LANGUAGE

Linguistic experts do not agree as to the origins of the Vietnamese language. Rather than being a homogenous language, it is an amalgam from Thai, Khmer, Muong, and some Malay languages. Moreover, half of the Vietnamese vocabulary is derived from Chinese. Because of China's millennium-long rule in Viet-

Hmong Tribe children in the Hoang Lien Mountains. The ethnic minorities in Vietnam are sometimes linguistically separated from the lowland Vietnamese. (Steve Raymer/CORBIS)

nam, the Chinese character-based writing system, known as *chu nho,* was used in Vietnam. By the 1200s, the Vietnamese scholars had adapted chu nho into the indigenous written language, and this script was termed *chu nom.* At that time, Vietnam's imperial court still used the Chinese script, but chu nom slowly gained in popularity both inside and outside the emperor's palace. When the sixteenth-century European missionaries established missions in Vietnam, they set out to create a more accessible written form of chu nom so that they might increase the effectiveness of their evangelistic efforts. Led by the Catholic cleric Alexander de Rhodes, a romanized system of writing chu nom was established, called *quoc ngu.* In the mid 1600s, a Latin-Portuguese-Vietnamese dictionary was published that paved the way for a greater use of quoc ngu by the Vietnamese and foreigners. Quoc ngu became the official language in Vietnam during the early twentieth century.

Spoken Vietnamese is a challenge to learn as it is a tonal language, with a total of six possible tones for some words. Thus, one simple word might have six different meanings based on how it is said. For example, the word *ma* has the following meanings:

ma – ghost
mã – horse
mạ – rice seedling
mả – tomb
mà – that
má – mother

Nonnative speakers must be careful how they say a Vietnamese word or they will be misunderstood. It is possible to insult someone when the intention is quite the opposite. Thus it is important to learn the tones and how they are pronounced. The six tones and their markings are as follows:

a A vowel with no marking is an even tone, and the speaker does not raise or lower his/her voice when pronouncing the vowel.

ã A person would pronounce this vowel by having the voice start just above normal, then lowering it slightly followed by a quick rise in the voice.

à   This is pronounced by a falling tone in the voice.
á   This is pronounced by a rising tone in the voice.
ả   This is pronounced by a tone that begins low, falls slightly, and
     then rises.
ạ   This vowel is pronounced by a low tone that falls and ends
     abruptly.

For individuals whose first language is not tonal, it is helpful to remember that much practice is needed when learning a tonal language. And while tones may seem like a foreign concept, English speakers often use tones to convey meaning. For example, most have a tendency to raise their tone at the end of a sentence where a response is requested.

These are twenty-nine letters in the Vietnamese alphabet, which are divided as follows:

aA = "a" as in [a]pple
åÅ = no sound by itself
âÂ = no sound by itself
bB = "bu" as in [bu]tter
cC = "gu" as in [gu]tter
dD = "yu" as in [yu]mmy
ðÐ = "du" as in [du]mmy
eE = "aya" as in [a ya]m
gG = "ge" as in [gi]rl
hH = "ha" as in [ha]mmer
iI = "e" as in m[e]
kK = "ka" as in [ca]mera
lL = "le" as in [le]mon
mM = "mo" as in [mo]ney
nN = "na" as in [Na]poleon
oO = "au" as in [au]gment
ôÔ = no sound by itself
½´ = "u" as in [u]tter
pP = "ba" as in [ba]ton
qQ = no sound by itself
rR = "ra" as in [ra]pport
sS = "sha" as in [sho]wer
tT = "da" as in [da]da
uU = "oo" as in sch[oo]l
ß¿ = guttural sound that combines sounds of several letters, similar
      sound to "eu"logy

vV = "the" as in the
xX = "the" as in [the]rmos
yY = "e" as in tr[ee]

Consonant clusters:

ch = as in [cha]pter
ǵi = as in [Za]ire
ǵh = as in [ǵu]tter
kh = as in [co]me
nh = as in nǵa or as in bri[nǵi]nǵ where the i is substituted with a
     short "a"
nǵ = as in nǵa or as in bri[nǵi]nǵ where the i is substituted with a
     short "a"
nǵh= as in [pa]ramour
ph = as in [bu]t
qu = as in [qua]si
th = as in [co]ver
tr = as in [tra]vail

There are twelve vowels in Vietnamese:

a = as in f[a]ther
å = as in f[a]ther, but the [a] is pronounced longer
â = as in fl[a]ck
e = as in fl[ai]r
ê = as in pat[é]
i = as in fl[ee]
y = as in fl[ee]
o = as in fl[oo]r
ô = as in d[ough]
½ = as in b[u]tter
u = as in b[oo]
ß = as in f[ue]l

Names

As is done in other East Asian cultures, Vietnamese given names follow the family name. For example, in the name Nguyen Co Thieu, Nguyen is the individual's family name and Co Theiu are the person's given names. Almost 50 percent of Vietnam's population has Nguyen as a family name. Other common family names include Vo, Tan, Le, Dinh, and Hoang. A Vietnamese woman retains her family name following her marriage but may be called by her husband's given name. In the West, a similar situation would be a woman who is married to a man named Jeffrey Smith and her friends calling her Mrs. Jeffrey. Vietnamese children are given their father's family name. Vietnamese also use the name of one's profession as a personal address. Thus, some people may be known as Mr. Lawyer, Miss Doctor, or Mr. Businessman.

Greetings

The philosophy of Confucianism runs deep in Vietnam, and the importance of maintaining proper relationships pervades all of society, particularly in the first stages of an association. First impressions are critical in Vietnam, and the manner by which one greets another sets the tone for the future relationship. The terms in common greetings are taken from kinship titles, for example, uncle, aunt, cousin, and little brother. Some of these salutations include:

chào ông	to an older or an important man
chào anh	to a younger man
chào bà	to an older or important woman
chào cô	to a younger woman
chào em	to a male or female child
chào ban	to a friend your same age

It is more formal to address someone by placing the person's name after the greeting. More of this subject is explored in the etiquette section of this chapter.

FOOD

Vietnam's cuisine, like its language, is heavily influenced by its neighboring countries. Nonetheless, the distinctive quality of the country's foods certainly makes this aspect of Vietnamese culture unique.

Rice is the staple crop of the Vietnamese. The fertile portions of the Red River delta, which were conducive to growing rice, first encouraged northern peoples to occupy Vietnam. The earliest social

Food can be purchased in open restaurants, air-conditioned restaurants, or from open-market vendors. (Catherine Karnow/CORBIS)

leaders in Vietnam were the individuals who controlled the largest rice paddies. Today Vietnam is the world's third leading exporter of rice, growing more than twenty varieties of this grain. Long-grain white rice is the most common strain used in Vietnamese meals. For most of Vietnam's history, only a privileged few could afford to eat the best variety of rice. Farmers usually sold the superior rice and survived on the cheaper, less tasty rice. It still remains a privilege to serve the best varieties of rice in Vietnam. Those who cannot afford the top-quality grain use additives such as nuts and leafy vegetables to make the rice more palatable.

Noodles are also used extensively in Vietnamese recipes. The most common noodle used is the thin rice noodle. Threads from bean plants are utilized to make noodles, and the adopted Chinese egg noodles are also served in Vietnam. Various Vietnamese Buddhist sects follow a vegetarian regimen, and so rice and noodles are essential for sustenance among these groups.

Pork and chicken are the most common meats in Vietnamese meals. Beef is a scarce commodity because large cattle ranches are not feasible in the limited space and resources of Vietnam. The Vietnamese often cook and eat every portion of the animal. Fish is also popular throughout Vietnam, as the entire western segment of the country borders the sea. Vietnam annually exports more than 150 thousand tons of live reef fish to China. They also export a large number of frozen fish products, such as shrimp and squid. Tuna is one of Vietnam's most lucrative export products.

Vietnamese enjoy a wide variety of fruits and vegetables. An indigenous fruit, known as durian, has received mixed reviews from those who visit the country. Durian's odor has been likened by some to that of an open sewer. Its smell is so malodorous that some hotels ban the product from its restaurants. Its taste is somewhere between a custard and an onion. Citrus fruit trees flourish in Vietnam as well as other fruits such as pineapple, mango, jackfruit, papaya, and banana.

Cultural differences between northern, central, and southern Vietnam extend to the diet the three regions enjoy. Chinese food is popular in the north, though all parts of Vietnam have adopted the Chinese chopsticks as eating utensils. Stir-fry is more popular in the north than in other portions of Vietnam, and northerners eat less fish than do the peoples of central and south Vietnam. One of Hanoi's most popular dishes is *pho bo,* which is a layer of thin rice noodles topped with a beef broth gravy, thin slices of raw beef, and hot spices.

Central Vietnam cuisine is a bit more complex, with multiple dishes accompanying any one meal. Because Hue was once the imperial capital, certain recipes associated with the royal court have been adopted by the surrounding villages. Potatoes, tomatoes, and similar vegetables are used in many of Hue's recipes. One of the most popular dishes in central Vietnam is pork sausages eaten together with rice cakes.

India's influence on Vietnamese food is most clearly seen in southern Vietnam. Curries and other South Asian spices are regularly used in south Vietnamese recipes. The large sugar cane plan-

Those along the coast of Vietnam supplement their income by selling fish. Fish provides iodine in the Vietnamese diet. (AFP/CORBIS)

tations in the Mekong Delta also facilitate the more extensive use of sugar in south Vietnam. One of the more popular dishes in Ho Chi Minh City is *chao tom,* a sugarcane stalk with shrimp. The fertile Mekong area also provides a greater variety of leafy vegetables for use in the south Vietnamese diet. In fact, meals are often wrapped in vegetable leaves, where the leaf is used as a plate as well as to add flavor to the meal.

The one recipe ingredient that is used the most often in all of Vietnam, however, is fermented fish, or *nuoc nam.* This food item is used in other portions of Southeast Asia but is given a different name. (For example, in the northern and central Philippines it is termed *bagoong.*) It is used as a dipping sauce or poured over rice, and it is a way of salting the otherwise bland steamed vegetables. Inhabitants along western Vietnam brew this concoction by following instructions handed down from past generations. Nuoc mam varies depending upon the type of fish it is made from. Nuoc mam made from anchovies is one of the most popular varieties.

To make nuoc mam, fish are layered in wooden barrels or, in some cases, large vats. Salt is placed between the layers of these fish, and the fish are left to decompose for at least three months. The sauce is removed and placed at the top of the barrels, and it ferments for at least another three months, at which point a nozzle is opened wherein sauce can ooze out to be used in meals. Nuoc nam is an acquired taste but is somewhat habit-forming once an individual learns to enjoy the flavor. It easily adds a unique flavor to a meal that might be otherwise tasteless.

The Vietnamese usually eat three meals a day. Breakfast is served rather early as the day often begins before the sun rises. Breakfast might consist of sticky rice served with some type of fish or other meat. Dough filled with pork and vegetables and then baked is a breakfast substitute for those who might need to grab a quick meal on their way to work. Lunch is served around 11:00 a.m. and is much more substantial than the lighter breakfast. Supper, which occurs later in the evening when the entire family is together, usually begins with a light soup followed by some type of meat or fish dish and then rice. Desserts are not normally a part of a meal, although sweet fruits might occasionally be served after the main course has been served.

If rice is the staple food of Vietnam, tea is the ubiquitous beverage in the land. Green tea is manufactured from tea leaves that are roasted immediately after being harvested. Black tea is made from partially fermented tea leaves. Dried flower leaves from jasmine and lotus plants are at times added to the tea for flavor and aroma.

One of the legacies of French colonial rule in Vietnam is the manufacture and consumption of coffee. This drink is particularly popular with Vietnamese men and is often part of the breakfast meal. An iced and sweetened French coffee, *ca-phe sua da,* is popular across the various sectors of Vietnam's population. Alcohol is also a very popular drink in Vietnam. Local beers include 333, Huda, Saigon Beer, and Halida. Foreign beers brewed in Vietnam include the Philippine beer San Miguel, and the Dutch brand

Heineken. Whiskey is served on special occasions, as is the locally brewed *ruou de,* or rice wine.

The following Vietnamese recipes are representative of the types of food served throughout the country:

Banh Pho Bo (Beef Noodle Soup)
This dish is best started early in the day, as the stock needs to cook for 6–12 hours. You can also prepare the stock a day or two in advance of serving the pho.

    3 large onions
    1 tablespoon peanut oil
    5 pounds beef and chicken bones, meaty combination
    4 ginger slices, julienne sliced
    2 carrots, julienne sliced
    1 small cinnamon stick
    1 star anise
    2 whole cloves
    1 teaspoon whole black peppercorns
    2 garlic cloves, smashed
    1/2 pound fresh bean sprouts
    1/2 pound beef sirloin, sliced very thin across grain, bite size
    1 green onion, finely sliced
    1/4 cup chopped cilantro
    4 serrano chiles, sliced (only wimps devein them)
    2 limes, cut into wedges
    8 ounces rice stick noodles
    3 tablespoons nuoc mam (fish sauce)
    freshly ground black pepper to taste

Slice two of the onions into 1/4-inch slices. Heat oil in a frying pan. Add the sliced onion and cook, stirring, until the edges brown. Remove and drain. Slice the remaining onion into paper-thin slices and set aside. Rinse the beef and chicken bones and place in a stockpot. Cover with cold water. Bring slowly to a boil. Reduce heat and simmer, uncovered. For a clear broth skim off foam. After 10–15 minutes, add browned onion, ginger, carrots, cinnamon, star anise, cloves, garlic, and peppercorns. Bring to a boil. Simmer the stock, partially covered for 6 to 12 hours, skimming regularly. If necessary add more water to keep the bones covered. Strain the stock, skim off, and discard any fat.

To serve, arrange the sliced beef on a platter. Garnish with reserved white and green onion. On another platter, arrange the bean sprouts, cilantro, chiles, and limes. Meanwhile, place the rice sticks in boiling water to heat. Reduce heat and allow rice noodles to soak for 30 minutes; drain. Place an equal portion of rice noodles in each soup bowl. Cover to keep warm. Heat beef stock to boiling. Season with fish sauce and pepper. Pour into a soup tureen or chafing dish.

At the table, place the soup on a portable warmer to keep hot. Offer each guest a bowl of warm rice noodles. Each diner adds some beef and onion to a bowl. Ladle the hot stock over the meat, stirring to cook the meat. Add the bean sprouts, cilantro, chiles, and lime to taste. Optional additions include fresh basil leaves and ground peanuts. Serves 6.

Chao Tom (Barbecued Shrimp Paste on Sugar Cane)
Although this dish can be baked in an oven, it is better grilled over charcoal. The dish may be prepared over two consecutive days. On day one, prepare the dipping sauce and condiments. The vegetable platter and shrimp paste can be assembled the following day. Fresh sugar cane is available at Caribbean markets; canned sugar cane is available at Asian grocery stores.

1 tablespoon roasted rice powder
1/4 cup scallion oil
1/4 cup crisp-fried shallots
1 tablespoon ground roasted peanuts
1 pound raw shrimp in the shell
1 tablespoon salt
6 garlic cloves, crushed
6 shallots, crushed
2 ounces rock sugar, crushed to a powder, or
1 tablespoon granulated sugar
4 ounces pork fat
4 teaspoon nuoc mam
freshly ground black pepper

peanut sauce (available in jars in Asian and specialty markets)
vegetable platter (carrot and celery sticks, raw leafy vegetables)
8 ounces rice-paper rounds (banh trang), 6-1/2 inches in diameter
12 pieces fresh sugarcane, or 12 ounces sugarcane packed in light syrup, drained
12 bamboo skewers, about 8-1/2 inches long, soaked in water for 30 minutes
vegetable oil, for shaping shrimp paste
8 ounces extra-thin rice vermicelli

Combine the roasted rice powder, scallion oil, crisp-fried shallots, and roasted peanuts. Set aside.

Shell and devein the shrimp. Sprinkle the salt over the shrimp and let stand for 20 minutes. Rinse the shrimp thoroughly with cold water. Drain and squeeze the shrimp between your hands to remove excess water. Dry thoroughly with paper towels. Coarsely chop the shrimp.

Boil the pork fat in water for 10 minutes. Drain and finely dice.

In a food processor, combine the shrimp, garlic, shallots, and sugar. Process until the shrimp paste pulls away from the sides of the container, stopping as necessary to scrape down the sides. The paste should be very fine and sticky. Add the pork fat, roasted rice powder, fish sauce and black pepper (to taste) to the processor. Pulse briefly, only enough to blend all of the ingredients. Cover and refrigerate.

Meanwhile, prepare the peanut sauce and vegetable platter. Cover the rice papers with a damp towel and a sheet of plastic wrap; keep at room temperature until needed. Peel the fresh sugar cane; cut crosswise into 4-inch sections. Split each section lengthwise into quarters. (If using canned sugar cane, split each section lengthwise in half only, then thread 2 pieces lengthwise onto a skewer.)

Pour about 1/4 cup of oil into a small bowl. With oiled fingers, mold about 2 tablespoons of the shrimp paste around and halfway down a piece of fresh sugar cane. Leave about 1-1/2 inches of the sugar cane exposed to serve as a handle. (If using canned sugar cane, there is no need to leave a handle. The skewers will serve as handles.) Press firmly so that the paste adheres to the cane. Proceed until you have used all the shrimp paste.

Prepare a charcoal grill or preheat the oven to broil. Steam the noodles, then garnish with the scallion oil, crisp-fried shallots, and ground roasted peanuts. Keep warm. Pour the peanut sauce into individual bowls and place the vegetable platter and rice papers on the table. Grill the shrimp paste on the sugar cane over medium coals, turning frequently. Or broil, on a baking sheet lined with foil, about 6 inches from the heat, for 3 minutes on each side, or until browned. Transfer to a warm platter.

To serve, each diner dips a rice paper in a bowl of warm water to make it pliable, then places the paper on a dinner plate. The rice paper is then topped with a variety of vegetables, some noodles, and a piece of the shrimp paste, which has been removed from the sugar cane. The rice paper is then rolled up to form a neat package. The roll is dipped in the peanut sauce and eaten out of hand. The remaining sugar cane may be chewed. Note: If neither type of sugar cane is available, use skewers. Shape the shrimp paste into meatballs and thread 3 or 4 on each skewer. Serves 4–6.

Crab and Asparagus Soup

    6 cups clear chicken broth (canned is fine)
    2 green onions, sliced into 1-inch pieces
    2 slices (1/4-inch thick) fresh gingerroot
    1 tablespoon chicken bouillon granules
    18 spears white asparagus, peeled
    6 ounces crabmeat
    2 eggs, beaten
    6 sprigs cilantro
    salt to taste

Combine chicken broth, green onion, gingerroot, and bouillon in a medium saucepan and bring to a rapid boil. Reduce heat, cover, and simmer 1 hour. Strain broth and remove any fat. Return to pan.

Cut asparagus spears into thirds; add to broth along with crabmeat. Simmer gently, uncovered, 10 minutes. Beat eggs in a small bowl. Slowly pour eggs into soup, stirring gently but constantly to stream egg threads. Divide soup into 6 bowls and garnish each with cilantro sprig. Serves 6.

Vietnamese Spring Rolls

    8 ounces boneless, skinless chicken breast
    2 tablespoons soy sauce
    1 tablespoon hoisin sauce
    1 tablespoon water
    2 teaspoons frozen orange juice concentrate
    1 teaspoon peanut butter
    1/2 teaspoon Asian chili paste
    1 teaspoon sesame oil
    2 teaspoons cornstarch
    8 dried shiitake mushrooms
    2 ounces cellophane noodles
    2 tablespoons peanut or safflower oil
    1 tablespoon fresh gingerroot, minced
    2 garlic cloves, minced
    3 green onions, minced
    1 red bell pepper, julienne sliced
    3 tablespoons fresh cilantro or parsley, chopped
    30 rice paper triangles or circles
    6 cups oil for deep frying

Cut chicken into 1-1/2 by 1/2-inch strips. In bowl, blend soy sauce, hoisin sauce, water, orange juice concentrate, peanut butter, chili paste and sesame oil until smooth. Stir in cornstarch. Add chicken and stir to coat; marinate for 15 minutes.

Cover mushrooms with warm water; soak for 15 to 50 minutes or until softened. Drain water and rinse mushrooms of any remaining sand; discard stems and slice caps into thin strips. Meanwhile, break noodles into pieces 1-1/2 inches long. Place in bowl and cover with water; soak for 5 minutes, then drain. In saucepan of boiling water, cook noodles for 5 minutes. Drain and rinse with cold water; drain well.

In wok or skillet, heat peanut oil over medium-high heat. Sauté ginger, garlic and onions for 30 seconds. Add red pepper and mushrooms; cook for 3 minutes, stirring. Add chicken with marinade; cook for 3 to 4 minutes or just until chicken is no longer pink inside. Stir in noodles and cilantro; let cool.

Dip rice papers, one at a time, into warm water to soften; lay out on damp tea towels in a single layer. Place about 2 tablespoons of mushroom-noodle filling in center of each triangular sheet (or 1/4 cup in each round sheet). Fold up bottom over filling; fold sides over and roll up tightly. Rolls can be covered with a damp tea towel in separate layers and refrigerated for up to 8 hours.

In wok or Dutch oven, heat 6 cups of oil over medium-high heat to 375° F. Fry rolls in batches for about 5 minutes or until crisp and golden on all sides. Drain on rack. Makes 16 large or 30 small rolls.

Note: Instead of deep-frying, the rolls can be steamed in an oiled steamer for 5 minutes, or baked for 20 minutes in 400° F. oven. Assembled spring rolls can also be eaten without being cooked.

ETIQUETTE

Whether due to Confucianism, Buddhism, or a past rooted in numerous travails, the Vietnamese are much less direct in conversations than are Westerners. Although the latter are likely to give a direct answer to a question, even if the reply is in the negative, the Vietnamese might lie rather than answer in the negative. For example, if a foreigner visiting Vietnam invites a Vietnamese person to an engagement that the invitee cannot attend, rather than turning down the request, the person may indicate that they will attend though they know quite well that they will not be able to. Even among family members, there is an understood meaning behind an affirmative answer that in reality implies the negative. In English, when someone is unsure about whether they can accept an invitation the phrase "I'll see" is often used. The Vietnamese have a similar phrase, but the parties know that the "I'll see" actually means no. It is much easier for the Vietnamese to say this rather than to respond with a blunt "no" to a request.

In relation to the above, it is uncharacteristic for the Vietnamese to display overt anger in public. Many Western business people have tried to use a blunt, aggressive approach in setting up enterprises in Vietnam. Stories are told of frustrated foreign business folk raising their voices in meetings with their Vietnamese counterparts. This is not an effective method for making a point in Vietnam. Virtue is demonstrated in one's ability to control his/her emotions, and the Vietnamese seek to be virtuous people. Moreover, patience is also a quality that is nurtured among the Vietnamese. Their patience has been demonstrated in their ability to endure lengthy foreign occupations and devastating wars. Western powers falsely assumed that the Vietnamese won previous wars because Vietnamese leaders had no qualms about sending millions of soldiers to their deaths. This is not true. Their victories are rooted in their persistence. This attribute also governs their interpersonal relationships. It is more polite to demonstrate patience than to display an air of anxiety.

It is also important to show proper deference when meeting someone for the first time and throughout the relationship. The hierarchy in affiliations is primarily dictated by age. Younger people are expected to demonstrate respect to the elderly both in the actions and the manner by which they address them. This transcends gender boundaries; younger men, for example, are expected to show reverence toward older women. In the business and government culture, the normal rules of hierarchy etiquette are bent so that one's position takes precedent over age and gender.

The giving of gifts is a common occurrence throughout Vietnam. Because of the pervasive Buddhist philosophy, there is a sense that the giver receives more benefits than the recipient. One's karma, or accrued merit, is enhanced by generosity, and so guests often bring a gift when invited to dinner. Appropriate gifts include fruit, plants, sweets, and candied ginger. Items that obviously come from outside Vietnam are also much appreciated by Vietnamese. Flowers are one of the most common presents that people give to each other, but there is a proper protocol that goes along with presenting someone with a bouquet. Pink roses represent romantic inclinations by the giver, and chrysanthemums are associated with funerals. Most other flowers are appropriate for expressing gratitude to someone. Knives are symbolic of fighting—something the Vietnamese wish to put in their past—and so people do not exchange knives as gifts. Soaps, deodorants, and perfumes are usually not given as presents because they may indicate that the recipient is malodorous.

There is a strong sense of reciprocity in Vietnam. One should avoid overwhelming an individual or family with gifts and favors because those that receive these benefits will feel an inordinate debt and will have to find some way to repay the kindness. For this reason, small, inexpensive souvenirs are appropriate because they demonstrate thoughtfulness but do not represent the placing of an unspoken obligation on the recipient.

Alcohol and cigarettes are part of business meetings. A high percentage of Vietnamese men smoke (currently, women who publicly smoke are often perceived as prostitutes). Foreigners who smoke should place their pack of cigarettes on a table with some of the individual sticks halfway out of the pack. Vietnamese smokers enjoy foreign brand cigarettes and will welcome the opportunity to accept an invitation to take these cigarettes. Nonsmokers should be prepared to endure a smoke-filled room rather than complain about the polluted air. One should also be aware that some of the local alcoholic beverages are quite potent. When serious drinking begins, the participants begin calling for *tram phan tram* (100 percent). The meaning of this phrase is similar to the English term "bottoms up." When tram phan tram is stated, the person drinking is obliged to completely drain the contents in the glass in front of him or her. Nonindigenous business people may substitute soft drinks for alcohol, but their Vietnamese counterparts may view them curiously or with greater reservation.

Vietnamese are more reserved than Westerners, and the primary goal in social relations is to not "lose face." There are various reasons as to why an individual may be shamed in a public situation. These include being accused that one is not properly caring for relatives; being scolded by a friend, colleague, relation, or supervisor; and failing to fulfill certain obligations, such as repaying a debt. Vietnamese are not as comfortable as Westerners in terms of making direct eye contact during initial meetings. Physical contact in public is also kept to a minimum, particularly between individuals who are not close friends. The casual pat on the back is not part of socially acceptable actions in Vietnam. These taboos apply for individuals who are not close friends. Direct eye contact is normal between close friends, and one often sees young men holding hands as they walk together, and young women doing the same. Young romantic couples also hold hands in public, though this is a relatively new practice in Vietnam.

HOLIDAYS

Proper etiquette extends to how one observes Vietnam's national holidays. There are five official holidays in Vietnam, and each is associated with certain sociocultural norms.

New Year's Day, January 1. Adopting this Gregorian calendar date as a holiday is a compromise the Vietnamese government made to be in step with the rest of the world. As it has become more globally connected economically, the Vietnamese government has followed the lead of other countries and now closes its institutions in observance of this date. There are limited, if any, public celebrations on this holiday.

Victory Day, April 30. This holiday commemorates the North's victory over South Vietnam. It is more politically correct to speak of this day as the observance of Vietnam's unification. The celebration that takes place on this day is limited to government holiday activities.

International Labor Day, May 1. This holiday is particularly appreciated because it means that the Vietnamese have two consecutive days of vacation. Vietnamese observe this holiday by hosting family picnics at public parks. Restaurants and stores usually stay open on May 1, and so it is also a time when people splurge by shopping and eating at their favorite restaurants.

National Day, September 2. On this date in 1945, Ho Chi Minh declared the founding of the Democratic Republic of Vietnam. For the Vietnamese this is their day to celebrate independence. Again, most of the celebratory activity on this day centers on government agencies. It is very appropriate to send gifts to government officials on National Day, and many foreigners exchange gifts with their joint venture partners. The day following National Day is also observed as the anniversary of Ho Chi Minh's death, though he expired the previous day. When he died in 1969, government officials did not tell the public so as not to spoil the National Day festivities. Ever since, then, Ho Chi Minh's death has been observed on September 3.

Tet, the Lunar New Year. It is difficult to adequately express the enormous social/cultural significance of Tet. The Lunar New Year changes from year to year, but it usually takes place in early February. The government asserts that Tet should be celebrated for three days, but many Vietnamese spend up to three weeks honoring this holiday. Preparation for Tet begins three months before its occurrence.

The complete name for the celebration is *Tet Nguyen Dan,* with *Tet* meaning festival. Tet is the Vietnamese adoption of the Chinese New Year, and there are similarities between the observances and activities of the related holidays. Employers usually give their workers annual bonuses, which often consists of a month's extra pay, several weeks prior to Tet. This allows the employees to purchase gifts for their family and friends. A traditional gift to children is a crisp new monetary note that is placed in a red envelope. Although the amount of money is small, the symbolism behind the gift is of great significance. The money represents a bright future for the recipient. If one is involved in business in Vietnam, it is important that all employees are given some type of present for Tet. It is also appropriate to send small gifts to the children and spouse of each worker.

Tet is also an important occasion in terms of reconciliation. One is not to begin a new year with a grudge against another person. Past animosity is to be replaced with friendly relations. One also seeks to be out of debt as he or she enters the New Year. New clothes are purchased in anticipation of the celebration, and many Vietnamese residing abroad return home to participate in Tet. Like the Gregorian calendar New Year's Day, Tet revelry begins at midnight of the lunar new year. Firecrackers and other noisemakers ring in the new year. Some superstition accompanies the enormous noise at midnight. There is a belief that as the old year is ushered out, so too are the gods that protected the family, particularly the kitchen gods that assured sufficient sustenance during the past year. Thus, between the time that the old gods leave and the new, benevolent gods enter the home, there is a period where evil spirits can come in and create chaos. The noise that is generated is meant to keep these malevolent spirits away.

Though people stay up late on Tet's eve, it is customary to get up early on the morning of Tet. The early morning hours of Tet are extremely significant. It is believed that the first sound that is heard portends either blessing or cursing for the next year. For some a rooster crowing means that there will be much toil for the next year, and a dog's bark represents a forthcoming year of bounty. Vietnamese believe that the first person to enter your house on Tet is responsible for the fortunes of that house for the next year. Thus the first person to pass through the door may be considered to be a hero at the end of the year, or might be accused of bringing bad luck upon the house.

Following the first day of Tet, games and regional competitions take place. These activities range from soccer tournaments to wrestling matches. There are also ceremonies for the dead, with offerings made for ancestors. The celebrations of Tet often culminate at the cemetery, where graves are swept and offerings are presented for the deceased. In connection with this practice, the Vietnamese repeat these graveyard visits every August but for a very different purpose. In August, the offerings for the dead are for the "wandering souls" who have no progeny to present appropriate reverence. This ensures that those that have died and are forgotten will receive acknowledgement, even if it is from people who are not directly related to them.

References
Bach, Ngô, and Gloria Zimmerman. *The Classic Cuisine of Vietnam.* New York: Penguin, 1986.
Brook, Timothy, and Hy V. Luong. *Culture and Economy: The Shaping of Capitalism in East Asia.* Ann Arbor: University of Michigan Press, 1999.
Chambers, Kevin. *Succeed in Business: The Essential Guide for Business and Investment in Vietnam.* Portland: Graphic Arts Center Publishing, 1997.

Cohen, Barbara. *The Vietnam Guidebook*. New York: Houghton Mifflin, 1991.

Curry, Jeffrey E. *Passport Vietnam: Your Pocket Guide to Vietnamese Business, Customs & Etiquette*. San Rafael, Calif.: World Trade Press, 1997.

Duffy, Dan. *North Viêt Nam Now: Fiction and Essays from Hanoi*. New Haven, Conn.: Yale University Council on Southeast Asia Studies, 1996.

Ellis, Claire. *Culture Shock! Vietnam*. Portland: Graphic Arts Center Publishing, 1995.

Engholm, Christopher. *Doing Business in the New Vietnam*. Englewood Cliffs, N.J.: Prentice Hall, 1995.

Faculty of Arts Quynh-Du. Ton-That@anu.edu.au. "Vietnamese Studies." Monash University. http://www.arts.monash.edu. 2000.

Ferro, Jennifer. *Vietnamese Foods & Culture*. Vero Beach, Fla.: Rourke Press, 1999.

Huu, Ngoc. *Sketches for a Portrait of Vietnamese Culture*. Hanoi: Gioi Publishers, 1997.

Kronowitz, Ellen L. "Creating New Images of Vietnam: Celebrating Tet in the Middle-School Classroom." *The Social Studies* 86, no. 1 (1995): 29–33.

Lê, Pham Thúy-Kim, and Kim-Oanh Nguyên. *Chúng Ta Nói: Conversational Vietnamese*. Seattle: University of Washington Press, 2001.

Murray, Geoffrey. *The Simple Guide to Vietnam: Customs & Etiquette*. Kent, U.K.: Cromwell Press, 1997.

Nghia, Le Huu. "On the Character and Main Context of Our Time." *Viet Nam Social Sciences* 3 (1999): 3–8.

Nguyen, Dang Liêm. *Advanced Vietnamese: A Culture Reader*. South Orange, N.J.: Seton Hall University Press, 1987.

Quy, Nguyen Duy. "Vietnamese Village Culture and Development." *Viet Nam Social Sciences* 1 (1999): 13–18.

Routhier, Nicole. *The Foods of Vietnam*. New York: Stewart, Tabori and Chang, 1989.

Scheela, W., and N. Van Dinh. "Doing Business in Vietnam." *Thunderbird International Business Review* 43, no. 5 (2001): 669–688.

Tran, Quoc Vuong. "Popular Culture and High Culture in Vietnamese History." *Crossroads* 7, no. 2 (1992): 5–38.

Trankiem, L., et al. "Doing Business in Vietnam: Implications for International Investors." *Journal of Transnational Management Development* 5, no. 4 (2000): 3–24.

Xuan, Viet. "Market Economy—Which Orientation?" *Viet Nam Social Sciences* 4 (1998): 15–25.

Vietnam-Related Organizations

Telephone calls to Vietnam require the use of the country code 84. A city code also is needed; the most common are 8, for numbers within Ho Chi Minh City, and 4, for numbers within Hanoi. Country and city codes are shown in parenthesis preceding the phone numbers in the addresses below.

BUSINESS AND ECONOMIC

Australian Business Group
Mondial Center, Room 304
203 Dong Khoi Street, District 1
Ho Chi Minh City, Vietnam
Tel.: (84-8) 822-7360
Fax: (84-8) 822-7408

British Business Group of Vietnam
25 Le Duan Street, District 1
Ho Chi Minh City, Vietnam
Tel./ Fax:(84-8) 822-5172

Department of Planning and Investment of Ho Chi Minh City
32 Le Thanh Ton Street, District 1
Ho Chi Minh City, Vietnam
Tel.: (84-8) 829-4988
Fax: (84-8) 829-5008 or (84-8) 829-0817
E-mail: ipdpi@hcm.vnn.vn
Website: http://www.hcminvest.gov.vn

French Council of Commerce and Industry of Vietnam
Saigon Trade Center
37 Ton Duc Thang Street, District 1

Ho Chi Minh City, Vietnam
Tel.: (84-8) 910-0308
Fax: (84-8) 910-0309

Japanese Business Association of Ho Chi Minh City (JBAH)
Sun Wah Tower, Room 1407
115 Nguyen Hue Street, District 1
Ho Chi Minh City, Vietnam
Tel.: (84-8) 821-9369
Fax: (84-8) 821-9370
E-mail: jbah@hcm.vnn.vn

Vietnamese Overseas Business Association in Ho Chi Minh City
147 Nguyen Dinh Chieu Street, District 3
Ho Chi Minh City, Vietnam
Tel.: (84-8) 930-1530
Fax: (84-8) 930-6737

GOVERNMENT/EMBASSY/ MISCELLANEOUS INFORMATION

American Chamber of Commerce in Vietnam
Hanoi Chapter:
Press Club 5/F
59 A Ly Thai To Street
Hanoi, Vietnam
Tel.: (84-4) 934-2790
Fax.: (84-4) 934-2787

Ho Chi Minh City Chapter:
New World Hotel, 3/F Room 324
76 Le Lai Street, District 1
Ho Chi Minh City, Vietnam
Tel.: (84-8) 824-3562
Fax.: (84-8) 824-3572

Like most countries doing business in Vietnam, the United States has organized Chambers of Commerce made of member companies. Larger Chambers of Commerce have a hired staff member who acts as executive director, whereas smaller Chambers may have only a volunteer staff. Chambers of Commerce often are good sources of information on the ease or difficulty in doing business in Vietnam. Oftentimes they can refer you to members who have detailed insight into start-up problems, the incidence of corruption, and other challenges of international business.

Asia-Europe Foundation (ASEF)
No. 1 Nassim Hill
Singapore 258 466
Tel.: (65) 838-4700
Fax: (65) 838-4719
Website: http://www.asef.org/

ASEF was established in 1997 with the aim of promoting engagement between the civil societies of Asia and Europe and forging mutual understanding between the two regions. Based in Singapore, the foundation reports to a board of governors representing the twenty-five member countries and the European Commission. ASEF is funded by contributions from member governments and their institutions, as well as private corporations, foundations, and individuals of ASEM countries.

Commercial Service—Hanoi
U.S. Commercial Center
31 Hai Ba Trung, 4th Floor
Hanoi, Vietnam
Tel.: (84-4) 824-2422
Fax: (84-4) 824-2421

Commercial Service—Ho Chi Minh City
U.S. Commercial Service
9F Saigon Centre, 65 Le Loi Boulevard, District 1
Ho Chi Minh City, Vietnam
Tel.: (84-8) 825-0409 or 836-0491

This agency assists those interested in trade missions and gaining information on industry sector analysis.

Communist Party of Vietnam
Website: http://www.cpv.org.vn
Country Profile for Vietnam
Website: http://www.abisnet.com

Embassy of Vietnam
1233 20th Street NW, Suite 400
Washington, DC 20036
Tel.: (202) 861-0737
Fax: (202) 861-0917
E-mail: info@vietnamembassy-usa.org
Website: http://www.vietnamembassy-usa.org/embassy/

Fulbright Program
Public Affairs Section—U.S. Embassy Hanoi
Rose Garden Tower, 6 Ngoc Khanh Street, Third Floor
Hanoi, Vietnam
Tel.: (84-4) 831-4580
Fax: (84-4) 831-4601
E-mail: fulbrightvn@fpt.vn

The worldwide Fulbright Program, established by the U.S. Congress in 1946, was created with the goal of increasing understanding between the people of the United States and the peoples of other countries by means of educational and cultural exchange. The U.S. State Department's Bureau of Educational & Cultural Affairs (ECA) is the principal administrator of the Fulbright Program. Because Vietnam does not host a Fulbright commission, U.S. Embassy/Public Affairs Section officers are responsible for program administration and coordination. Recipients of Fulbright scholarships conduct research for six months to one year in Vietnam.

**Library and Education Assistance Foundation
for Vietnam (LEAF-VN)**
Website: http://www.leaf-vn.org/

LEAF-VN strives to help the Vietnamese people achieve excellence
in education by providing assistance in developing the country's
library systems and services.

Ministry of Industry
54 Hai Ba Trung Street
Hoan Kiem, Hanoi, Vietnam
Tel.: (84-4) 825-2852 or 826-7870
Fax: (84-4) 826-9033

This ministry's goal is to encourage local and foreign firms to
establish factories in Vietnam.

Ministry of Trade
31 Trang Tien
Hanoi, Vietnam
Tel: (84-4) 824-2124 or 825-3881
Fax: (84-4) 826-4696

Vietnam's Ministry of Trade attempts to promote the country's products, attract investment, and regulate business. Generally Vietnamese seek foreign investment and the opening of foreign manufacturing and other projects because this expands employment
while increasing trade and tax revenues. You may want to use the
ministry to check the information you are getting from other
sources and to contact it as a source for further data.

Vietnam Veterans of America Foundation
1725 Eye Street NW, Fourth Floor
Washington, DC 20006-2412
Tel.: (202) 483-9222
Fax: (202) 483-9312
Website: http://www.vvaf.org/

Annotated Bibliography of Recommended Works on Vietnam

The following material is presented in the same order as the narrative section of this book. Every effort has been made to include accurate and readable sources that should assist those readers who want to know more about Vietnam. These sources are, for the most part, general in nature. For more specialized subjects, readers should refer to the more detailed bibliographies at the end of each chapter. A few websites also are noted; these have been carefully chosen in light of the ever-changing nature of Internet addresses.

GEOGRAPHY AND HISTORY

Duiker, William J. *Historical Dictionary of Vietnam*. Metuchen, NJ: Scarecrow Press, 1989. 269 pp. (available in hardcover only, currently out of print). Professor William J. Duiker is arguably the foremost American scholar on Vietnam. This book provides wonderful vignettes of the people who have played a role in shaping Vietnam. Richly detailed and meticulously researched, the *Historical Dictionary* is an important resource for anyone who wishes to understand particular people and events in Vietnam's past. It is a reference work and is found in college and university libraries.

Duiker, William J. *Ho Chi Minh: A Life*. New York: Hyperion, 2000. 695 pp. (available in hardcover and paperback). The *Washington Post* noted in its review of *Ho Chi Minh* that "It is the most authoritative account of Ho's life we are likely to have for a long time to come." What makes this definitive biography so useful is that Duiker is able to masterfully weave Vietnam's history in with Ho Chi Minh's life. One way to study history is through the lens of a major figure, and this book gives a reader an overall history of Vietnam during the twentieth century.

Jamieson, Neil L. *Understanding Vietnam.* Los Angeles: University of California Press, 1993. 428 pp. (available in paperback). This book provides a wonderful context for understanding Vietnam's history and society. Playing on the theme of Yin and Yang and the idea of Vietnam's obsession with harmony and balance, Jamieson demonstrates how the Vietnamese kept this delicate system in place and how it came apart during World War II. This is a book that if published in the 1950s might have given U.S. military and foreign advisers a better foundation for making decisions in this Southeast Asian country. Students will enjoy this work because it looks at history from the perspective of the everyday Vietnamese citizen.

Karnow, Stanley. *Vietnam: A History.* New York: Viking Press, 1983. 784 pp. (available in paperback). Journalists often make the best writers of history. This is the case with Karnow's Pulitzer Prize–winning *Vietnam: A History.* Stanley Karnow lived in Paris in the 1950s as a U.S. foreign news correspondent during France's fight for dominance in Vietnam. He had access to archives and individuals that had firsthand experience in Vietnam. Although this book is primarily about the U.S.-Vietnam War, the chapters concerning Vietnam's earlier history are written in a very clear manner, and he provides a wonderful context for understanding the war. A ten-hour video series entitled *Vietnam: A Television History* was based on Karnow's work. These videos are also extremely helpful in understanding the war between Vietnam and the United States.

Marr, David G. *Vietnamese Tradition on Trial 1920–1945.* Los Angeles: University of California Press, 1984. 450 pp. (available in paperback). This book approaches the history and society of Vietnam by demonstrating that Western imperialism had a profound effect on Vietnam. As noted in the title, the author first sets forth what Vietnamese tradition is, and how it was challenged by foreign influence. As he explores Vietnam's tradition, Marr explains the basis of Vietnamese culture and how this is rooted in centuries of tradition.

Taylor, Keith W. *The Birth of Vietnam.* Los Angeles: University of California Press, 1983. 397 pp. (available in paperback). One of the most complicated subjects in Vietnamese history is the early period in the formation of the state. Taylor is leading U.S. scholar on the early history of Vietnam. He wrote this book for college students, but it also is a useful reference for high school students who want to learn how Vietnam was born into the family of nations.

VIETNAM'S ECONOMY

Unlike the more established economies, Vietnamese officials continue to struggle to give people more economic freedom without compromising the socialist ideology where capitalism is downplayed. The most effective way to keep updated on Vietnam's economy is by regularly reading a journal that focuses on this issue. Three journals that help casual observers understand Vietnam's economy are *The Far Eastern Economic Review, AsiaWeek,* and *AsianWeek.* The following sources are also helpful in understanding Vietnam's economy.

Fforde, Adam, and Stefan de Vylder. *From Plan to Market: The Economic Transition in Vietnam.* Boulder, CO: Westview Press, 1996. 24 pp. (available in paperback). This book provides an overview of how Vietnam's economy changed during the last quarter of the twentieth century. It explores why some of the changes have been planned whereas others have been unforeseen. The authors try to write so that readers with limited background on this topic can understand the material.

Photius, http://www.photius.com. This Internet site is effective because it lists some of the important economic indicators on its opening web page, including Vietnam's gross domestic product (GDP); the GDP divided according to the nation's agriculture, industries, and services; inflation rate; labor force; unemployment rate; and major import and export products.

Vietnam Economic Information Network, http://www.vneconomy.com. The Internet is particularly helpful for individuals learning about Vietnam's economy. This particular site has links to material on Vietnam's economy, the agriculture-rural development, Vietnam's stock market, and currency exchange rates.

Williams, Michael C. *Vietnam at the Crossroads*. New York: Royal Institute of International Affairs, 1992. 104 pp. (available in paperback). This is the best one-volume introduction to Vietnam's economy for those who are not economists. Williams is able to take very complicated concepts and make them understandable; in fact, the book can be understood by high school students. He also presents a brief background to Vietnam's history since the end of the U.S.-Vietnam War.

VIETNAMESE INSTITUTIONS

Chifos, Carla Marie. *Southeast Asian Urban Environments: Structured and Spontaneous*. Tempe, AZ: Arizona State University Press, 2000. 326 pp. (available in paperback). Vietnam, like other Southeast Asian countries, is trying to control the growth of its urban communities and the institutions in those communities. Hanoi and Ho Chi Minh City are magnets for unemployed farmers and for young people who are seeking to overcome their boredom with country life. Chifos's book examines how the growth of these cities is affecting all of Vietnam's society.

Glewwe, Paul, and Harry Anthony Patrinos. "The Role of the Private Sector in Education in Vietnam: Evidence from the Vietnam Living Standards Survey." *World Development* 27, no. 5 (1999): 887–901. This article is particularly helpful for those who are interested in Vietnam's education system. The authors present a case for increasing private education in Vietnam. Although many statistics accompany this study, the article is written in a clear fashion and the statistical numbers are clearly explained.

Kerkvliet, Benedict, and Doug Porter, editors. *Vietnam's Rural Transformation*. Boulder, CO: Westview Press, 1995. 272 pp. (available in paperback and hardback). Vietnam experienced radical economic and social changes during the mid-1980s. This book is the first English study on what those changes have meant to the various institutions in Vietnam. Although the contributors acknowledge that there has been improvement in real income for the Vietnamese people, this volume also illustrates that there have been some difficult consequences of these changes. These include a growing disparity between the rich and poor, the decline in education services, and the disillusionment that many Vietnamese have with the government and the Communist Party. This is a solid introduction to the changes that Vietnam has gone through during the last decades of the twentieth century.

Kolko, Gabriel. *Vietnam: Anatomy of Peace.* New York: Routledge, 1997. 200 pp. (available in paperback and hardback). Gabriel Kolko, a Canadian scholar, wrote this book after having spent some of the 1980s in Vietnam. His thesis is that communist North Vietnam had a marvelous opportunity to make Vietnam a vibrant society after 1975 but squandered its chances. Kolko describes the various institutions in Vietnam and how each one was adversely affected by the policies of the Socialist Republic of Vietnam.

Woodside, Alexander. "The Triumphs and Failures of Mass Education in Vietnam." *Pacific Affairs* 56, no. 3 (fall 1983): 401–427. Woodside clearly explains the history of Vietnam's education system and why Vietnam needs to make fundamental changes in its current classroom structures.

VIETNAMESE SOCIETY AND CONTEMPORARY ISSUES

Epstein, Michael. *Vietnam: A Book of Changes.* New York: W. W. Norton, 1996. 170 pp. (available in hardback). A number of books explore Vietnam through pictures, but Epstein's work stands out with regard to his use of pictures in telling a story. Text accompanied by more than eighty photographs take the reader on a journey through contemporary Vietnam. The elegance and the honesty with which the author presents Vietnam in this volume is unparalleled.

Hayslip, Le Ly, and John Wurts. *When Heaven and Earth Changed Places: A Vietnamese Woman's Journey from War to Peace.* New York: Plume, 1989. 368 pp. (available in paperback). The cinematic version of this book, released in 1993, did not do justice to the passion with which Le Ly Hayslip wrote her auto-biography. This volume is extremely readable and provides an overview of how Vietnam was affected by the U.S. presence there during the 1960s and 1970s. It also offers an insight into the Vietnamese experience in the United States.

Hiebert, Murray. *Vietnam Notebook.* Hong Kong: Review Publishing, 1994. 216 pp. (available in paperback). Murray Hiebert, a correspondent for *The Far Eastern Economic Review,* pooled his stories on Vietnam for this volume. The thirty-eight short chapters in this work represent a wide range of material. Among the issues Hiebert takes on are minorities in Vietnam, the growing population, a spiritual renewal in Vietnam, the return of overseas Vietnamese, and the education crisis.

Marr, David G. *Vietnamese Youth in the 1990s.* Sydney: Macquarie University, 1996. 52 pp. (available in paperback). The 1990s was a time of dramatic change in Vietnam. This was especially true with regard to the younger generation. Globalization brought in foreign television shows and movies along with rap music and other aspects of Western culture. In his study, Marr demonstrates how these changes have affected Vietnamese young people and what the future holds for a generation that has grown up with peace.

Templer, Robert. *Shadows and Wind: A View of Modern Vietnam.* New York: Penguin Putnam, 1998. 384 pp. (available in paperback and hardback). This book is a must for anyone studying modern Vietnam. In his seventeen chapters, Templer takes the reader through a Vietnam that has changed due to war, disillusionment, economic failure, and globalization. The author writes in a very appealing manner and offers a valuable introduction for those who have no background to Vietnam.

VIETNAMESE CULTURE, CUSTOMS, AND ETIQUETTE

Chambers, Kevin. *Succeed in Business: The Essential Guide for Business and Investment in Vietnam.* Portland: Graphic Arts

Center Publishing, 1997. 240 pp. (available in paperback). This book is included in this section because Kevin Chambers has spent a good deal of time clarifying Vietnamese political and social life. His chapter on culture and communication is especially effective.

Curry, Jeffrey E. *Passport Vietnam: Your Pocket Guide to Vietnamese Business, Customs, and Etiquette.* San Rafael, CA: World Trade Press, 1997. 95 pp. (available in paperback). As part of the Passport Series, this book is a solid introduction to the intricacies of social interaction in Vietnam. It will be especially helpful for those who plan to visit Vietnam and for those interested in conducting business in the cities of Hanoi and Ho Chi Minh.

Ellis, Claire. *Culture Shock! Vietnam.* Portland: Graphic Arts Center Publishing, 1995. 263 pp. (available in paperback). This book opens with an overview of Vietnam's history that lays the groundwork for chapters on "Culture Shock," "Communication," "Socializing in Vietnam," and "Business Etiquette." It takes a rather in-depth look at these subjects and so is not a quick read. The author writes on these complicated subjects in a very clear manner. The book can be used as a reference work at a junior high level.

Ferro, Jennifer. *Vietnamese Foods & Culture.* Vero Beach, FL: Rourke Press, 1999. 42 pp. (available in paperback). This short book is helpful in that the author intermingles Vietnamese recipes with Vietnamese history and explains why certain foods are prepared at certain times of the year. She includes a discussion of Vietnamese holidays and describes how food and etiquette are intertwined in the keeping of those holidays.

Murray, Geoffrey. *The Simple Guide to Vietnam: Customs and Etiquette.* Kent, UK: Cromwell Press, 1997. 81 pp. (available in paperback). This book was written with the traveler in mind. The ten brief chapters introduce the reader to Vietnam and to the social norms of the country. The chapter on social situations is particularly helpful for those who wish to learn Vietnamese etiquette.

Index

About the Author

Shelton Woods was born in Southeast Asia and lived there for fifteen years, growing up immersed in the various cultures and languages of Southeast Asian highlanders. In 1994 he received his Ph.D. in Southeast Asian History from the University of California at Los Angeles. His books include *Vietnam: An Illustrated History* and *A Broken Mirror: Protestant Fundamentalism in the Philippines.* Dr. Woods currently serves as Associate Professor of history and Associate Dean at Boise State University. He lives in Boise with his wife, Karen, and their son, Lindsay.